NORTHWEST
Readers

Other Titles in the Northwest Readers Series

Series Editor: Robert J. Frank

The Collected Poems of Hazel Hall, edited by John Witte

Nature's Justice: Writings of William O. Douglas, edited by James O'Fallon

A Richer Harvest: The Literature of Work in the Pacific Northwest, edited by Craig Wollner and W. Tracy Dillon

Wood Works: The Life and Writings of Charles Erskine Scott Wood, edited by Edwin Bingham and Tim Barnes

Badger and Coyote Were Neighbors

Melville Jacobs on Northwest Indian Myths and Tales

Edited by
William R. Seaburg

and

Pamela T. Amoss

Oregon State University Press

Corvallis Oregon

The paper in this book meets the guidelines for permanence and durability of the Committee on Production Guidelines for Book Longevity of the Council on Library Resources and the minimum requirements of the American National Standard for Permanence of Paper for Printed Library Materials Z39.48-1984.

Library of Congress Cataloging-in-Publication Data
Badger and Coyote were neighbors : Melville Jacobs on Northwest Indian Myths and Tales / edited by William R. Seaburg and Pamela T. Amoss.—1st ed.
    p. cm.—(Northwest readers)
Includes bibliographical references and index.
ISBN 0-87071-473-2 (pbk. : alk. paper)
1. Indian mythology—Oregon. 2. Indians of North America—Oregon—Folklore. 3. Indians of North America—Washington—Folklore. 4. Indian mythology—Washington. 5. Indian mythology—Northwest Coast of North America. 6. Indians of North America—Northwest Coast of North America—Folklore. 7. Jacobs, Melville, 1902-   I. Seaburg, William R. II. Amoss, Pamela. III. Series.
E78.O6 B33 2000
398.2'089'970795—dc21

00-008046

**OREGON STATE
UNIVERSITY**

Oregon State University Press
101 Waldo Hall
Corvallis OR 97331-6407
541-737-3166 • fax 541-737-3170
http://osu.orst.edu/dept/press

Series Preface

In 1990 the Oregon State University Press issued its first two books in the Northwest Reprint Series, *Oregon Detour* by Nard Jones, and *Nehalem Tillamook Tales*, edited by Melville Jacobs. Since then, the series has reissued a range of books by Northwest writers, both fiction and nonfiction, making available again works of well-known and lesser-known writers.

As the series developed, we realized that we did not always want to reissue a complete work; instead we wanted to present selections from the works of a single author or selections from a number of writers organized around a unifying theme. Oregon State University Press, then, has decided to start a new series, the Northwest Readers Series.

The reasons for the Northwest Readers Series are the same as for the Northwest Reprint Series: "In works by Northwest writers, we get to know about the place where we live, about each other, about our history and culture, and about our flora and fauna."

RJF

To the memory of

Melville Jacobs and Elizabeth D. Jacobs

Contents

Acknowledgments   ix

Melville Jacobs: An Introduction to the Man and His Work   1
Bibliography of Melville Jacobs   31

Toward a Theory and Method of Oral Literature Research
1 Oral Literature   38

2 A Few Observations on the World View of the Clackamas
Chinook Indians   64

3 Humor in Clackamas Chinook Oral Literature   75

4 Genres in Northwest States Oral Literatures   88

5 Areal Spread of Indian Oral Genre Features
in the Northwest States   94

Oral Traditional Texts with Interpretations
6 Badger and Coyote Were Neighbors (Clackamas Chinook)   104

7 The Old Man and His Daughter-in-law. Her Fingers Stuck
Together (Clackamas Chinook)   119

8 She Deceived Herself With Milt (Clackamas Chinook)   125

9 Wildcat (Klikitat Sahaptin)   132

10 Sun and His Daughter (Klikitat Sahaptin)   146

11 Coyote's Journey (Upper Cowlitz Sahaptin)   163

12 Mink, Panther, and the Grizzly Sisters
(Mary's River Kalapuya)   183

13 The Sagandahs People (Miluk Coos)   201

14 An Historical Event Text from a Galice Athabaskan in Southwestern Oregon (Galice Creek Athabaskan)   210

Oral Traditional and Ethnographic Texts

15 Coyote, Eagle, and the Wolves (Upper Cowlitz Sahaptin)   224

16 The Basket Ogress Took the Child (Clackamas Chinook)   238

17 Coyote and Skunk. He Tied His Musk Sac (Clackamas Chinook)   255

18 A Girls' Game (Clackamas Chinook/Chinook Jargon)   260

19 Ethnographic Texts on Spirit Powers and Shamanism (Santiam Kalapuya)   262

20 Some Shakers Find the Body of My Brother's Child (Santiam Kalapuya)   278

21 The Origin of Death (Upper Coquille Athabaskan/Chinook Jargon)   282

22 Small Bird Hawk Had His Head Cut Off (Hanis Coos)   284

23 The Girl Who Had a Dog Husband (Miluk Coos)   288

24 The Person That Halloos (Miluk Coos)   292

25 The Young Man Stepped on Snail's Back (Miluk Coos)   295

References Cited   296

Index   302

Acknowledgments

We are most grateful to colleagues and friends who have helped us in the rather lengthy process of selecting, editing, and setting a context for this sample of Melville Jacobs's folklore studies. We thank Jacobs's former students: M. Dale Kinkade, Robert Theodoratus, Thom Hess, and Virginia Gill Powers; his former University of Washington colleagues, Simon Ottenberg, Laurence C. and M. Terry Thompson, and Harold Amoss; and folklore scholars Dell and Virginia Hymes. We thank Laurel Sercombe and Susanne J. Young for their thoughtful readings of the manuscript; the staff at the Whatcom Museum of History and Art, especially the former Director, Mary Pettus, who encouraged us to pursue the project; and the archivists at the University of Washington, who helped us locate things of interest in Jacobs's papers and notebooks. We benefited greatly from Barbara MacLean's willingness to cast a disinterested but friendly eye over an early draft. We are particularly indebted to the Northwest Reader Series Editor, Robert J. Frank, of Oregon State University, for asking us to assemble a collection of writings by Jacobs. When we fell behind schedule in our preparation of the book, Editor Warren Slesinger patiently got us back on track and walking—if not running—toward our goal. Managing Editor Jo Alexander has steadfastly assisted us to the finish line. And, of course, we cannot begin to repay the contributions of our long-suffering families and housemates. To each of these individuals we are indebted.

All unattributed photographs are courtesy of William R. Seaburg. Correspondence cited from Melville to Elizabeth Jacobs are in Seaburg's possession. Correspondence cited between Melville Jacobs and Franz Boas is from the Franz Boas Collection, American Philosophical Society Library, Philadelphia.

We acknowledge permission to reproduce portions of this book from the following publishers:

The American Folklore Society for "A Few Observations on the World View of the Clackamas Chinook Indians," *Journal of American Folklore* 68:283-89 (1955).

The University of Chicago Press for two chapters from *The Content and Style of an Oral Literature: Clackamas Chinook Myths and Tales* (1959): "Badger and Coyote Were Neighbors" (pp. 27-36) and

"Humor" (pp. 178-86). We also thank Chicago for material that appeared in the *International Journal of American Linguistics:* Volume 34:183-91 (1968), "An Historical Event Text from a Galice Athabaskan in Southwestern Oregon"; the English translations of texts from *Clackamas Chinook Texts, Part 1*, Volume 24.2 (Part I) (1958), "Coyote and Skunk. He Tied His Musk Sac" (pp. 13-18); and in *Clackamas Chinook Texts, Part 2*, Volume 25.2 (Part II) (1959), "The Old Man and His Daughter-in-law. Her Fingers Stuck Together" (pp. 310-12), "She Deceived Herself with Milt" (pp. 348-50), and "The Basket Ogress Took the Child" (pp. 388-409).

The Institute of Folklore Research for "Areal Spread of Indian Oral Genre Features in the Northwest States" from the *Journal of the Folklore Institute* 9:10-17 (1972).

The University of Washington Press for interpretations of "The Old Man and His Daughter-in-law. Her Fingers Stuck Together" (pp. 202-5) and "She Deceived Herself with Milt" (pp. 243-47) from *The People Are Coming Soon: Analyses of Clackamas Chinook Myths and Tales* (1960). We also thank Washington for material from the University of Washington Publications in Anthropology (UWPA) 7.1 (1936) *Texts in Chinook Jargon*, the English translations of "The Origin of Death" (pp. 26-27) and "A Girl's Game" (pp. 12-13); from UWPA 8.1 (1939) *Coos Narrative and Ethnologic Texts*, the English translations of "The Person That Halloos" (pp. 51-52) and "The Young Man Stepped on Snail's Back" (pp. 54-56); from UWPA 8.2 (1940) *Coos Myth Texts*, the English translations of "Small Bird Hawk Had His Head Cut Off" (pp. 235-38) and "The Girl Who Had a Dog Husband" (pp. 159-62); from UWPA 11 (1945) *Kalapuya Texts*, the English translations from "Santiam Kalapuya Ethnologic Texts" (pp. 51-72), [includes "Shakers Find the Body of My Brother's Child" (pp. 52-55)].

The Wadsworth Publishing Company for one chapter from *Pattern in Cultural Anthropology* (1964): "Oral Literature" (pp. 319-45).

The Jacobs Fund of the Whatcom Museum Society for permission to use a previously unpublished conference paper by Jacobs, "Genres in Northwest States Oral Literatures," as well as chapters from a previously unpublished and untitled manuscript. Selections printed from this work include "Wildcat," "Sun and His Daughter," "Coyote's Journey," "Mink, Panther, and the Grizzly Sisters," "The Sagandahs People," and "Coyote, Eagle, and the Wolves."

Melville Jacobs
An Introduction to the Man and His Work

Melville Jacobs, 1954
(photo by Alfred A. Witter, Seattle)

Introduction

In 1926 Melville Jacobs left New York City and drove west across America to begin his life work, the recording and analysis of the fast-disappearing languages and oral traditions of the Native Americans of Oregon and Washington. He was not the first of an unlikely cadre of city-bred Jewish intellectuals to devote their careers to salvaging and interpreting the life ways of America's first peoples. His mentor, Franz Boas, had set the pattern and his students, Sapir, Lowie, Kroeber, Goldenweiser and others, followed. There are many ironies in the partnerships that developed between these cultivated urbanites and the old Indian men and women who patiently taught their complex and difficult languages and shared their rich legacy of myths and tales. That it should be children of a denigrated and threatened European caste, newly established in America, who would take responsibility for preserving the heritage of America's equally denigrated and threatened earliest inhabitants, has a certain poetic symmetry. But the symbolic associations were probably lost on the investigators themselves. For them, the enterprise was simply hard work under trying conditions. The languages were totally exotic; the rural settings in which they worked were as alien as the languages and folklore they collected. Fieldwork for most of them began as daunting and continued to be onerous no matter how long they worked or how successful they became. Robert Lowie, from the first generation of these students of Franz Boas, had been forced to grow a beard on his maiden fieldtrip because, as he confessed to his seminar students many years later, he had never shaved himself when he lived in New York, but had always gone to the local barber (Harold Amoss, personal communication, 1999).

Although by the 1920s the second generation of Boas's students, including Jacobs, were American born and raised, they shared much of the discomfort of their predecessors in adjusting to the rustic settings in which American Indians lived. Anyone who knew Melville

Jacobs, fastidious in dress and grooming, cultivated and witty, always had difficulty imagining him coping with bad roads, seedy hotels, and truck-stop food. In January 1930 he wrote to Bess Langdon, the woman who would become his wife, describing his trip to Oregon from Seattle:

> *I had a mad ride down: a blizzard near Tacoma, freezing blasts about Centralia, a suddenly frozen glassed road surface of rain about Kelso, torrents near Vancouver, a billion needles of hail crossing the Columbia, a blind frozen windshield the last score miles, a near wreck in Portland. ...*
>
> *Today, I found my Indians awaiting me. Not a minute's waiting: I recorded treasures, at once, from Mrs. H. [Victoria Howard, Jacobs's Clackamas Chinook informant]. I had nearly lost her: an automobile sent her to the hospital some weeks ago. She is all patched up and fine for work now. Her nuisance husband has had gout or dropsy or worse since I left him last August, and seems to have recovered for my especial benefit. The road is clear; all I need is Shaeffer's ink, and a sense of humor to put some meaning into the drudgery* (letter, Jacobs to Langdon, 29 January 1930).

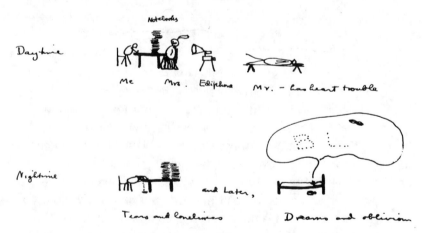

Drawings from a letter from Melville Jacobs to Bess Langdon (19 March 1930)

When Jacobs prepared his students for fieldtrips, he always warned them not only how difficult Native American languages were, but also how dismal the settings would be, how lonely they would feel, and how such discomfort and frustration were the essential rites of passage for the professional. Nevertheless, this remarkable man, totally unsuited by personality and background to do what he did, managed by a combination of strong intellect and stronger will, and with the cooperation of equally remarkable Indian people, to amass and preserve a genuine treasure of Native American languages and traditions. Furthermore, he was a leader in the drive to convince the scholarly world that Native oral traditions deserved the same kind of respect, and would reward the same kind of careful analysis, previously accorded only to the written treasures of the western canon.

The selections in this volume from Jacobs's writings were chosen to illustrate his folklore research. We deliberately excluded the more technical linguistic works, the works on race, and his book reviews covering the wide range of his interests—from folklore, to race, to the history and sociology of the Jews. We concentrated on his analysis and interpretation of American Indian folklore, which he himself believed to be his true contribution to anthropology. We have arranged the material in three sections. First are five articles and chapters that illustrate his theoretical orientation. Two of them focus specifically on the Clackamas Chinook oral traditions, because it was in the interpretation of the Chinookan texts that Jacobs attempted to demonstrate the merits of applying his structural-psychological model to Native American folk literature.

Section two consists of nine examples of Jacobs's discursive style of text interpretation. The stories are taken from the Clackamas Chinook, Mary's River Kalapuya, Klikitat Sahaptin, Upper Cowlitz Sahaptin, Miluk Coos, and Galice Athabaskan languages. We have included Jacobs's translations of the stories and his interpretations. Five of the text interpretations are published here for the first time.

Section three presents eleven additional stories representing a range of genres which Jacobs collected, and drawn from the Native American groups he worked with.

Overview of Jacobs's Academic Career

Melville Jacobs was born in New York City on 3 July 1902, the only child of Alexander and Rose Blau Jacobs. "Both parents were second-generation Americans of Bavarian Jewish ancestry, but without strong religious identification" (Thompson 1978, 640). Jacobs's Jewish background undoubtedly played at least some part in his concern with racial issues; he published several articles and reviews on race in the 1940s (Jacobs 1941a, b; 1942; 1944; 1946a, b) and wrote, but never published, a book-length study on racism. His interest in human variation may have developed long before his encounter with anthropology because as a boy he loved to go on his own to watch the immigrants pour off the ferry from Ellis Island.

Jacobs studied history and philosophy at the College of the City of New York (BA 1922) and American history at Columbia University (MA 1923). At CCNY Jacobs fell under the influence of a remarkable teacher, Morris Raphael Cohen. A philosopher of science with a particular interest in the philosophy of history, Cohen, like Jacobs (and like Franz Boas) was a Jew who acknowledged his ethnic roots but looked beyond Judaism for his intellectual and ethical foundations. Cohen was part of the milieu of Jewish intellectual tradition in and around New York, perhaps best exemplified by the Ethical Culture movement, whose adherents combined an extraordinary devotion to learning with an edifying zeal for social service (Hollinger 1975, 17-18; Frank 1997, 734). Although Cohen has no following among contemporary philosophers, he was extraordinarily influential during the first third of the twentieth century.

Cohen was an early and enthusiastic promoter of the middle way between the extremes of pragmatism and idealism. He liked to quote Tennyson in saying that whenever thought and fact are joined, thunder rolls (Hollinger 1975, 60). Cohen's commitment to the marriage of theory and fact carried him to the conviction that knowledge obliges action. No small part of his efforts was directed to sharing the blessings of education and enlightenment with the common people. To this end he was a leader in establishing and teaching at the "Breadwinners' College"—a night school program for working people. Not surprisingly, Cohen not only served as an intellectual ideal, but also offered the young Jacobs a role model of scholarship in service of society—a role Jacobs played during his early years teaching English to immigrants in a special evening program in New York. When he joined the faculty at the University of Washington, Jacobs continued to bring the benefits of scholarship to a wider public through lectures to community groups. Jacobs was interested in, and read widely in, various scientific disciplines, which was the foundation for a "long and successful series of radio talks ... for the University: the Science News Broadcasts were aired weekly from 1934 to 1951, except for an interruption during World War II" (Thompson 1978, 642). His decision to join the Communist Party (around 1935) can also be best understood as an attempt to work toward a more just society. He abandoned all these efforts only after his traumatic encounter with the Canwell Committee in the late 1940s convinced him that his tarnished public image would no longer reflect credit on the ideas he espoused.

Jacobs's interest in history and philosophy had a lasting influence throughout his career as an anthropologist. Evidence for this can been seen, for example, in the careful documentation of his fieldnotes, photographs, and sound recordings. Working with the Jacobs Collection papers in the University of Washington Library's Division of Manuscripts and University Archives is gratifying in no small part because of his respect for provenance information. Names, dates, and origins are almost always carefully noted. As late

Melville Jacobs's home for June, July, and August 1927 at Morton, Washington, while he worked on Táitnapam grammar and mythology.

Melville Jacobs in camp in Morton, Washington, 1927.

as the mid 1950s, Jacobs was assigning Cohen's treatise on logic to his advanced seminar on anthropological theory (Robert Theodoratus, personal communication, 1999).

Jacobs entered the Anthropology Department at Columbia University in 1924, where he studied under Franz Boas along with such fellow students as Ruth Benedict, Melville Herskovits, George Herzog, Margaret Mead, and Gene Weltfish. Boas first sent him to the field in 1926 (in eastern Washington) to study the Sahaptin language, and his PhD dissertation, *A Sketch of Northern Sahaptin Grammar,* was published in 1931. Although Jacobs's subsequent contributions to Amerindian linguistics include large linguistic files on many now-extinct western Oregon languages (much of which remains to be analyzed and published; Seaburg 1982), a structural sketch of Chinook Jargon (1932), a delineation of the areal spread of sound features in the Indian languages of the Northwest (1954), and numerous texts in phonetic transcription and translation, he thought of himself primarily as a cultural anthropologist rather than a linguist.

In 1928, upon Boas's recommendation, Jacobs was appointed Associate in Anthropology at the University of Washington, and he remained at the University, with the exception of occasional visiting appointments elsewhere, for his entire career. Jacobs attained the rank of Assistant Professor in 1937, Associate Professor in 1945,

Melville Jacobs, June 1928.
(photo by James Brandon [Ahkla],
Eskimo of Nome, Alaska)

and Full Professor in 1952. Jacobs died of cancer on 31 July 1971 in Seattle, Washington, one year short of retirement.

Jacobs was almost thirty when he married the woman who would be his emotional and intellectual partner for the rest of his life, Elizabeth Derr Langdon (née Elizabeth Louise Derr). Petite, red-headed, with a wicked sense of humor, Bess, as she was known, seems to have enchanted Jacobs completely. In one of his letters to her he comments on some incident when she felt she may have seemed unfriendly,

> But you did not look either stony-eyed or casual! You never do. You looked your own quietly vibrant controlled self, and I am learning that it means many lovely things, and I prefer it to Isidora Duncanning and such like ecstatics. You must always purse your lips, put on green headlights, toot the horn for right of way, keep the windshield swipe spiffing and carry on, and I shall clatter behind happily in my own fliver (sic) way (letter, Jacobs to Langdon, 19 March 1930).

After their marriage in 1931 Bess also became an important part of Jacobs's field investigations. She went with him into small towns

Elizabeth D. and Melville Jacobs, 1952

in Oregon and Washington where, thanks to her own rural Idaho background, she felt at ease though he did not. She even persuaded him to take in wrestling events, one of the few entertainments offered locally, as a way of unwinding from the rigors of fieldwork. While he worked on language and the painstaking grammatical analysis of texts, Bess recorded stories and ethnographic data—primarily in English—from several Native groups (Seaburg 1994). Her work with a speaker of Nehalem Tillamook Salish culminated in *Nehalem Tillamook Tales* published in 1959, many years after they were collected. Having her with him made such a difference to Jacobs that in the 1950s he confided in some of his students that he would never again do field research without her. Even years after Bess had embarked on her own professional life as a psychiatric social worker, she was the only person to whom Jacobs submitted his work for editorial criticism.

Perhaps the most telling evidence of Bess Jacobs's commitment to Melville Jacobs's work comes in her determination to realize the dream they both had of endowing a fund to support the research they believed in. Childless and without close ties to any younger kin, they had originally determined to leave their estate to the Anthropology Department at the University of Washington, but Jacobs's growing disenchantment with the direction of scholarship in the department led him to look for an alternative venue. Fellow linguist Larry Thompson, and his wife, M. Terry Thompson, were instrumental in finding a place where Jacobs believed both his small monetary legacy and his precious basket collection would be properly appreciated. Susan Barrow, the dedicated and ambitious director of the Whatcom Museum of History and Art in Bellingham, Washington, immediately saw the advantages of accepting the baskets and creating a structure for disbursing the Jacobs money for research on Native Americans.

Jacobs worried about money all his life. He was the child of frugal parents who as a young adult experienced all the disquieting forces of the Great Depression of the 1930s. Early in his academic career he began to save for his retirement. Later, with Bess's help and encouragement, they began systematically buying rental properties. Shortly after his death in 1971 she began funding small research grants on an annual basis. She appointed a board of Jacobs's colleagues and former students to advise her. Under the auspices of the Whatcom Museum the original board continued to operate after her death when her estate became available for annual grants. The fund was considerably enlarged upon the death of Jacobs's mother, Rose Jacobs, who lived to a great age and who left her estate to the fund. Thanks to careful management, the Jacobs Research Fund has been able to continue making small annual grants for research with Native peoples of North America in the fields of cultural anthropology and linguistics.

Jacobs came to the University of Washington on a special arrangement set up between his mentor, Franz Boas, and then University president M. Lyle Spencer. In one of his letters to Spencer, Boas said that Jacobs was "by far the best man I have had for many years." Both Jacobs and his fellow student Thelma Adamson were to teach part of the year and do fieldwork part of the year. Their salaries would be paid by the University and the Committee on Research in Native American Languages, which Boas chaired. Adamson relinquished her position after one quarter but Jacobs remained. In the meantime the University hired Leslie Spier to direct both the anthropology program and the Washington State Museum on campus, a post vacated by T.T. Waterman. As part of the package, Erna Gunther, Spier's wife and also an anthropologist, was hired to teach in the program. When in 1930 Spier left both the University and his marriage, he negotiated an understanding that the administration would continue to employ Gunther in the role he was vacating. Jacobs may not have been entirely pleased about having Erna Gunther put into a position senior to him. Whatever chagrin he experienced then was nothing to the distress he experienced when a little more than a year later his very place at the University was jeopardized by stringent cost-cutting measures forced on the institution by the depression. As a junior person, Jacobs was vulnerable. Furthermore, although in later years he was an entertaining lecturer, his early students complained that he was a lackluster teacher. In 1929 the University of Washington for the first time instituted student evaluations of teachers. Jacobs's evaluations were not flattering. Furthermore, when the administration asked department head Gunther to evaluate Jacobs's performance in the classroom, she wrote that although she had tried to advise him how to improve, he had not cooperated and remained a poor teacher (Gunther papers, Burke Museum). Although Jacobs managed to rescind the initial decision to let him go, he undoubtedly knew that Gunther had been willing to sacrifice him. He never forgot it.

There were other reasons for his animus. He had no patience for the atheoretical style of ethnography that Gunther favored, nor did he share her vision of how the department should develop. In a 1936 letter to Boas, Jacobs complained that Gunther did not battle for money to publish his Coos texts because "she wishes to build our position and prestige with publication of material that is far more widely in demand" (letter, Jacobs to Boas, 1936). In the middle 1950s, when Gunther, after some twenty years in harness, neared retirement age, Jacobs and several colleagues were successful in their efforts to have her replaced as chairman.

A change in department leadership did not ultimately create the kind of climate for his work that Jacobs had in mind. New faculty who joined the department in the dramatic expansion of the late 1950s had little interest in traditional Americanist descriptive linguistics, folklore, or indeed, Native Americans. Ironically, just as Jacobs was beginning to publish his more seminal works in the field of folklore analysis, he found himself increasingly isolated and disaffected from many of his colleagues. Fortunately, he had found an intellectual community elsewhere on the University campus. He regularly lunched at the Faculty Club with a group of historians— with whom, thanks to his early training and predilections, he found he had much in common.

The influence of an anthropological scholar is often judged by the number of the students he or she produced. Franz Boas is, of course, the standard against which others are measured. Unlike

Boas, Jacobs could claim few students who followed the intellectual path he set forth. Nevertheless, Jacobs profoundly influenced succeeding cohorts of graduate students at Washington in two significant ways. First, he drove home an abiding respect for proper phonetic recording of terms in the native language. Second, he convinced even the more skeptical that the oral traditions of pre-literate people would reward careful analysis by revealing the unacknowledged areas of conflict within the fabric of culture.

In 1948 the University of Washington experienced a wrenching debate over alleged Communist infiltration. Melville Jacobs, who with Bess had belonged to the Communist Party from approximately 1935 to 1945, found himself, with several other University faculty members, subpoenaed to appear before the Canwell Committee. The Canwell Committee had been created two years earlier by the state legislature to determine to what extent public and private institutions within the state were being manipulated or controlled by Communists to advance the interests of the Soviet Union. After a year of investigating the Pension Union, a pro-labor political group formed to support the rights of pensioners, the Committee turned its attention to the University of Washington where, it was rumored, "many" Communists or Communist sympathizers were ensconced within the faculty. According to Jacobs's own account, when first summoned to the University President's offices for informal interrogation, he sought legal advice and was counseled to deny his earlier membership in the local Communist Party. Under subpoena, during public hearings before the Committee, he admitted joining the Party but claimed he had left it some years before. He refused to answer questions on other people he might have known as Party members. Asked why he had joined, Jacobs cited two factors that had influenced him: the disruptions and suffering caused by the Depression and the rising threat of Nazism. Although Jacobs did not allude to it, his friendship with Harold Eby and Garland Ethel, both also called before the Committee, undoubtedly explains in part his decision to join the Communist Party. Even more important, Bess Jacobs was equally committed to what they all perceived as the Party's worthwhile social and economic agenda.

Along with five other professors—Herbert Phillips (Philosophy), Ralph Gunlach (Psychology), Joseph Butterworth, Harold Eby, and Garland Ethel (all of English), Jacobs was subjected to disciplinary action by the University's Committee on Tenure and Academic Freedom. Once more, as it had in 1931-32, Jacobs's career dangled from a thread. And once again, he and his supporters argued persuasively for his salvation. But unlike his earlier experience which had proceeded quietly under the cloak of confidential personnel action, this threat was acted out in the full glare of publicity on and off campus.

The Canwell encounter seems to have changed the direction of Jacobs's life, in the sense that he abandoned his commitment to public service and withdrew into a narrow scholarly world, concentrating his energies on the hope that his legacy of research and publication would provide his justification. At the Tenure Committee hearing Jacobs was asked if a resurgence of Fascism might not lure him to rejoin the Party. He replied,

> *I have been through a lot, especially in recent months. ... I am not twenty-five or thirty-five any longer. I have taken enough of a beating that I think it will have to be a world or national situation much more shot through with danger and fear for me ever to want to touch either the Democratic or Republican Party, let alone the Communist Party. I have a certain amount of time left in which I can get my scientific obligations complete, to get my research work out, and do what I want to do. ... In my present frame of mind, something would have to happen to some of the cells in my cerebrum before anybody could persuade me ever to touch politics with a ten-foot pole after what I have been through* (Countryman 1951, 241).

For the rest of his life he remained anxious and suspicious of public involvement. Five years after his collision with Canwell, Jacobs refused to write letters of recommendation for students applying for Fulbright awards, convinced that a letter from him would be a kiss of death. Once, in the middle 1950s at a student party at the Jacobs's home, one of the more inebriated guests struck up the "Internationale." Jacobs became terribly agitated and begged him to stop immediately before the sound carried to his neighbors. Fifteen years later, on a visiting summer appointment at the University of Colorado in Boulder, he was still nervous enough to decline an attractive summer rental because the owner was the former wife of a known Communist sympathizer.

The decision to withdraw from public service undoubtedly cost Jacobs much satisfaction and self-respect. That he never abandoned his ideal, the scholar who contributes directly to illuminating the understanding of the general public, is revealed in his final evaluations of his early mentor, Franz Boas. A few months before his death in 1971 Jacobs said that if Boas had done nothing else his unremitting "tub thumping about the lack of evidence for racial inferiority" was a lasting contribution (Amoss [1971]).

Jacobs on Anthropology

Perhaps because of his early indoctrination by Cohen, first and foremost Jacobs saw himself as a scientist and anthropology as a scientific enterprise. But his assessment of anthropology as an empirical science was not sanguine. In his *Pattern in Cultural Anthropology* (1964, 6) Jacobs says:

> But advances in cultural anthropology are uneven or timorous. They occur in the presence of galling barriers of frequently badly trained personnel, rigidities about methodology, myopias and fundamentalism about theory, and entrapment by father figures of dwarf size.

A central theme which runs through every chapter of this survey is its emphasis upon the newness, inchoateness, and immaturity in methods of research and state of global knowledge of cultural expressions.

For Jacobs, structural linguistics was a social science whose structuralist methodology could profitably be emulated by anthropology (certainly folklore)—at least in part. He had reservations even about linguistics. Jacobs's discussion of methodology in folklore is replete with references to the 'structuring of components in an expressive system,' 'contrastive classes of units,' 'discovery ... of correct units, classes of units, and their patternings and functions,' and so on, often with explicit comparison to classes of contrastive phonemes and their allophones, morphemes and allomorphs. The following passage is typical of Jacobs's use of structural linguistic analogies:

> I suggest, therefore, that oral literature style classes functioned so like the form classes of a grammar that

> *they may offer productive analogies for processes*
> *involved in formation and maintenance of grammatical*
> *form classes. Style classes of oral literature, and all oral*
> *literatures have had their structurings and their numerous*
> *stylistic form classes, are already manageable evidences,*
> *at hand in quantity, which look strikingly like earlier*
> *stages of crystallization of grammatical form classes*
> (Jacobs 1964, 109).

In Jacobs's estimation, much of cultural anthropology was at the pre-structuralist stage of science; thus, much of what passed for cultural anthropology was worthless for the advancement of anthropological theory.

Fieldwork in the Northwest States

During his early years at the University of Washington, Jacobs engaged in intensive field research in cultural anthropology, folklore, music, and linguistics, primarily among western Oregon Native American groups. "From 1928 to 1936 Jacobs's tenure at Washington permitted him to conduct field researches during six months every year. His field research interests from 1926 to 1939 were largely to salvage everything possible, in cultural anthropology, folklore, native music and linguistics, in [western] Oregon American Indian groups that were on the verge of extinction" (from Jacobs's unpublished 1971 "Notes for an obituary").

Jacobs conducted several "reconnaissance" missions in western Oregon, searching for informed culture bearers with whom to work. In an informative three-page letter to Boas (27 April 1931) Jacobs noted, "This last week end I indulged in a northwest Oregon reconnaissance. Permit me to list for you all the information I now have about native survivors in this region." He lists, with some discussion, thirty-one possible consultants. In 1935 he again reported to Boas, "In order to plan our field labors for the summer and autumn I have made three scouting trips into western Oregon during the last month" (letter, 11 May 1935). Probably a regular aspect of all of Jacobs's fieldtrips was the checking out of leads on potential Native speakers, especially of languages thought to be extinct (Seaburg 1994, 44-45).

One of the constraints on Jacobs's fieldwork was the uncertainty or scarcity of funds. During the Great Depression, when departmental appropriations for fieldwork were greatly reduced, Jacobs depended upon Boas and the American Council of Learned Societies's Committee on Research in Native American Languages for such support. In a letter to Boas (17 October 1932) Jacobs explained the financial situation at the University of Washington:

> About 400 dollars was forgotten or left or otherwise salvaged in the drastic slashing of expenses, and is being used by Mr. [Verne] Ray and myself for field work before April 1. We consider ourselves astonishingly lucky to have this money to work with, and we are inclined to fear that it may be a long time before we will see another sum like it available for field researches.

On 6 March 1933 (letter) Jacobs wrote to Boas, indicating that "disaster in our funds might be forestalled if money could be matched against University of Washington money as we did these past four years." Boas responded on 13 March with a promise of $500 for ethnographic and linguistic work in western Oregon provided that the University of Washington supplied the balance. On 1 June (letter) an embarrassed Jacobs wrote to Boas that the University was "not able to find a full 500 clear for field researches as such, to counter your sum for field researches" although he was counting on "well over 200" from the departmental budget. He ends his letter by saying,

> I am indeed surprised and pleased that so much was done for me, at a time that witnesses drastic salary slashes and even more drastic slashes in every other aspect of the work of the university. In addition to finding [two months' additional salary] money for me, they are as usual permitting me the remarkable opportunity to absent myself with salary from now until January 1, with use of the museum car, for any researches I may be interested in undertaking. I had not expected so much again this year.

In a short note (5 June 1933) Boas replied in his usual laconic fashion: "I do not need, I think, to be concerned with the details of the money to be furnished by the University of Washington. Your proposal, as planned, is quite satisfactory to me."

Jacobs followed his mentor Boas in the tradition of extensive fieldwork and obsessive data collection and in this sense can be considered Boasian. Both anthropologists gathered more data than they were able to get published in their lifetimes. Nonetheless, Jacobs published nine volumes of ethnographic and folklore texts and translations.

Like Boas, Jacobs felt that the recording of myth and ethnographic dictations in the Native language produced the least amount of investigator-induced distortion. Hence, many of Jacobs's monograph-length publications are in the form of texts and translations. Native language texts also provided linguistic data for grammatical and lexical analyses as well as a sampling of a group's oral traditions. In the Introduction to *Clackamas Chinook Texts, Part 1* (1958, 4), Jacobs defended the recording and printing of texts:

> Since the retirement of Dr. Franz Boas during the middle 1930s few anthropologists followed his example, and

Melville Jacobs and Annie Miner Peterson, his Coos consultant, 1934, Charleston, Oregon, with Jacobs's newly made electric phonograph recorder.

that of some of his students, in printing texts and translations, either folkloristic or ethnographic. I think that important factors in attenuation of interest in text documentation include the failure, by most anthropologists, to assess the potentials in texts, and the lack of comprehension of the need for presenting the most firmly founded supports for descriptive, interpretive and theoretical writing in anthropology. In my Clackamas reports I hope to show that we can produce and bolster firmly many formulations regarding interpersonal relationships, components of personality structure, ethical standards, humor, and literary style, for an extinct group where the principal documentation is a body of folkloristic texts rather than field observations of other kinds.

In some respects Jacobs had an advantage over Boas. First, he did not have to travel so far to get to the field and, thanks to Boas's plan, Jacobs had a reliable source of support in the field. Second, and more importantly, thanks to the arrangement Boas made for him with the University, he was able to conduct some of his fieldwork during the winter months. This was helpful because the Indian groups with whom Jacobs worked had strong taboos against relating myth texts during the summertime.

Like his mentor Boas, Jacobs amassed much more material than he was able to publish. He had always planned to use his retirement years to write the ethnography of western Oregon. Many of the Native American groups with whom Jacobs worked were represented by only a few survivors and little or no information had been gathered on their lifeways. Jacobs believed he was in a position to combine his own field materials with what other information was available to produce a definitive treatment.

Fieldwork Methodology

How Melville Jacobs conducted his linguistic fieldwork can be surmised from an unpublished manuscript (ca. 1945) entitled, "Handbook for Field Recording of Primitive Languages." The first few days are spent phonetically recording "native names of body parts, animals, birds, fish, insects, house parts, numerals, and other ordinary vocabulary words" (763). More complex materials, such as short sentences illustrating features of grammatical structure, are elicited next:

> each evening after hours of studying through the slips secured with his interpreter earlier in the day, he prepares scores or hundreds of phrases or sentences for which he plans to secure his interpreter's translation into the native language. Each day's study thus fertilizes the next day's labors (Jacobs ca. 1945, 764).

After four or five weeks the consultant is "encouraged to launch into connected speech," usually in the form of "simpler and shorter folktales" (765).

All of the myth and tale texts Jacobs collected were originally elicited as part of his linguistic investigations. He noted in several of his published collections that all of the texts were volunteered by his consultants. In *Northwest Sahaptin Texts, 1* (1929, 243) Jacobs wrote: "Joe [Hunt] has been anxious to have me preserve what he believed worth preserving. I have not suggested things or stories to dictate; I have asked him to tell what he wished to tell." Jacobs continues with a brief description of how the text dictation with Mr. Hunt proceeded:[1]

> His dictation is mechanized to perfection; he watches my pen and utters word after word; it is done at a very high speed. I am convinced that this sort of dictation is ideal for every purpose except one: it makes for occasional phrase and sentence artificiality, distortion and repetitiousness such as would not appear in normal fluent myth and story narration; I see no way of obtaining dictation from Joe other than the way in which he has already given me this material; indeed, it is on the whole unusually fine dictation.

From the perspective of late twentieth-century anthropologists, Jacobs's refusal to encourage his students to tape record the field materials they collected is a source of great regret. In fact, his attitude about using recording devices to preserve Native language material is puzzling. He himself used early devices, such as the Ediphone wax cylinder recorder, primarily to record songs and music, during fieldtrips from 1926 to 1934. In 1934 Jacobs ordered a portable electric phonograph recorder built for him by Mr. Philip A. Jacobsen of the Department of General Engineering at the University of Washington, with help from his assistant, Mr. Orin Johnston. Its construction was made possible by a grant-in-aid of $242.50 from the National Research Council. As with the Ediphone records, though, most of the acetate disc phonograph recordings from 1934-1939 were of Indian musical traditions rather than folklore texts (Seaburg 1994).

By the 1950s when he was directing the research of Sally Snyder on Coast Salish (Skagit) folklore and Pamela Thorsen on the Nooksack Coast Salish language, he was very much opposed to the use of the tape recorder. He was afraid, he said, that Thorsen would be tempted to slight the painstaking process of writing text as the informant dictated. It was not clear why he did not encourage Snyder to make Skagit recordings of the stories she was collecting in English. Jacobs himself admitted that a slow and unnatural delivery was the price of his method.

There is no doubt that Jacobs developed a respect, and even affection, for individual Native American people. About Victoria Howard he wrote,

> I might note at this point, a conviction that has been growing upon me with increasing intensity since I commenced working with Mrs. H. It is that here is the unsurpassably intelligent and sublimely loquacious informant. Her dictation, too, is nicely distinct, perfectly timed for the most rapid dictation and never a moment hesitant ... (Jacobs field notebook 59 [1929-1930]).

The next year, writing to Bess from the field, Jacobs says,

> Mrs. [Howard] dictates too marvelously; Mr. [Howard, Victoria's husband] is dying of heart trouble, I fear; he was pretty bad today. Mrs. looks at him with profound

*worry, then turns to me with a line of humour such as I
have never tasted before; she is incredible. I shall stay
with her as long as I can stand the loneliness of nights
here (letter from Jacobs to Langdon, 19 March 1930).*

Despite what he admired in his consultants, Jacobs seemed to
lack appreciation or understanding of the contemporary Native
culture in their everyday lives.[2] To him such "acculturated" lifeways
were only a pale shadow of what had been. His evaluation of the
Indian Shaker Church, which began in the 1880s among Puget
Sound Indians as a classic revitalization movement, is representative
of his attitude. As he saw it, Shakerism lacked the validity and
integrity of the aboriginal spirit quest religion and was, therefore,
not interesting. Nevertheless, when his consultant chose to dictate
texts about Shakers, Jacobs dutifully recorded them. See "Some
Shakers Find the Body of My Brother's Child" in this volume.

Although Jacobs often lamented that, because the old Indian
cultural systems were dead, he had not been able to observe the
context necessary to illuminate the full meaning of the stories—
audience reaction, interplay between raconteur and listeners, fuller
exegesis by both audience and raconteur, etc.—he never attempted
to collect folklore in a setting where the cultural tradition was still
lively and where he would have had access to the information he
lacked for his Northwest Coast narratives. He did, however, at least
consider undertaking such research. In 1954 the ethnomusicologist
Richard Waterman came to Washington fresh from fieldwork
among Australian Aborigines, where he and his wife had observed
a lively tradition of storytelling still embedded in its social and
cultural context. Inspired by these descriptions, Jacobs confided in
some of his students a plan to go to Australia and collect texts. He
even envisioned buying a trailer that would provide a comfortable
base for himself and Bess while they worked with the folklore of
Aboriginal peoples. The project never came to pass. Possibly the real
difficulties of tackling a totally new language gave him pause. It is
equally likely that the anticipated hardships of fieldwork deterred
him.

Editing and Publishing of Folklore Texts

Jacobs was not particularly punctilious about the translation process itself. Unlike many linguist-folklorists, he seldom called attention to the difficulties of translating particular passages in his texts. His English translations seem to be based on close interlinear renditions in English by the consultants rather than on an intimate knowledge of the grammar of the particular Indian languages involved.

One potential problem with Jacobs's published translations involves his frequent parenthetical remarks. They represent different kinds of information. Sometimes they clarify ambiguous anaphoric reference, i.e., to which character does this "he" or "she" refer? At other times they represent presumed shared cultural knowledge, knowledge that everyone in a Native audience would have and that therefore had not been made explicit by the storyteller. In yet other instances, Jacobs's parenthetical remarks are his textual interpretations. For example, in "Mink, Panther, and the Grizzly Sisters," in this volume, Jacobs translates "… sure enough here Grizzly (his fat sister-in-law) arose before him." Jacobs makes the assumption that because Panther's Grizzly sister-in-law becomes momentarily caught in his doorway, it is because she is fat. In his interpretation of this motif, he states, "The woman is noted as corpulent." But in fact the text says nothing about Grizzly's corpulence. It could just as easily be argued that stuck-in-the-doorway symbolized the huge size of the Grizzly and triggered not laughter at the expense of fat women but fear at the potential threat of a large and dangerous Grizzly person. Jacobs's inclusion of "fat" in his parenthetical comment is a matter of interpretation; it is neither text-based nor clearly a case of shared cultural knowledge. The problem is that the reader may come to view such frequent parenthetical comments as a clarification of the translation rather than Jacobs's interpretation, which they sometimes represent.

Although Jacobs followed Boas in emphasizing folklore, it is in the analysis and interpretation of folklore that the student and teacher went their separate ways. One of Boas's primary concerns in folklore was in demonstrating how folktale plots and motifs diffused throughout a contiguous geographical area, such as the Northwest Coast. Boas maintained that "folklore elements had combined in different ways in different areas" and he "cited indications of their recombinations in order to combat the theory that similar elements originated independently many times" (Jacobs 1959c, 125). In folklore, Boas's method "was primarily diffusionist and historical" (Jacobs 1959c, 126). In conversation with students and colleagues, Jacobs admitted that he had vigorously rebelled against all this. He had found, he claimed, much more inspiration for his real interest in expressive culture in Paul Radin's work than in Boas's (Amoss [1971]).

Jacobs was highly critical of most folklore research, from its beginnings in the nineteenth century through the 1960s. The discipline's shortcoming were delineated—repeatedly so—in Jacobs's publications, perhaps nowhere more forcefully than in his 1964 outgoing presidential address to the American Folklore Society, "A Look Ahead in Oral Literature Research" (Jacobs 1966). Jacobs argued that folklore was still in "a natural history phase" of intellectual development because it lacked an adequate theory to guide the collecting, analyzing, and arranging of folklore data. For Jacobs,

> *knowledge is ultimately theoretical knowledge, and it is in constant process of growth. It is not orderly piles of so-called 'facts.' Facts, that is, evidences, serve only as buttresses for portions of ever-expanding systems of theoretical knowledge. The tragedy of contemporary folklore scholarship is that it still focuses upon facts of just a few old kinds and the means for and merits in collecting them, without illumination from theory that tells what kinds of facts are very likely most worth seeing next.*

Folklorists had been content to collect texts and versions thereof, arrange them into tale-types, catalogue their motifs or other such macro-units and, for the historico-geographically inclined, attempt to determine tale-type origins, spread, and changes as the result of diffusion. Jacobs argued that such exercises were utterly devoid of any theoretical import. Jacobs proposed a different agenda for folklore research.

In matters of theory and interpretation, Jacobs departed radically from his Boasian roots. We can dub Boas's theory of folklore the 'mirror image' or 'reflective' theory. Boas said, "Since the tale is an artistic unfolding of the happenings in human society, it must reflect the habits and conflicts of life of the society in which the narrator lives" (Boas 1930, 93) and "the essential features of a society and culture 'appear distinctly mirrored' in their folktales" (Jacobs 1959c, 131). As Jacobs pointed out, Boas failed to account for the fact that not all aspects of a culture show up in folktales; only some aspects are chosen, others are ignored. Jacobs developed what may be called the "projection" theory of folklore, a melding of the image of a movie projection onto a film screen and the psychological process of projection.

In essence, Jacobs's theory of interpretation was that story content "included projections of points of stress in the society; that is, events and social relationships portrayed in an oral literature connected with relationships which were unsatisfactorily resolved by social structure and custom. … [F]olktales express a great many incidents and relationships, but only a few are stressed" (Jacobs 1959c, 130). In other words, Jacobs was concerned with "ascertaining [folklore's] function in the psychological life of the community" (Thompson 1978, 643).

The psychological model which Jacobs used was psychoanalytic. We see this in his discussion of latent and manifest content and in his use of such psychodynamic concepts as projection, displacement, regression, identification; oral, anal, and sadistic personality types, and the like. Yet Jacobs's psychoanalytic interpretations were not uncritical applications of Freudian theory. Nor were they esoteric, jargon-laden, nor particularly dogmatic. In fact, he was selective in his choice of mechanisms "salvaged from the grandiose structure of psychoanalytic theory to become central components of a special theory for oral literature" (Jacobs 1964, 326-27). And at all times Jacobs was concerned with relating the folklore of a people to the values and attitudes, the systems of personal relations, the world view of their society. Jacobs, then, committed himself to interpreting the folklore texts which he had so painstakingly collected in careful phonetic transcription.

It is interesting to note that Jacobs, like Boas, did not systematically interrogate his consultants in the field about the meaning of the folklore he collected. Boas apparently felt that texts recorded in the original language provided an "inside view" of the culture which was free from investigator bias—at least more so than intrusive investigator questioning, with answers which no doubt included what Boas called "secondary explanations" or "secondary rationalizations". Later, Jacobs came to see the lack of detailed, systematic follow-up field questioning of folklore meaning as a lamentable omission in his field research strategy. The following is typical of Jacobs's frequent admonition to folklorists to combine text recording with post-recital detailed question-and-answer sessions with the storyteller. Regarding world view as one kind of expressive content found in a people's oral literature, he says: "After a dictation and its translation, a field worker ought to direct questions which draw out native commentary so as to fill in depictions of perceptions of the universe or multiverse. ... Partial expressions of world view which were latent or explicit in oral literature recitals require comparison with full perceptions yielded in ethnographic and other expressive analyses" (Jacobs 1964, 331). Jacobs came to believe that these post-recital inquiries were almost as important as the text recording itself.

Assessments of Jacobs's Folklore Research and Publications

Jacobs's ambitious and audacious assault on Clackamas Chinook folk traditions, a groundbreaking experiment in the application of unitary theory to a body of non-western literature—as he himself modestly characterized it—created more than a little interest, not always laudatory, among folklorists, anthropological or traditional. All praised his industry and linguistic skills in recording, translating, and publishing the impressive collection of myths, tales, and ethnographic texts. Most were favorably impressed by his judicious application of Freudian theory to the characters and events in the stories. It was clear from the outset that Jacobs was far too sophisticated an ethnographer and far too knowledgeable about the global variations in family structure and infant socialization to force village-dwelling hunter-gatherers into the procrustean beds of Freud's Viennese bourgeoisie. The criticisms therefore did not deal with his use of psychoanalytic theory but rather with his slighting traditional linguistic anthropological theoretical concerns. Although Jacobs himself said he worked from "multifactorial premises" citing historical, psychological, linguistic and aesthetic aspects to be considered, his critics argued that whatever attention he paid to psychological and aesthetic evidence, he was lacking in devotion to historical and linguistic evidence.

For the literatures of people without writing, history can only be deduced from comparisons of analogous story variants from neighboring groups. Addressing this concern, Sven Liljeblad took umbrage at Jacobs's disdain of the classic folktale tale-types and motifs. He complained that such neglect led Jacobs to ignore other versions of the stories from other parts of North America, and indeed, other parts of the world, where raconteurs attached different significance to the characters of the stories and their adventures. The story, "Black Bear and Grizzly," that Jacobs claimed represented deep-seated fear of powerful women to the Clackamas, was interpreted among the Shoshone youth as an adventure in which the youthful hero prevails against heavy odds. If the same story could be so differently interpreted in other cultural groups, Jacobs's contention that it rose from the repressed angst the Clackamas felt about strained social relationships could hardly be supported (Liljeblad 1962).

Anthropological folklorists, most of whom had themselves struggled with at least one difficult Amerindian language, also faulted Jacobs for slighting the grammatical, syntactic, and lexical aspects of the corpus. In his review of *The Content and Style of an Oral Literature,* Stanley Newman remarks,

> In view of the breadth and thoroughness of the study, I find it puzzling that Jacobs, despite his meticulous recording of the stories in the native language, should discuss the elements of Clackamas style entirely through English translation. Furthermore, he flatly expresses the conviction that an analysis of the linguistic features in the narratives would have negligible value ... (Newman 1960, 81).

In his 1964 presidential address to the American Folklore Society, Jacobs responded to Newman's criticism:

> One fundamental point must be insisted upon. ... Linguistic features and sets of them are rarely or never going to be shown to comprise a large percent of the significant features which comprise an oral literature style. When I wrote a few years ago about style in Chinook oral literature, several reviewers claimed that linguistic factors must be, had to be, of noteworthy

*importance in that style. Their bland certainty suffered no
doubts in the light of the fact that they had not analyzed
style in Chinook or any other oral literature. ... It is true
that recitalists manipulate linguistic features for stylistic
purposes, and very likely do so in every utterance. But
the principal apparatus of a stylistic kind in most myth
and tale literatures is to be found in nonlinguistic
devices ... (Jacobs 1966, 423).*

Dell Hymes, an enthusiastic supporter of Jacobs's folklore project,
and a close student of related Chinookan dialects, showed how
attention to lexical elements would have solved some open
questions in Jacobs's exegesis (1965, 330). He also showed how
attention to versions of stories from surrounding groups would have
actually strengthened Jacobs's interpretations. For example, local
differences in the organization of the story and the delineation of
characters proved that for the Clackamas, if not for other groups
who told the tale, "Black Bear and Grizzly" was, in fact, a grim
meditation on the hostility simmering just under the surface of the
social order.

Faithful though he was to analyzing the stories as projections of
the tensions in the social and cultural world of the community,
Jacobs often seemed oblivious to the very real concerns these same
folk had about the non-human world in which they were immersed
(Liljeblad 1962). For example, in denying that animal characters
represented anything of the natural world, he overlooked the fact
that animal actors were chosen for their assigned roles by people
who were close and unsentimental observers of nature (e.g., Grizzly
bears *are* ferocious and unpredictable and they do, on occasion, kill
black bears). Focused as he was on the role of the stories in
sublimating tensions generated by internal conflicts and
inconsistencies in the social fabric, Jacobs seems to have ignored the
possibility that the myths and tales might have had political
implications, not only for justifying relationships of subordination
and power within the village group, to which he does allude, but
also for bolstering claims to resources coveted by other local groups.
In this he was typical of most anthropologists working in the Pacific
Northwest in the 1950s and 60s. Perhaps because nothing
remained of aboriginal polity, most ethnographers made little effort
to reconstruct regional intergroup power relations. At the same
time scholars working elsewhere in the world were finding clear

political functions assumed by myths and tales (Leach 1954, 264 passim).

All critics, directly or indirectly, took issue with what they saw as Jacobs's rather cavalier discounting of any universal quality in the creation and dissemination of myths. The great myths of the unlettered peoples of the earth, like the great myths of written traditions, express more than the parochial concerns of a particular people at a particular time and place. As Hymes noted without specific reference to Jacobs:

> *Interpretation that seeks only an individual voice, the*
> *author's or the interpreter's, falls short as well.*
> *Interpretation that attends only to what is culturally*
> *defined, excluding both the mode of existence of the*
> *work and the personal voice ... yields only a surface*
> *image, however much it talks of underlying depth*
> *(Hymes 1981, 8-9).*

While Jacobs's defenders might feel that his attempt to apply the purportedly pan-human principles of western psychoanalytic theory to these works indicated that he did, indeed, appreciate their universal quality, his critics argued that whatever the value of his analysis, it remained limited. Hymes, in particular, urged the need to complement Jacobs's psychological interpretations with both historical comparative and close linguistic analysis (1965, 330).

Almost half a century has passed since the appearance of Jacobs's major work, the volumes of Chinook texts and the two books of analysis and commentary. It is now possible to reassess both his contribution and the merit of the criticisms leveled against his work.

During his lifetime, Jacobs saw very little effort to emulate or surpass his achievements. Of his students, there was only one who devoted herself to his agenda, Sally Snyder. Gifted and diligent, Snyder produced a doctoral dissertation that applies Jacobs's theoretical approach to the literature of another Northwest Coast group, the Salish-speaking Upper Skagit of western Washington State (1964). Like Jacobs, Snyder was fortunate in finding a number of good storytellers, among them a superior narrator, Lucy Williams, who dictated a substantial corpus of over one hundred stories. Although Williams and most of Snyder's other storytellers were fluent speakers of Skagit, Snyder recorded all the stories in English, so that her legacy lacks the powerful combination of interpretation buttressed by texts in Native language that distinguishes Jacobs's folklore work. Unfortunately, Synder's work is not widely known because she died before managing to publish either the texts or her interpretations.

The inadequacies of Jacobs's approach discussed by his critics in the 1960s seem as telling now as they did then. The significance of his groundbreaking effort to apply a consistent explanatory model, a socio-psychological theory, to a corpus of Native American oral literature remains, but his approach has been superseded by more sophisticated approaches that incorporate the psychological explanation with other types of interpretation. His careful and dedicated recording of the last legacy of the Clackamas, however, continues to grow in stature as Native and non-Native alike appreciate more fully the value of what has been saved.

Conclusion

In a short essay it is not possible to do justice to the complexity of such a scholar as Melville Jacobs. There are many facets of his life and work which we have not touched upon. In several important areas he was and remained a product of his Boasian intellectual upbringing. In other areas—most notably in his concern for scientific theory, psychological processes, and interest in oral literature interpretation—he went beyond the Boasian tradition.

Perhaps Jacobs will best be remembered for his careful collection and documentation of Pacific Northwest Native oral traditions in the Native languages, with translations into English whenever possible. But Jacobs ultimately was not content merely to collect and publish oral traditions; he was willing to face the arduous task of consistently interpreting these texts for the benefit of the discipline of folklore and for a non-Native audience's appreciation. Even when the editors disagree with his interpretations, we are forced to rethink texts in ways impossible without the intellectual stimulation he provided.

Editors' Notes

1. See "Wildcat" and "Sun and His Daughter" in this volume for texts dictated by Joe Hunt.
2. For a postmodernist view of Jacobs's relationship with Howard, see Senier (1997).

Bibliography of Melville Jacobs

Omitted are encyclopedia articles as well as newspaper reviews and articles.

1929. *Northwest Sahaptin Texts, 1.* University of Washington Publications in Anthropology 2.6, 175-244. Seattle: University of Washington Press.

1931. *A Sketch of Northern Sahaptin Grammar.* University of Washington Publications in Anthropology 4.2, 85-292. Seattle: University of Washington Press.

1932a. "Notes on the Structure of Chinook Jargon," *Language* 8:27-50.

1932b. "Northern Sahaptin Kinship Terms," *American Anthropologist* 34:688-693.

1933a. "Review of *The Changing Culture of an Indian Tribe*, by Margaret Mead," *Commonwealth Review* 15:53-55.

1933b. "Review of *The Carrier Language*, by A. G. Morice," *Washington Historical Quarterly* 24:150-152.

1934. *Northwest Sahaptin Texts* (English translations). Columbia University Contributions to Anthropology 19.1, 1-291. New York: Columbia University Press.

1936a. *Texts in Chinook Jargon.* University of Washington Publications in Anthropology 7.1, 1-27. Seattle: University of Washington Press.

1936b. "Review of *Nez Percé Texts*, by A. Phinney," *Pacific Northwest Quarterly* 27: 85-86.

1936c. "Review of *Quileute*, by M. J. Andrade, and *Quileute Texts*, by M. J. Andrade," *American Anthropologist* 38:314-315.

1936d. "Review of *Chinook, A History and Dictionary of the Northwest Coast Trade Jargon*, by E. H. Thomas," *Pacific Northwest Quarterly* 27:180-181.

1937a. *Northwest Sahaptin Texts* (Indian text). Columbia University Contributions to Anthropology 19.2, 1-238. New York: Columbia University Press.

1937b. "Historic Perspectives in Indian Languages of Oregon and Washington," *Pacific Northwest Quarterly* 28:55-74.

1937c. "Review of *Anthropology*, by A. Goldenweiser," *Frontier and Midland* 17:298.

1938. "Review of *The Amerindians*, by D. M. McNicol," *Pacific Northwest Quarterly* 29:213-214.

1939. *Coos Narrative and Ethnologic Texts.* University of Washington Publications in Anthropology 8.1, 1-126. Seattle: University of Washington Press.

1940a. *Coos Myth Texts.* University of Washington Publications in Anthropology 8.2, 127-260. Seattle: University of Washington Press.

1940b. "The Teaching of Anthropology in the Secondary Schools," *University of Washington College of Education Record* 6:49-53. (Reprinted partially in *University of Chicago School Review* 48:323-325 [1940].)

1940c. "Review of *Nootka Texts: Tales and Ethnological Narratives*, by Edward Sapir and Morris Swadesh," *Journal of American Folklore* 53:284-286.

1940d. "Review of *Race, Language and Culture*, by Franz Boas," *Tempo* 1:116-117.

1940e. "Review of *Handbook of American Indian Languages, Part 3*, ed. Franz Boas," *American Anthropologist* 42:329-331.

1940f. "Review of *Handbook of American Indian Languages, Part 3*, ed. Franz Boas," *Pacific Northwest Quarterly* 31:97-98.

1941a. "A Survey of Pacific Northwest Anthropological Research, 1930-1940," *Pacific Northwest Quarterly* 32:79-106.

1941b. "Racism and the Teacher," *University of Washington College of Education Record* 8:12-16.

1941c. "Review of *Race: Science and Politics*, by Ruth Benedict, and *The Economic Life of Primitive Peoples*, by M. J. Herskovits," *American Teacher* 25:30.

1942a. "Jewish Blood and Culture," in *Jews in a Gentile World*, eds. I. Graeber and S. H. Britt, pp. 38-55. New York: Macmillan.

1942b. "Review of *The Cheyenne Way*, by K. N. Llewellyn and E. A. Hoebel," *Pacific Northwest Quarterly* 33:223-225.

1943. "Anthropology's Major Contributions at the Present Turn of History," in *Victory for What?* Pp. 53-56. Seattle: University of Washington Bookstore.

1944a. "The Future of Colonies and Dependencies," *Washington Alumnus* 33:16-17.

1944b. "Our High School Libraries and Racism," *University of Washington College of Education Record* 11:22-27. (Reprinted by Bureau for Intercultural Education, New York, 1945.)

1945a. *Kalapuya Texts*. University of Washington Publications in Anthropology 11, 1-394. Seattle: University of Washington Press.

1945b. Letter in The Classification of Jewish Immigrants. *YIVO*:29-32.

1946a. "An Anthropological View of Colonial and Race Questions," in *If Men Want Peace: The Mandates of World Order*, eds. J. B. Harrison, L. A. Mander, and N. H. Engle, pp. 97-111. New York: Macmillan.

1946b. "An International Auxiliary Language," *World Affairs* 109:44-48.

1946c. "The Negro People of the United States," *Washington Alumnus,* 36:19-20.

1946d. "Racism: A Program for Action," American Council on Race Relations, Pacific Coast Clearing House Release No. 8, pp. 1-8.

1947a. (with Bernhard J. Stern) *Outline of Anthropology*. New York: Barnes and Noble.

1947b. "Mental Hygiene, Anthropology and Racism," *Mental Health Today* 6:3-5.

1947c. "Cultures in the Present World Crisis," *Human Relations* 1:228-239.

1947d. "Review of *The Theory of Human Culture*, by J. Feibleman," *Interim* 3:44-45.

1947e. "Review of *Indians of the Pacific Northwest*, by Ruth Underhill," *University of Washington College of Education Record* 13:64.

1948a. "Further Comments on Evolutionism in Cultural Anthropology," *American Anthropologist* 50:564-568.

1948b. "Sense and Nonsense About Race," Proceedings of the Institute on Cultural Factors in Social Work, pp. 4-9. Portland, Ore.: Council of Social Agencies.

1948c. "Review of *When Peoples Meet*, rev. ed., eds. A. Locke and B. J. Stern," *Humanist* 8:131-132.

1948d. "Review of *A History of the Jews*, by S. Grayzel," *Annals of the American Academy of Political and Social Science* 255: 210.

1949a. "Mental Health of the Pacific Northwest Indians," *Mental Health Today* 8: 6-18.

1949b. "Review of *An Analysis of Coeur d'Alene Indian Myths*, by Gladys Reichard," *American Anthropologist* 51:308-309.

1949c. "Review of *An Analysis of Coeur d'Alene Indian Myths*, by Gladys Reichard," *Review of Religion* 13:425-426.

1949d. "Review of *In Search of a Lost People: The Old and the New Poland*, by J. Tenenbaum," *Annals of the American Academy of Political and Social Science* 263: 225-226.

1949e. "Origins of These Stories," in *When Coyote Walked the Earth, Indian Tales of the Pacific Northwest*, ed. Corinne Running, pp. 69-71. New York: Holt.

1949f. "Letter on Supplementary Survey Reviews," *American Anthropologist* 51:529.

1950a. "Foreword," in *The Snoqualmie-Duwamish Dialects of Puget Sound Coast Salish*, by C. E. Tweddell. Melville Jacobs, ed., pp. iii. University of Washington Publications in Anthropology 12, 1-78. Seattle: University of Washington Press.

1950b. "Review of *The Earth is the Lord's: The Inner World of the Jew in East Europe*, by A. J. Heschel," *Annals of the American Academy of Political and Social Science* 270:197.

1950c. "Review of *YIVO Annual of Jewish Social Science*, Vol. 4, Yiddish Scientific Institute, 1949," *Annals of the American Academy of Political and Social Science* 270:197-198.

1950d. "Review of *Jerusalem*, by T. Weiss-Rosmarin," *Annals of the American Academy of Political and Social Science* 272:296.

1951a. "Review of *Israel Revisited*, by R. McGill," *Annals of the American Academy of Political and Social Science* 273:300.

1951b. "Review of *The Hebrew Impact on Western Civilization*, ed. D. D. Runes," *Annals of the American Academy of Political and Social Science* 275:206.

1952a. "Psychological Inferences from a Chinook Myth," *Journal of American Folklore* 65:121-137.

1952b. (with Bernhard J. Stern) *General Anthropology*, second and rev. ed. New York: Barnes and Noble. (First ed. publ. in 1947 as *Outline of Anthropology*.)

1952c. "Review of *A Social and Religious History of the Jews*, by S. W. Baron," *Annals of the American Academy of Political and Social Science* 281:237-238.

1952d. "Review of *A Partisan History of Judaism*, by Elmer Berger," *Annals of the American Academy of Political and Social Science* 283:235.

1952e. "Review of *Navaho Grammar*, by Gladys Reichard," *Pacific Northwest Quarterly* 43: 306-307.

1953a. "Review of *Gambling Among the Yakima*, by G. R. Desmond," *American Anthropologist* 55:750.

1953b. "Review of *Ancient Judaism*, by Max Weber," *Annals of the American Academy of Political and Social Science* 286: 242-243.

1954a. "The Areal Spread of Sound Features in the Languages North of California," in *Papers from the Symposium on American Indian Linguistics*. University of California Publications in Linguistics 10, 46-56.

1954b. "Review of *The Makah Indians: A Study of an Indian Tribe in Modern American Society*, by Elizabeth Colson," *Pacific Northwest Quarterly* 45:36-37.

1955a. "A Few Observations on the World View of the Clackamas Chinook Indians," *Journal of American Folklore* 68:283-289.

1955b. "Review of *Struggle for Tomorrow: Modern Political Ideologies of the Jewish People*, eds. B. J. Vlavianos and Feliks Gross," *Annals of the American Academy of Political and Social Science* 297:159-160.

1956. "Review of *The Coast Salish of British Columbia*, by Homer G. Barnett," *Oregon Historical Quarterly* 57:179-180.

1957a. "Language Families and Important Written Languages," in *Encyclopedia Britannica World Atlas*. Plate 16.

1957b. "Titles in an Oral Literature," *Journal of American Folklore* 70:157-172.

1957c. "Review of *Native Accounts of Nootka Ethnography*, by Edward Sapir and Morris Swadesh," *Journal of American Folklore* 70:287-288.

1957d. "Review of *Mythology and Values, An Analysis of Navaho Chantway Myths*, by Katherine Spencer," *Midwest Folklore* 7:240-242.

1958a. *Clackamas Chinook Texts, Part 1*. Indiana University Research Center in Anthropology, Folklore, and Linguistics Publications 8. Bloomington: Indiana University.

1958b. "The Romantic Role of Older Women in a Culture of the Pacific Northwest Coast," *Kroeber Anthropological Society Papers* 18:79-85.

1959a. *The Content and Style of an Oral Literature: Clackamas Chinook Myths and Tales*. Chicago: University of Chicago Press.

1959b. *Clackamas Chinook Texts, Part 2*. Indiana University Research Center in Anthropology, Folklore, and Linguistics 11. Bloomington: Indiana University.

1959c. "Foreword," in *Nehalem Tillamook Tales*, by Elizabeth D. Jacobs. Melville Jacobs, ed., pp. iii-iv. University of Oregon Monographs: Studies in Anthropology 5. Eugene: University of Oregon Books.

1959d. "Folklore," in *The Anthropology of Franz Boas*, ed. Walter Goldschmidt, pp. 119-138. American Anthropological Association, Memoir 89.

1959e. "Review of *Morphology of the Folktale*, by Vladimir Propp," *Journal of American Folklore* 72:195-196.

1959f. "Review of *Indians and Other Americans*, by Harold E. Fey and D'Arcy McNickle," *Pacific Northwest Quarterly* 50:161-162.

1959g. "Review of *From Ape to Angel*, by H. R. Hays," *Isis* 50:501-502.

1960a. *The People Are Coming Soon: Analyses of Clackamas Chinook Myths and Tales*. Seattle: University of Washington Press.

1960b. "Thoughts on Methodology for Comprehension of an Oral Literature," in *Selected Papers of the Fifth International Congress of Anthropological and Ethnological Sciences*, ed. Anthony F. C. Wallace, pp. 123-129. Philadelphia: University of Pennsylvania Press.

1960c. "Humor and Social Structure in an Oral Literature," in *Culture in History: Essays in Honor of Paul Radin*, ed. Stanley Diamond, pp. 181-189. New York: Columbia University Press.

1960d. "Review of *Indian Portraits of the Pacific Northwest: Thirty of the Principal Tribes*, by George M. Cochran," *Pacific Northwest Quarterly* 51:85.

1960e. "Review of *The Indians of British Columbia: A Study of Contemporary Social Adjustment*, by H. B. Hawthorn, C. S. Belshaw, and S. M. Jamieson," *Oregon Historical Quarterly* 61:353-354.

1961a. "Review of *Indian Legends of Canada*, by Ella E. Clark," *Pacific Northwest Quarterly* 52:117.

1961b. "Review of *The House of the Seven Brothers: Trees, Roots and Branches of the House of Ste-tee-thlum*, by Mary A. Lambert," *Pacific Northwest Quarterly* 52:163.

1961c. "Review of *Seeking Life*, by Vera Laski," *Western Folklore* 20:132-133.

1961d. "Review of *The Men Called Master: The Cahuilla Indians*, by Harry C. James," *Western Folklore* 20:134-135.

1961e. "Review of *American Folklore*, by Richard M. Dorson," *Pacific Northwest Quarterly* 52:71-72.

1962a. "The Fate of Indian Oral Literatures in Oregon," *Northwest Review* 5:90-99.

1962b. "Areal Descriptions in Anthropology," *Pacific Northwest Quarterly* 53:156-158.

1962c. "Review of *Legends of the Mighty Sioux*, compiled by workers of the South Dakota Writers' Project, Works Project Administration," *Western Folklore* 21:206-207.

1963. "Comments on 'Sociopsychological Analysis of Folklore,' by John L. Fischer," *Current Anthropology* 4:277-279.

1964a. *Pattern in Cultural Anthropology*. Homewood, Ill.: Dorsey Press.

1964b. "Indications of Mental Illness Among Pre-Contact Indians of the Northwest States," *Pacific Northwest Quarterly* 55: 49-54.

1964c. "Review of *Indian and Eskimo Artifacts of North America*, by Charles Miles," *Pacific Northwest Quarterly* 55:188.

1964d. "Review of *Sepass Poems: The Songs of Y-Ail-Mihth*, recorded by Eloise Street," *Pacific Northwest Quarterly* 55:89-90.

1965. "Review of *The Sioux: Life and Customs of a Warrior Society*, by Royal B. Hassrick," *Western Folklore* 24:214.

1966a. "A Look Ahead in Oral Literature Research," *Journal of American Folklore* 79:413-427.

1966b. "Foreword," in *The Anthropologist Looks at Myth*, ed. John Greenway, pp. vii-viii. Publications of the American Folklore Society, Bibliographic and Special Series, 17. Austin: University of Texas Press.

1966c. "Report of the Delegate to the American Council of Learned Societies," *Journal of American Folklore Supplement*, Annual Report of the American Folklore Society, pp. 22-23.

1966d. "Review of *Letters from Edward Sapir to Robert H. Lowie*," *Pacific Northwest Quarterly* 57:38.

1966e. "Review of *War Chief Joseph*, by H. A. Howard and D. L. McGrath," *Western Folklore* 25:214.

1966. (ed-comp.) special issue of the *Journal of American Folklore* 79 (311), The Anthropologist Looks at Myth.

1967a. "Our Knowledge of Pacific Northwest Indian Folklores," *Northwest Folklore* 2: 14-21.

1967b. "Report of the Delegate to the American Council of Learned Societies," *Journal of American Folklore Supplement*, Annual Report of the American Folklore Society, p. 31.

1967c. "Review of *Indian Lives and Legends*, by Mildred V. Thornton," *Pacific Northwest Quarterly* 58:211.

1968. "An Historical Event Text from a Galice Athabaskan in Southwestern Oregon," *International Journal of American Linguistics* 34:183-191.

1970a. "Resources in Kalapuyan Languages," *International Journal of American Linguistics* 36:67.

1970b. "Review of *An Introduction to American Folklore*, ed. Tristram Potter Coffin," *American Anthropologist* 72:434-435.

1971a. "Review of *Morphology of the Folktale*, by V. Propp," *American Anthropologist* 73:897-898.

1971b. "Review of *American Indian Periodicals in the Princeton University Library: A Preliminary List*, by Alfred L. Bush and Robert S. Fraser," *Pacific Northwest Quarterly* 62:158.

1972. "Areal Spread of Indian Oral Genre Features in the Northwest States," *Journal of the Folklore Institute* 9:10-17.

Toward a Theory and Method of
Oral Literature Research

1

Oral Literature

Jacobs favored a radical departure from the approaches to oral literature current in the 1950s and 1960s. The following chapter is reprinted from *Pattern in Cultural Anthropology* (1964, 319-39), a college textbook designed by Jacobs as "an effort to present an orientation rather than a patchwork survey" (p. v). To save space, we omitted the final sections of this chapter: Prose Versus Poetry, Aesthetic Evaluation of Oral Literature, and Suggestions for Further Reading. This overview serves as an excellent orientation to Jacobs's approach to theory and method in oral literature research. Many of the ideas presented here are further developed in the following selections on method and theory.

Introduction

Fragments of plot and motif content in myth and tale recitals, penned by scribes and authors and doubtless, in many respects, different from oral versions offered to live audiences, are available from a few wealthy civilizations such as China, India, Mesopotamia, Egypt, Greece, and Rome, in some instances for as much as two millennia before the Christian era. But not one oral literature, whether from ancient cultures or modern food-gatherers and other nonliterate peoples, is represented in a large and reliable sample of its content until about the 1880s. If little content expressed in perhaps thousands of orally transmitted literatures survives, just about nothing remains of their features of style before the 1880s because missionaries, travelers, and other scribes embellished and censored without concern for content and canons imbedded in spoken originals. Until later decades of the nineteenth century, literate people of western civilization regarded dramatic recitals, orations, rituals, or prayers by unlettered elders of less wealthy and, therefore, less glamorous civilizations as worthy of recording only if fitted out in the style of written Euro-American literature of the time.

Today, faithful written and tape records of stylized verbal expressions, together with a fairly wide range of recorded recitals in each culture, offer insufficient source materials for development of a structure of oral literature theory, although they permit its initiation. Such a structure will exhibit features both of content and style, fabrics which they display, probable causes of their origin and maintenance, and ways in which they operated in the lives of their recitalists, audiences, and society.

Professional folklorists, so-called, of the past eighty or more years interested themselves in setting up new standards of accuracy in recording and sampling. They stressed analysis into plots and macrosegments termed "motifs." They also dedicated themselves to archiving and cross-indexing such materials. And they studied, with devotion worthy of a more revealing pursuit, regional and world distribution of their plots and motifs, the latter largely in order to attempt deductions about centers of origin and routes of dissemination. They were completely accepting of the merit of such historical reconstructionist ventures and never questioned the meagerness of contribution which historicism of that kind could make to a system of theory about oral literatures. But they were not really interested in a scientific theory about any one or all of the verbal arts. They were interested in history or, rather, historical perspectives in folklore, and in problems such as discovery of paths and times of diffusion of tales and components of tales from the Middle East or India. This is, in unfair brevity, the historico-geographical "school" of folklore. Its scholarship has already provided perhaps millions of field notebook pages of accurately recorded tale texts, mostly from modern European raconteurs but also from some nonwestern peoples. Hundreds of monographs and maybe thousands of papers, in a variety of folklore and other scholarly journals, set forth historico-geographical studies that have been made.

In spite of such monumental and, in many respects, admirable production, a structure of scientific theory, about content, forms, and processes in the world's oral dramatic literatures and other oral arts has progressed little farther than it had developed in the 1880s. So little theoretical advance is curious in the light of universal fascination in myths and folktales and in the numbers of cautious scholars who have been collecting and examining them. Surely, eighty years and thousands of devoted field workers and students might have produced something more than literal reports, plot, tale type and motif catalogs, stacks of maps, and guesses about routes of plot and motif borrowing. Unlike the minuscule amounts of effort applied to study of ethnomusicology, non-western dance, and humor, numbers of admirably painstaking scholars did work in folklore. They labored in an era of great progress in so-called "hard" and "behavioral" sciences. But it appears that since most of them were trained in history, languages, and literature, they rarely became acquainted with developments of method and theory in more advanced fields of scientific inquiry. They, were essentially perspiring collectors, drudging archivists, and aspiring historians, not scientists in pursuit of adequately validated statements designed to fit into a theoretical system. The devastating thought is that the motifs, plots, and tale types which interested them had extremely little to do with a developing scientific theory about dramatic oral literature. Meaningless macrosegments of content were the be-all and end-all of almost one century's specialists in folklorist researches. Oral literature is, then, backward as a science, although it possesses extraordinary amounts of descriptive, catalog, and comparative items. Their utility for construction and validation of a system of theory about oral literature is no longer a moot question. There is no doubt that they are largely waste effort. Not much is known about nonwestern oratory, rituals, and other oral art forms. A majority of historico-geographical folklorists had little interest in them.

To be sure, a number of theories, spun during the past hundred years, have purported to account for ultimate origins of oral literature plots, themes, motifs, tale types, and actors. Historico-geographical folklorists maintained a nodding acquaintanceship with these theories, occasionally cited and criticized them graciously, but in effect ignored them. Let us comment about them briefly after a glance at anthropological folklorists who valiantly supplemented, in researches among nonliterate peoples, the European folklorists' accumulations, catalogs, and maps.

Anthropological Folklore

After the 1860s and until about 1940, numbers of anthropologists and linguists, principally Americans, who were conducting field studies among nonwestern peoples, recorded folktales. They perceived that texts recorded in a precise transcription of sounds of a nonwestern language were not only required in scientific linguistics but produced superior results, in most instances, for purposes of folkloristic studies. There are over one hundred published volumes of such texts and many more are still unpublished notebooks. Well over half of them are from a small percentage of the groups of American Indians north of Mexico, a circumstance which arises from leadership given in such researches after the 1890s by Columbia University's Professor Boas. Most nonwestern language groups, thousands to be sure, in Asia, Oceania, Africa, and Latin America are wretchedly, or not at all, represented in this form. Recordings made directly from interpreters who were able to use English, Spanish, or other European languages are many for Indian groups north of the Rio Grande and spare for most other parts of the world.

Little of all such data gathering, in nonwestern language text-with-translation or in a European language through interpreters, offers the richness in alternate versions which characterizes notebooks and publications of historico-geographical workers in their field collections among European storytellers. Alternate versions are potentially important but enervatingly time consuming for field workers. And such versions have slight use in a vacuum of theory, regarding processes of origin, maintenance, remodeling, and the designing of projective expressions which relieve tensions and conflicting sentiments.

Oral literature collections by anthropologists and linguists usually offer admirably recorded single versions of only an extremely small percentage of a repertoire of myths and tales. In most instances, the fate of work done by such field workers is that it yielded far too small a sampling for purposes of advancing oral literature theory.

Almost all collectors ceased their field effort after recording and translating dictated words. They did not know what else they ought to do. After all, they faithfully recorded a recital itself and they supposed that their work as collectors was then done. During a century, no field collector appears to have operated with a kit of tentative hypotheses which required elaborate question and answer follow-up to elicit correlated matters in a society and culture. Questions later put to interpreters were usually linguistic and sometimes, more recently, on Freudian matters, but did not go far toward supplying answers which helped in the progress of oral literature knowledge.

The most dedicated and precise field collecting is accompanied by an aura of ineffectuality when it is not guided by questions answers to which may shed light on sociocultural and psychological correlates of recitals. Hundreds of linguists, anthropologists, and Europe-oriented folklorists recorded tale dictations with an exactitude and integrity which, if oral literature had possessed a system of theory, might have granted spectacular scientific returns. As it is, most collections are small, lack variants and, above all, are devoid of relevant commentary elicited in question and answer follow-up. The key to scientific progress is in use of judgment, as well as resources of theory during interrogation of informants and interpreters.

Assessment of what has been achieved, therefore, amounts principally, to the following. Anthropological folklore discovered—a most important finding—that oral literatures, whether collected among economically backward food-gatherers or in any other kinds of societies, possessed features of content and form which warrant acceptance of merit and suggest intensive studies of new kinds. Complexities which require unraveling probably exceed those which scientific linguists have been exposing in the world's nonwestern language structures. Features of content and form were often manipulated with excellence, projected with subtlety and imagination, and responded to with critical and mature understanding. Accumulation of indications of such kinds may have provided one of the notable achievements of the past century's work in behavioral sciences. It serves no purpose to assert, nor is it longer plausible, that there was something distinctively primitive, in the sense of simple or inferior, about any, or all oral literatures. Affirmations of such a kind are patently defensive mechanisms which operate to bolster the often diminishing self-regard of protagonists of so-called "higher civilizations."

Folklore's Theory Fringe

Few active field collectors have offered hypotheses regarding origins of oral literature content. Contributors of such theories were principally students who examined Classical Mediterranean and European mythologies and reports published by modern field workers. Historical and literary scholars, that is to say, amateurish observers whose perceptions were unaffected by field research experiences, originated most of the speculations regarding ultimate beginnings of oral literature expressive content. From the point of view of scientific method, results of their efforts have been as petty as the writings of most persons who brashly characterized themselves as chemists and had never passed over the threshold of a chemistry laboratory. It is difficult to find an area of scientific inquiry in which publishing houses have printed so much presumptuous guesswork couched in elegant and lyrical measures or so many postulates that have been unusable for purposes of advancing knowledge. Science fiction authors have very likely offered more constructive stimulation to scientists than have all the psychoanalytic and literary bibliophiles who have presumed to tell a large reading public about the nature of mythology and folklore. In addition, a culture-hungry public which would enjoy some enlightenment about folklores the world over finds little in even the best university and large city bookstores which serves a function other than to mislead them.

A few nineteenth-century scholars proposed that folklore plots and motifs originated in one or another impressively luxurious center such as the Near East or India. They indicated that the rest of humanity, less favored by wealth, slavery, military power, and temple plazas with great stone structures gradually accepted, by a process of borrowing, plots, motifs, and tale types supposedly spawned in environments of enchanting urban living, dancing girls, priestly processions, mysterious rituals, earth goddesses, and commerce. One might almost come to the conclusion that plots, motifs, and tale types traveled arm in arm with merchants transporting herbs, cosmetic ointments, spices, and dyes, and were greeted with gusto by heathen bards in many Old World regions.

Satisfactory reasons for the literary seminality of a certain few homelands were never forthcoming. Indeed, publications of oral literatures from other regions, especially from North American Indian districts, presently showed that every country was arrestingly creative in oral literature content, style too, although Pan-East Indian diffusionists appear not to have concerned themselves with what, to them, were very likely only lowlier kinds of creatures, savages, and barbarians. Nor were they often interested in items of folklore content which were found in the Americas but not in the Old World. Spreadings of features of content from the wealthiest Old World centers and from economically least impressive districts, that is, from areas of food-gatherers, remain to be assessed, a task not yet possible because field reports are too uneven.

Some decades ago, a phalanx of writers argued that "primitive peoples," a term which everyone then employed without a quiver of misgiving, projected human and zoomorphic figures into phenomena of nature such as sun, moon, stars, meteors, eclipses, storms, tides, floods, and forest conflagrations, and presently wove plots about these figures and occasions. Such a naturistic theory of origin of content assumed folklorists' ability to speculate plausibly about first causes of components of content which thousands of persons had subsequently transmitted and remodeled during long periods. But neither proof nor disproof of naturistic origin was ever possible for a single actor personality, social relationship, or other expressive feature. Probably, the widespread stylistic trait in oral literatures which is an explanatory accounting for heavenly bodies persuaded protagonists of the theory that they were on the right track. A naturistic theory of origins soon lost support because it patently violated principles of scientific evidence and it seemed improbable to most scholars whatever their canons of thinking. Few active field workers were able to regard it seriously at any time. Today, it is also evident that plot, tale type, and motif origins are only the smallest part of the business of a scientific theoretical structure for oral literatures.

Members of the early twentieth century group of Freudian sectarians, perhaps only one of whom, Dr. Geza Roheim, entered upon nonwestern researches which provided oral literature from field sources, also engaged in scholarly disquisitions upon ultimate beginnings of folklore content. Many of these psychoanalytic writers had humanistic kinds of education in European gymnasia and universities and, therefore, were familiar with Greco-Roman mythology and religion. These theoreticians proposed that expressive items originated—once again the nineteenth century compulsion to fixate upon beginnings—in much the manner in which dreams bubble through from unconscious wellsprings into conscious awareness. Latent drives and conflicts, with an especial frequency of feelings around Oedipal situations, were disguised by a variety of distortional mechanisms such as rationalization and displacement. Nevertheless, manifest dream and myth content may be analyzed to reveal mechanisms and originating drives. Content in both dreams and myths comprised manifest expressions of latent feelings and conflicts. Again, proof or disproof of merits of such generic theorization about origins, as well as evidences for processes of maintenance and remodeling of content down through the ages, cannot be obtained for items which are more than a generation old. Most oral literature material is, of course, of indeterminable antiquity. A system of theory regarding which relevant observations and evidences cannot be provided is of small value unless its plausibility is superior to any other theoretical system. Obviously, validation or disproof of statements of the theory may be expected for mechanisms of dream work. But oral literature displays distinctive content, far more numerous or elaborate stylizations, a wider range of religious and other social functions, maybe some special mechanisms, and doubtless a great deal more than dream portrayals, for all its surface similarity to them—which Freudian writers rightly perceived. Many myths of nonwestern peoples do exhibit arrestingly dreamlike characteristics.

A group of literary, historical, and psychoanalytic scholars, with virtually no allies who conducted folkloristic field researches, have made a remarkable impact not upon workers of scientific bent but upon mid twentieth-century literary critics, principally in that spirited sect of facile arbiters known as the New Critics. Their deities or father figures include the Zurich psychoanalyst C. G. Jung, the famous and prolific protagonist of the long discredited nineteenth-century form of the comparative method applied to religion, magic, and folklore, Sir James G. Frazer, and some recent essayists and writers in literature itself. The group have urged that myth plots, and some of them have thought principally about Greco-Roman mythology, might be traced, if data were available, to rites practiced by earlier peoples. This ritual-to-myth evolution-oriented theory, of course, explains nothing about origins of rites, reasons for processes in embroidery and remodeling of plots around them, or causes for their retention. Most myths and tales recorded in text and translation from nonwestern peoples exhibit no signs if superficially read, and no indications if deftly probed, of ritual origins. The theory patently tells little or nothing about origins and subsequent fashionings of actor depictions, social relationships, humor, features of world view, ethical items, or other components of oral literature collections. The theory asserts nothing about the many features of style in each such collection, a curious omission in a portfolio of postulates which comprise the faith of the New Critics whose alleged interest in close analysis of style in verbal arts of western civilization is almost their most distinctive attribute. The theory offers no statements about functioning of an oral literature in a people's daily conversations or in their formal myth recitals. One gets an uneasy impression that protagonists of ritual-to-myth theory are little interested in any myths except creation and other highly esoteric or dreamlike materials. But when an anthropological folklorist ill-advisedly permits himself to be drawn into a discussion of their theory with them, they seem impelled to be severely consistent with the theology of their cult, to bow reverently in the direction of Frazer (who stimulates few genuflections among scientists), and to insist that all folkloristic data must be assumed to constitute a kind of detritus laid down long ago by rituals of ancestral people. Nineteenth-century kinds of unverbalized premises and habits of mind are obvious in the cult: evolutionary stages for which evidences are unobtainable, survivals which cannot be demonstrated, disinterest in minutiae of behavior, fixation upon creation myths, and failure to attend to patternings and stylizations. In spite of wholly anachronistic premises of the theory, thousands of literature professors who are unacquainted with methodological or other advances in the behavioral sciences since the Spanish-American or Boer Wars are lecturing today in favorable terms about an unproven, unprovable, and wholly improbable doctrine. It itself appears to offer a solitary available example of a ritual-to-myth process.

The same literary rank and file have managed to intertwine a pseudo-psychological premise with their ritual origin surmise. The splinter sect of Freudians created by C. G. Jung a half century ago later identified a limited number of themes or plots, so-called "archetypes," which supposedly received development at the hands of folklore recitalists everywhere. The postulate is that native raconteurs just could not resist formulating out of dark racial-feeling fabrics. They got started by some kind of biological jet propulsion and one after another archetypal plot poured out of them. These archetypal plots or themes have fastened, like a series of polyps on vocal cords, upon the heartstrings[1] of great numbers of contemporary specialists in literature criticism. Some of the cultist professors are confident, although they are acquainted principally with Old World myths, that the properly centered interest of folkloristic theory, whether it apply to Eskimos,

Fuegians, Ilocanos, Zuñis, or Zulus, is the discovery of such archetypal elements, even as the probing revelation of them is the virtuous professional obligation of a critic who subjects novels or poetry to close content analysis. The critic then examines how an author, or a raconteur in the instance of an oral art, has manipulated his archetypal themes. Close analysis is, of course, admirable, if that which is analyzed out is not principally, inevitably, and invariably one of Dr. Jung's archetypal social relationship conflicts with its early hypothetical ritual expression in some pre-Greco-Roman or other vanished tribal groups, preferably indeed groups which basked in the silvery light of Bachofen's matriarchate. Scientific workers in anthropology long ago relegated that state of feminine dominance to the scrap heap of bad guesses, but not so the New Critics. In spite of the awesome irresponsibility and absurdity of the New Critics' theology and their pathetic loyalties to Bachofen, Frazer, Jung, and a cluster of living idols, their support of close analysis stands as a valuable contribution. Ritual-myth and archetypal premises, Jung, and other deities of the New Critics receive no acceptance in scientific quarters.

When Boas, that most assiduous collector of precisely recorded anthropological folklore, suggested somewhat weakly about forty-five years ago that a folklore collection mirrored the life of a people who had expressed it, he meant only that ethnographic items of technology, economy, social organization, and religion sometimes received verbalization in myth and tale recitals [(Boas 1916)—Eds.]. He never sought an answer to an important question why some groups projected a great amount of their sociocultural life into myth recitals and other groups projected exceedingly little of it. He observed that there were such differences in amounts of what was mirrored, but he was unable to explain why the differences occurred. Today, a social scientist might state simply that the contrasts appear to be effects of multiple causes. In certain instances, it is a matter of different literary styles rather than something on a level of varying kinds and quantities of content expressed, although items of content functioned as stylistic features. More of this later.

Apart from a rigorous professional field worker such as Boas, dabblers in theorems about origin of content presented statements to which cross-cultural evidence could not be applied in validation or criticism. Unfortunately, Boas resembled others in leaving most features of content, style, and connected sociocultural phenomena untouched by theory. A grievous consequence for oral literature in the 1960s is its spare system of scientific hypotheses, one which is almost embryonic by contrast with growth achieved in other specialist fields in the behavioral sciences. Oral literature theory now contains principally evidences about the fact of dissemination of content, and it had mountains of evidences of that kind fifty or more years ago, provided both by careful European workers on folklores of Old World peoples and by Boas and his followers in their work on nonwestern oral arts. There are few correlated evidences or even thinly-supported statements about processes of any kind in oral literature creativity, maintenance, and functioning. In other words, 150 years after pioneering by the Grimm brothers in recording European fairy tales, a theory of oral literature content and style has barely begun to be fashioned.

However, a group of mechanisms limned by Freudians and called by now familiar terms such as "projection" and "displacement" can be salvaged from the grandiose structure of psychoanalytic theory to become central components of a special theory for oral literatures. These mechanisms can be set beside the process of dissemination. In fact, diffusion requires a vast amount of reexamination in order to determine what different kinds of processes are lumped clumsily, in fact concealed, under the gross heading.

Content Analysis

Within the past century chemistry, zoology, linguistics and other fields of inquiry were released to forge ahead, in some respects with sensational rapidity, toward systems of mature scientific theory after judicious appraisals and selections of their most likely minimal units and classes of units had been made. Elements and, later, the isotopes of elements in chemistry; chromosomes and, then, genes in zoology; phonemes, allophones, and morphemes in linguistics have so far served reliably and radiantly as hypothetical conceptual units which, in the current state of knowledge of each such field, permit devising many statements regarding structuring, process, and change.

Composites such as tale types, plots, and motifs which professional historico-geographical folklorists long cited, cataloged, and reified, paralyzed if they did not effect a garroting of interest in process other than who borrowed what and when.[2] The end product has been a kind of immature historicism, not a structure of theory about content and style, certainly not a step toward a mature system of theory about oral literature. Sound historians venture to locate major and minor factors, psychological and otherwise, which account for events they record. Legitimate scientific curiosity about causes, development, and maintenance of oral literature content was left to simplifications and guesswork by dithyrambic origin hunters who lacked awareness of scientific method and whose conceptual units of tale types and motifs were much too bulky. Before 1930, perhaps only one folklorist, Vladimir Propp, had stipulated that motifs, plots, and tale types were not the segments of folklore recitals with which to conduct scholarly researches. He failed to offer sets of superior units for content analysis, although, in a remarkable study of the structure of Russian fairy tales, he anticipated a modern kind of analysis of one aspect of oral literature style. He was able to do this because of his discovery of one class of smaller content units which had stylistic functions. His units were successive scenes in a fairy "play" and he called the scenes, curiously, "functions" [(Propp 1958)—Eds.]. Alan Dundes calls them "motifemes" [(Dundes 1964)—Eds.].

The avenue leading to selection of proper segments or units of content is indicated only upon discovery of what was expressed in an oral literature. For example, it is surprising that historico-geographical scholars perhaps never disclosed the many indications that oral literatures phrased and copied from neighboring literatures items that concerned social relationships, behaviors, and feelings which the borrowing sociocultural system failed to handle comfortably. Where there are written literatures, authors evidently select for writing out and printing discussions of relationships, personality types, values, and other interests concerning which they and their society are bothered: these are matters which are not otherwise customarily disposed of, adjusted, or tidied up with an extreme of efficiency in sociocultural life. In Western culture, script writers and directors place on the movie screen relationships, personalities, and values about war, love, and loneliness which represent infelicitous areas of contemporary life. That which receives projection onto the screen, for purposes of ventilation and emotional release, is often deeply disturbing. In every modern industrial nation, many different things are so projected onto printed pages in novels, short stories, or poetry, into newspaper cartoons, joke forms and other kinds of humor, song lyrics, and phrases of rites and rituals. Myth and tale screens of nonliterate peoples functioned in analogous ways. The basic processes, which appear in emotional needs and conflicts and their resolution by way of projection, displacement, identification, and ventilation, are universal.

The variety of materials which have been placed in many guises on oral literature screens, that is, which were expressed in oral literature recitals, require segmentation and classification. Plot, tale type, and motif concepts of folklore scholars have long impeded such classification because each encloses voluminous content of expressive significance. "Motifemes" are also overloaded with content. Such content must be further sliced into clear-cut small units and groupings of units that are meaningful because they point to processes that explicate oral literature behavior. Each such unit, and each such set of units, can then be shown in its connections with stresses and discomforts in the social system. A scientific attack upon processes which determined structurings, complexities, and vagaries in millions of myths and tales the world over must commence with the most promising expressive units and classes of units, those which can be tied in not with the entirety of a society and culture as in the Boasian mirror reflection theory but with sectors of sociocultural life which operated unsatisfactorily for a people who recited, discussed, changed, and listened.

Main classes of items of content included a great range of social relationships, usually hundreds of actor personalities, humor, cosmology, and world view, religion, value ideals, and almost always some interspersed songs. Each of these classes, and others too, has to be arranged in subclasses. Literary readers are herewith asked to note that archetypal themes do not comprise an employable class or subclass of content items, if for no other reason than that each such Jungian agglomerate is ridiculously massive. It is much too complex for possible scientific handling.

Each principal class of expressive content receives brief comment in paragraphs which follow.

Almost all myths or tales, other oral arts too, cited one or several types of *social relationship*, each of which may receive further subdivision in terms of behaviors and feelings expressed in the relationship. A tentative list of relationships includes these: premarital maneuvers; marital (monogamous, polygamous, polyandrous; deserted mate; tricked mate); incestuous; parent-child; siblings; leader-people; uncle or aunt-child; kidnapper-child; religious functionary-people; ogre or ogress-people; upper class-lower class; freeman-slave; in-laws-people; comrades; community-community; elder-people. Eliciting of full ethnographic background is a requirement for comprehension of these relationships and reasons for their placement on an oral literature screen.

Unlike other oral arts, a corpus of myths and tales contained a small group of principal male, another small group of principal female *actor personalities.* Their labels and lineaments as animal, bird, flower, fish, ogre, or other kinds of creatures served in various ways which included expression of animistic supernaturals, totemic animal ancestors, and so on. Basically all of them were human or humanlike. Human thinking, feeling, and relationships were projected into each of them. Each of these principal actors might appear in two or three to a dozen or dozens of myths. Community perception of the personality of each such actor constituted a composite of that actor's behaviors in all myths or other recital forms in which he appeared. Artistry in recital arose in selection and manipulation of facets of that perception. And a recitalist himself responded to year-round discussions within his community about such matters.

The small groups of leading actors were supplemented by many times as many minor actors, a few of whom sometimes constituted effective cartoon-like caricatures. Most of the minor actors were mere stage props. An oral literature field worker must elicit as extensive as possible commentary on every actor, leading or minor, in order to fill in otherwise unphrased perceptions of them had by a community. For it was just such unverbalized perceptions, the many things which a recitalist did not articulate but which his community understood very well, which contained fundamental features of an oral literature and which permit unraveling of its processes of expression of content. Verbal presentation by a recitalist offered only a stylized selection of actor personality traits. In analyses of expressive content, elicitation of commentary after a recital is methodologically almost more vital than the record of words of the recital itself, although the latter is indispensable, of course, especially, so for style analysis.

Actor personalities did not necessarily, or perhaps even often, mirror personality structures in a society. Oral literature actors tended to be composites, stereotypes, incongruous eccentrics, caricatures or projections, anthropomorphizations indeed, of value ideals. It is, therefore, impossible to deduce average and variability in a society's personalities from its oral literature's actor personalities. Only intensive ethnographic research permits assessment of similarities in oral literature actors and real people. Behavior and feelings in relationships exhibited by actors also were no mirror reflection of daily life. They appear to have comprised a selection of facets of life which stirred emotional turbulences. The realistic novel of modern western civilization is only to a degree realistically accurate in its depictions of how people live, feel, and relate to one another. But it is far closer to the reality of its society than any body of oral literature from nonliterate peoples. A decisive characteristic of content analysis is, then, determination of what was selected for placement on an oral literature screen, why it was chosen, and why everything else was passed over. Actually, much was.

The next principal feature of oral literature expressive content is *humor.* It was manifested in funny songs, comical vocal mannerisms, humorous features of physique and personality ascribed to actors, clownlike and other actors who were ipso facto amusing, laughable archaic verbal expressions and expletives, and funny situations. These and other types of humorous expressions punctuated myths and tales,[3] although not all of them. In some regions, myths were much more laughter-generating than tales. The opposite may have characterized other regions. Humor attached to expressive content which was itself incongruous, and it functioned stylistically to lighten tragedy, or ease long-continued tension. It, therefore, served for purposes of both content and style. …

Values, another long-neglected area of inquiry, except among religionists and philosophers, received oral literature expression in many ways. However, in some cultures very few myths or tales constituted centrally materials which were referred to or recited in order to offer sanction of an ethical principle. Myths might be wholly devoid of moralistic motivation. Or, ethical content in them might be no more than latent. Tales might constitute frank lessons in ethical precepts. An idealized actor personality might function as an example of an ethically most attractive person whose worth was highlighted by his tragic destiny—a kind of existentialist manipulation of plot.

The method of eliciting value ideals which received covert or manifest articulation is primarily by interrogation after a field recording. But significance of those values was in their relationship to a larger body of ethical statements and it can be gleaned only in ethnographic research. A principal task is to determine causes for expression of some values and omission of others from an oral literature. A starting hypothesis is that ideals which received inclusion, in one or another manner, in myths and tales dealt with those especially tense spots in maturation, relationships, and behavior which a sociocultural system failed to handle smoothly or to internalize fully in people. Expression of values in other oral arts very likely arose in the same way.

The next main kind of expressive content treats of portions of *world view*, that is cosmology, attitudes toward alien peoples and their sociocultural systems, and history and prehistory—pseudo history from the point of view of scientific historiography. Items of such kinds usually received expression incidentally in things actors said and did. After a dictation and its translation, a field worker ought to direct questions which draw out native commentary so as to fill in depictions of perceptions of the universe or multiverse, of space and time, propinquity and worth of alien peoples, supernaturals, deities, districts from which humans and other creatures came and to which they departed upon death, and so on. Partial expressions of world view which were latent or explicit in oral literature recitals require comparison with full perceptions yielded in ethnographic and other expressive analyses. Only then may it appear why certain components of world view were present in oral literatures and other items were left out.

At this point, a reader, a traditional folkloristic collector too, may be inclined to protest that oral literature research as conceived here is not primarily tale or other oral art collecting at all. It seems to be regarded as a special kind of ethnographic research. Orientation is in a direction of scientific theory rather than the folklorists' traditional data-gathering and historico-geographical perspectives. A reply to such a complaint is affirmative, except that in oral literature field research which is conducted as it ought to be, a great amount of sheer recording of myths, tales, and other oral art forms does go on. Folklorists and ethnographers have done little of the many-sided kind of collecting which is demanded, doubtless because they lacked time for it. And naturally ethnographers had self-assigned problems for which they had to harvest masses of evidence, without exhausting themselves in oral literature interests.

Let us continue with remaining kinds of content which received expression in oral literatures.

Religious content need not be discussed for those sociocultural systems where the topic can be subsumed under world view. On the other hand, it is prudent to suggest that items of religious ideology and behavior which were projected onto myth and tale screens constituted, in all likelihood, unconscious selections of precisely those portions of religion which stirred deepest concerns. Where rites do not appear to have tied in with a people's greatest anxieties, a myth and tale screen was almost a blank in its depiction or even citation of rites. A notable example of this phenomenon is in Boas' collections of myth texts from northerly Pacific Northwest Coast peoples. It is not possible to reconstruct ceremonies of those societies from their myths. On the other hand, animistic supernaturals constituted most provoking problems and such beings were cited endlessly.

In most myth and tale literatures, *musical compositions,* usually solo songs of actors, interrupted narration. Close analyses of words, vocal mannerisms, and purely musical features of songs may reveal significant things. In any case, each song must be accorded commentary in subsequent interrogations, and a folklorist does not have to be a practiced ethnomusicologist to ask most of the relevant questions. Incidental employment of myth or tale songs in everyday life has been common the world over. Their functions in such roles may be of interest, too. In instances where a field worker lacks a tape recorder and is doing research in the manner of most anthropological folklorists before 1950, that is, a phonetic-phonemic transcription in longhand, it is still indispensable that each song be recorded mechanically. If a tape recorder is unavailable, it is necessary to use some other mechanical device, maybe even old-fashioned equipment such as a wax cylinder Dictaphone. Songs can be dubbed onto tape for musicological analysis at a later time.

Style Analysis

No hard and fast line separates content and style because most classes of features of oral literature style constituted repetitive or other manipulations of items of expressive content.

Scientific linguists who have lately professed interest in literary style seem to be outraged at a suggestion that linguistic factors in oral literature styles were sometimes petty or negligible by contrast with nonlinguistic expressive devices. However, since not one linguist has offered a full-length stylistic analysis of a nonwestern oral literature, a preference by linguists for kinds of factors which they descry and highlight is intelligible, if not praiseworthy. Actually, large numbers of kinds of phonetic, morphological, and semantic items have functioned for stylistic purposes in nonwestern oral arts, a great many more of such linguistic items in some literatures than in others. An important theoretical point is that there were oral literature styles that were marked by few linguistic features which effected distinctive stylistic results.

Familiar linguistic devices included sound changes to express pity, diminutive size (e.g., *an eeedle bit* for *a little bit*), large size, and duration; duplication and reduplication to express them too (e.g., *big big* for *very big*). Classes of melodic contours or intonational patterns, also special vocal mannerisms and timbres, might be limited to myth or other stylized utterances.

Morphological devices which served stylistically were of the greatest variety, although only a tiny number may have received selection, so to speak, in any one oral art form. Obviously those which were selected and distinctive for literature style were classes of items whose members appeared in a literature in a frequency different from their frequency in everyday speech (e.g., *thee, thou, ye*, archaic pronominal vestigia in English). Moribund or archaic grammatical form classes or individual forms may have offered fairly frequent features of style. A grammatical feature which now may be familiar to many scientific linguists was a special tense for remote eras or the age of myths. Classes of special honorific or personifier morphemes might attach only to humanlike beings who were myth actors.

Unlike some oratory, myths might feature especially abbreviated discourse units, without subordinate phrases, such as successions of short staccato-like subject-predicate-object sentences. Syntactic features might display frequencies in oral literature performances different from their frequencies in informal discourse.

Classes of vocabulary and semantic features which were reserved for oral literature references and recitals were legion. There might be special names for myth actors, archaic morphemes for things and actions peculiar to myths, and almost always inventories of idiomatic phrase or sentence expressions (e.g., *once upon a time*) which belonged properly to myth recitals although referred to, in addition, in casual speech.

In brief, each oral art co-opted and assigned, in customary locations in individual myths or types of myths or in other oral arts, a limited array, sometimes an extremely small one, of purely linguistic traits from the great numbers of structural features and semantic units at hand in a language. Texts and translations of both recitals and conversations permit identification of linguistic traits which served in formal recital style.

Years hence, it may be possible to generalize warrantably that distinctive linguistic features of food-gatherers' recital styles (myths, tales, oratory, ceremonials) were much fewer than in some wealthier societies which included literature, governmental, juridical, and priestly specialists. Too little text-and-translation resource materials from wealthier and socially-stratified societies are available to warrant that deduction today. In any case, its service would not be so much a statement integral in a system of theory as a reminder to ascertain contrasted processes in oral expressions in the two very differently structured classes of sociocultural systems. The statement, which is of a kind dear to the heart of sociocultural neo-evolutionists, is too broad in its coverage to point to important dynamics within those sociocultural systems. Scientific theory deals with such dynamics, preferably in a temporal or historical frame if that frame is meaningfully specific.

All remaining characteristics of oral literature style involved selections, placements or orderings, and repetitions of items and classes of content, or other features. Most of them were vividly expressive, possibly surprisingly so. Brief comments follow on each of a limited selection of them, although the types presented constitute a list which could he multiplied. Recitalist audience behavior; beginnings, pauses, continuations, and endings; pattern numbers such as three, four, or seven; a class of items that expressed location; a class that expressed time explanatory devices; plot devices; structuring of act, scene, or episode sequences ("motifemes" are included here); headings, titles, or manner of ready reference; depictive inclusions and omissions; selected items of psychological commentary; speed of action, vocal technique and mannerisms, repetition, rhythm, and intensity. Again, many other kinds of mechanisms which employed expressive content served stylistically.

It is important to understand that all accurately and sensitively recorded oral arts, not least those in technologically simple societies, have displayed a great many classes of stylistic features and each such class might include a huge array of unitary items. The task is to identify every one of the classes and its component units and to attempt to determine their origin—usually a futile pursuit although the effort is worthy—and their functions—a difficult business sometimes. But they can and must be pinpointed by means of close content and style analyses, especially those conducted in a field situation because necessary interrogations are possible only there.

Paragraphs which follow take up those stylistic classes which are comparatively most expressive, and with only brief comments because the subject is sufficiently big to justify a treatise. However, there is one class of stylistic material which is distinctive in its breadth of content coverage. This class treats of the several genres found in each oral literature [see "Genres in Northwest States Oral Literatures" in this volume—Eds.]. A genre is, to be sure, an over-all structural or architectural type which has characteristic classes of content and classes of stylistic features. Genres will be spoken of after comments on other classes of features of style.

A formal recital of a myth or tale in a nonwestern society usually differed from protean everyday references to myths and tales in requirements regarding physical and vocal behavior of recitalist and audience. Children, adults, or both in an audience might be required to sit or recline in prescribed fashion. Audience members, maybe only the children, might have to intone each phrase after a recitalist, or utter an affirmative or other syllable after each phrase or larger segment of discourse. Some styles of oratory and ceremonial had similar canons.

Almost all myth performances had stylized beginnings and endings which functioned like English's "Ladies and gentlemen" and "Once upon a time," and "Thank you for your kind attention" and "Then they lived happily ever after." Many, maybe most, such formulae were in familiar morphemes or words but were not otherwise functionally meaningful. Some were as meaningless as "abracadabra." Myths that were so long that they must he halted and resumed the following night might be accorded stylized junctural phrasings at the close of the first evening and the beginning of the next session. Dramatic literatures might have stylized prologues in addition to formal initial phrases, and stylized epilogues with a stylized closing phrase.

Pattern number appears to have constituted a stylistic feature or class of features in most oral arts the world over, although districts here and there omitted it. Where it occurred, a myth or tale actor had, for example, three wives, shot three arrows, took three steps, crossed three streams, or was one of a set of three siblings. Persons and actions had to be cited in threes or, in other literatures, pairs, fours, fives, or sevens. A literature might have two, three, or more pattern numbers, that is, a class of them, each member of the class tied to something distinctive. For example, in one small coastal Oregon district, recitalists in Tillamook Salish hamlets had to enumerate four items if female actors or actions by females, five if male actors or actions by males.

The next few classes of items from which a recitalist must select were locational, temporal, and depictive. ...

In an oral literature, references to locations might comprise a class from which just one or two items could be or, rather, must be selected. For example, a recitalist of a tale might have to say "he left the village," or "he paddled into the stream." He might have to follow with "he went along the trail" or "he went upriver" or "he went downriver." If travel was on land, the next required phrase might be "he came out of the woods and into a clearing." Classes of such locational words or phrases were as watered out in expressive content as "and then" in English. But its stereotyped members or units, and one or another of a class of them often had to be used, functioned to move action along from place to place.

A class of features which expressed time was common, possibly even universal, in oral literatures. "Pretty soon," "after a long while," "the next morning," "presently," and a great number of others may be cited. Some oral literatures might have lacked a specific item such as "long, long ago," others required it. Some lacked "a long, long time afterward" but might require the recitalist to say only "presently," no matter what the context. The point is that a literature style usually offered a recitalist a ready-made kit of time expressions and depending on context he used, indeed he must use, one or the other item in that set.

One might go as far as Whorfians [(Whorf 1956)—Eds.] to deduce that a recitalist was so hemmed in by special temporal or other required classes of items available that his[4] own and his audience's perceptions of dramatic action were somehow shaped by this one segment of the style. Did oral literature style ever really shape perceptions, just as grammatical form classes have been claimed to have been determinants of perceptions? On the other hand, it is possible that fullness of knowledge of a way of life, heritage, and oral art itself must have been such, in both recitalist and audience, that restriction to stylized temporal items probably functioned only as a convenience for purposes of steady utterance. Although a speaker or recitalist cerebrated intensively, his ready-made devices permitted him to move along frictionlessly. Anyhow, no Whorfian seems to have come forth with a claim that thinking was molded by oral literature style classes in their structuring and functions. Maybe it is injudicious to suggest another neighborhood for exploration and lucubrations by such philosophical souls.

A linguist might elect to speak of classes of "zero" items, that is, potentially depictive allusions which a recitalist never mentioned. For example, if context pressured a recitalist to say something about a myth actor's good looks, he was able to select only one or two items from a small inventory of anatomical features, the only ones which were ever explicitly commented upon in that culture and its oral arts. Features of anatomy which remained unexpressed, unselected, possibly not even thought of, were always legion in every culture. Most peoples the world over ignored long eyelashes, although Europeans have long been rather sensitized to them and have had them mentally at hand for citation. The inventory of anatomically depictive items which could be referred to differed remarkably from culture district to district and, of course, from oral literature area to area. In one area, a recitalist might be able to mention light complexion and one or two or three other body characteristics like high forehead, buttocks, ankles, or feet. In another area he alluded to height. In another, to long straight hair; in another, wavy hair. In another area, to thickness of lips. In another, to long eyelashes, of course. A culture's selection of anatomical items which were tension-generating, highly regarded, or to be verbalized in a given context connected with the class of beauty items which were available for mention by myth recitalists.

Allusions to weather and landscape were also rigidly set. Most things that might be said about them were not said at all. It has to be ascertained if people perceived them without a cultural outsider's prodding. Many oral literatures lacked a style class of items which referred to "nature." And so their recitalists never mentioned foliage, flowers, brooks, or waving grass. Oceanian districts displayed styles which did pressure recitalists to cite particulars of "nature." Most western North American Indian recitalists never alluded to a single such feature. In each region, oral literature style analysis must not merely structure, that is, enumerate and arrange items in this facet of style. It must venture to account for their presence and maintenance, a task likely to be foredoomed to failure although, at least, it must be tackled.

Explanatory items have a long history in folkloristic writings. The familiar European "and that's why" there is a rock, waterfall, or mountain, and the widespread accounting for sun, moon, constellations, and stars by metamorphosis of tale actors into such celestial figures, have resulted in assertions that myths developed to account for features of nature. But secondary or tagged on functions of most explanatory items are now well-established. A recitalist's statements about the origin of this or that were primarily stylistic. They interrupted a plot so as to break suspense. Or they served to underpin components of world view or, on a smaller scale, supply some sort of security-granting account of items of local botany, geology, zoology, or geography. Explanatory elements were often of utmost unimportance for world view or security. But they served, primarily so, as stylistic punctuation. They functioned, too, as a special kind of plot device, of which more, presently. They broke continuity as digressions which distracted within plots. Or, when appended at the close of plots, they offered releases of another sort by weakening identification with people who had been plot actors and by lessening empathy for such actors' feelings in intense social relationships. Summary formulation about so-called "explanatory myths" themselves and about all explanatory pauses, asides, or closings is that their principal role was stylistic, their secondary role explanatory.

Plot devices in myths and tales suffered the sad fate of being construed by generations of folklore epigoni as central kinds of content for purposes of their scholarship. Innumerable monographs have assembled examples of one or more plot devices, which folklorists have called "motifs" and which number many hundreds around the globe. As noted above, the dedicated savants of traditional folklore scholarship exhibited interminably the geographical distributions of motifs, principally from the Atlantic Ocean to India and beyond, in a vain conviction that they were adding something of worth to knowledge. What are these motifs, which are far removed from the expressive core of oral literature although they constitute fundamental classes of stylistic machinery? An example or two will suffice. In several regions a myth actor ascended to the sky on a ladder made of arrows which connected. This motif has been primarily a plot device, one might almost suggest a short cut, although a spectacular one, which allowed a hunter or archer to get from below to above. Expressive content hinged actually upon his unexampled skill in archery or his supernatural ally or capacity.

A second example of a motif which is better treated as a plot device, and which, incidentally, has turned up in every continent, has been the so-called "magic" or "obstacle flight." A principal actor, with whom audience might identify, fled a hateful or terrifying creature but must quickly devise obstacles, tremendous ones, to slow up the evil one's pursuit. A thimbleful of water thrown back over the shoulder became a lake or sea. A rock or some dirt cast back became a mountain or range of mountains. A stick became an almost impenetrable forest. The plot device functioned to slow pursuit of an Oedipal or other feared being, to build and relieve tension around him.

Plot devices of many kinds might be collected under a generic heading of "magical" or "miraculous resuscitation." For example, corpses returned to life by merely stepping over them or uttering a stylized formula. The function of the device was evidently to get the deceased back to the living, quickly and excitingly so for the sake of the plot.

Folklorists who have been preoccupied with these and a hundred other plot devices and their geographical distributions have not perceived more essential content which was expressed in social relationships, actor personalities, and features of humor, world view, and ethics. Materials with which they should have been dealing largely evaded their scrutiny. A great many overt stylistic items such as motifs, which in each instance included expressive content too, became their main business. Almost a century's professional folklorists never comprehended that they were writing about components of style rather than about what they supposed was the most vital content which was expressed in oral literatures.

Additional characteristics of style are of importance, too. Many, if not most, oral literatures contained myths and tales which displayed comprehensive structurings—in his study of Russian fairy tales, cited above, Vladimir Propp called the components in one type of structuring "functions." However, gross or architectural structural matters can be managed nicely by borrowing captions such as skits, acts, scenes, entr'actes, prologues, and epilogues from Euro-American theater. Propp was really citing a single type of play, a genre, which always had seven scenes, each a selection from a set of possible items. Structuring in terms of acts and scenes may be inappropriate for some myth and tale repertoires and, naturally, it is unlikely to fit nonwestern oratory, incantations, prayers, and other types of oral arts. But it does constitute demonstrable stylistic segments, expressive content segments of course, in many or most dramatic myth or tale recitals. A recitalist might not be able to point, in so many words, to act 1, scene 4, or act 7, scene 2. Nonetheless, he had to frame his presentation in successive segments or macrosegments which were much like acts and scenes of Euro-American theater.

Distinctive genres in the corpus of oral literature of a nonliterate people present as troublesome a question as other contrastive features of style because folklorists, anthropological and others, have almost entirely ignored genres. But nonwestern peoples were always sharply aware of their genres and maybe always had names for them. Natives usually could indicate some of the main structural characteristics of each genre, kinds of content which tended to be included in it, and its special social, educational, or religious functions. Manifestations of genre are, in fact, easier for an outsider to identify than many other facets of style because traits which marked a genre comprise, even to him, visible and gross rather than hidden and small features.

Recitals might include a genre of myths about remote eras and another genre of myths dated as less remote. Ascription of lesser antiquity might be the solitary distinctive feature which marked this second genre. In all other stylistic respects, it might be identical with the first. Another genre might include formally recited tales distinguished by absences of a group of stylized devices which had to be employed in myth recitals. A global count of genres which could be characterized would doubtless add up to a huge total. A single society might possess as few as two oral literature genres, myths contrasted with tales, but genres of other oral art forms, as in rites, always appeared, too.

Just as nativistic cults effervesced in hundreds of nonwestern locales after the threatening advent and entries of Euro-Americans and the compulsive certainties which sometimes rendered missionaries attractive to people who had become unsure of themselves, so, too, new genres quickly boiled and bubbled through myth, tale, ritual, and other oral art forms inherited from the precontact era. Euro-Americans and missionaries were precipitating factors in the puzzlement which accompanied undermining of world view, values, relationships, and humor. Accordingly the Bible itself, or rather the perceptions and misunderstandings of Christian religious ideology and practice, provided features of new oral literature content. These introduced ideas stirred imaginations with resultant rationalizations and defenses in frequently impressively skillful efforts to reconcile native with Euro-American orientations. Such defensive maneuvers effected new projections on oral literature screens. And so an old myth genre might be supplemented by a kind of genetically related genre whose structure was much the same, but whose expressive content included novel features, especially some altered actor personalities and behavior and features of world view, ethics, and humor. For example, actors who were startlingly like older myth dramatic personae might be captioned Jesus and the Devil and only in some respects resembled Christians' delineations [see "Coyote's Journey" in this volume—Eds.]. New items of world view might depict a heaven and a hell, although the sketchings might by no means be similar to Dante's. New humor might include a lack of fit in citation of a supernatural who paused for his five o'clock tea.

Other postcontact genres might contain borrowed West African, French, or Spanish tales, depending on the provenience of new arrivals and how they presently related to original inhabitants of a district. Expressive content borrowed from tales told by such newcomers might become quickly remodeled and offered in the stylistic garb of a precontact genre. For example, early nineteenth-century French Canadians told tales of French origin to western Oregon Indians. The tales were rapidly and completely remodeled in style so as to be presented in the tale genre of the Indians. Expressive content was extremely mangled and the medieval French stresses and depictions largely lost.

Literary critics rightly seek stylistic devices of a great many kinds. They also look for what they call "texture." They enumerate and account for effective utilization of metaphors, similes, and symbols. Analysts of nonwestern oral arts have much to learn from pundits whose literary world is one in which solitary authors express themselves in writing and whose creative efforts do not tie in as directly with community discussions as do recitalists who record for anthropologists. The dynamics of creativity in content and style differed considerably in the diverse social settings which produced expressive forms. But classes of features which appear in a literate society's written arts should be sought in oral arts also. It is correct to presume that most such classes will turn up, at least in a few districts.

Editors' Notes

1. The original publication has "heartsprings," but the Editors have determined that this was a typographical error and so have taken the liberty of substituting "heartstrings," which the structure of Jacobs's metaphor seems to demand.
2. As in note 1, the Editors have corrected the original "paralleled" to read "paralyzed," since the former makes no sense in the sentence.
3. See "Genres in Northwest States Oral Literatures," in this volume, for the distinction between myth and tale.
4. Following what was earlier considered good style, Jacobs uses the masculine pronoun for the recitalist here, despite the fact that a significant number of his finest recitalists were women. Although he conformed to the casual male biases of literary style, Jacobs himself was a staunch advocate of equal rights and status for women. One of his former students dubbed him "a feminist" (Wayne Suttles, personal communication, 1985).

2

A Few Observations on the World View
of the Clackamas Chinook Indians

As with other areas of expressive content, worldview received only partial—and often incidental, indirect, or latent—expression in a culture's oral traditions. Jacobs believed it was important for a fieldworker to "direct questions which draw out native commentary so as to fill in depictions of perceptions of the universe or multiverse, of space and time, propinquity and worth of alien peoples, supernaturals, deities, districts from which humans and other creatures came and to which they departed upon death, and so on" (Jacobs 1964, 331). The article reprinted below originally appeared in the *Journal of American Folklore* 68:283-89 (1955). The Native text and translation appeared later (Jacobs 1958: 75-80). Subsequently, Jacobs revisited this same text (1960a: 58-64).

For further discussion of Clackamas Chinook worldview see Jacobs 1959b, 195-99). For a more general discussion of worldview see Jacobs 1964, 366-79). The Clackamas Chinook lived on the lower reaches of the Willamette River, upstream from the present location of the city of Portland. Decimated early by introduced diseases (Boyd 1999), they are not well represented in the ethnographic record. For a general description of Chinookan peoples see Silverstein (1990); also Ruby and Brown (1976) and Rubin (1999) for a more popular treatment. Almost all of what is known about Clackamas cultural life comes from the stories and texts Victoria Howard dictated to Melville Jacobs.

Years ago my Clackamas Chinook informant, Victoria Howard, who died in 1930, dictated in the native language and then translated a short myth which at the time seemed to me dull, possessed of slight meaning, and bleakly ritualistic—a kind of abracadabra. Her own title for the myth was "Coyote Made Everything Good." The personal name for the Coyote of this myth differed from the names for the several Coyote actors of other myths. The inference is that the Coyote referred to here played no role in the other myths which I collected. The narrator asserted her inability to recall the entire myth. What she gave was therefore only a fragment of a story, the text of which will be published elsewhere. It is sufficient to proceed with the translation, followed by an analysis of certain portions of its content, which I wish to suggest is much more revealing than I supposed when I first noted it. Brackets enclose additions which clarify meanings; the remainder is a close translation.

They would say at about this time [March], now things in the ground are growing. Perhaps this present moon [month], or maybe the next one when it [the moon] will be standing [will be visible], the very first camas [flat like buttons] have come.

  It [this camas] said [to a fish person, maybe Salmon, which also appears at the same time of year], "Goodness! Were it not for me [the people would die]. I hold their breath [I keep the people alive then]. Long time ago your people died of starvation." He [Salmon person] said, "Indeed. What kind of looking person is talking?" They [the people] told him, "She is kind of flat and gray-white." "Oh. Poor fellow. Her name [is to be] camas. That is what they will be eating."

  Soon then another said, "It is [I am] visible now. Were it not for me [the people would die of starvation]. I keep their breath [I keep them alive during this season]. Long, long ago they might have starved to death." They [the people] said, "Who is speaking? What is that one's appearance like?" They [the people] said, "To be sure. Seems to be long-faced and flat." "Oh [Salmon said in pity]. Poor thing. But she is really speaking the truth. Her name is cat ear [a small long white camas]. They will dig her out, they will eat her [raw], and then they will also bake her in ashes" [after blooming]. "Oh indeed."

Thereupon another [root] spoke. "She is [I am] visible [now]. Were it not for me, your people would have starved to death long ago." "Oh [said Salmon]. Who is speaking? What is that one's appearance like?" They [the people] replied to him [to Salmon], "Yes. Her head is kind of round." "Oh indeed [said Salmon]. Poor thing. Her name is camas [the staple type of camas]. Everyone will eat her. They will boil her [with hot rocks]; they will bake her; they will cook her on hot rocks [in an underground oven]."

Shortly then another said, "Now I am visible. Were it not for me [the people would die of starvation]. I hold their breath [and save their lives]." "Oh [said Salmon]. Who is speaking?" "Yes [the people replied]. Her hair is kind of black. It is tied in a bunch on top. She is a widow." "Oh no! She is just saying that [untruthfully]. They will not eat her; she tastes bitter. When you put her in your mouth, she will make you vomit. She is medicine merely. Once in a while when a person has become ill, they will then mash her, they will drink her juice. Her name is. ..." That is all [about her].

Soon then another one [a root] spoke. "It is visible now [I am visible]. Were it not for me [the people would be dying], I hold your people's breath [I save them from starvation]." "Oh [said Salmon]. What kind of person is speaking?" "[He is] someone who is sort of long." "Aha. Poor fellow. His name is wild carrot. He is speaking the truth."

Soon again then another one said, "He has become [I am now] visible. Were it not for me [the people would die of hunger], I hold your people's breath [I keep them alive]." "Oh. What kind of appearance does the person have who is speaking?" "Yes. He has long legs." "Oh. Yes. Poor things. Their name is wild carrot. They will eat them. They will boil them. They will make boiled mash-cakes [with them]."

Soon afterwards then he [another creature] said, "He is [I am] visible [about April]. Were it not for me [the people would die], I hold your people's breath [I keep them alive]?" "Indeed. Who is the one who is speaking? What is his appearance?" They [the people] replied to him [to Salmon], "Yes. He looks sort of gray." "Oh. Poor thing. His name is grouse. They will eat him. They will make [grouse] soup [for] a sick person, he will drink it."

Soon now then another one said, "He is [I am] to be seen [now]." "Oh. Who speaks? What is his appearance?" "Yes. The same as that [aforementioned one] again." "Oh. Poor thing. They will eat her, they will eat her eggs too. She is good for all sort of things. Her name is grouse."

Soon again then one said, "He is [I am] visible. Were it not for me [the people would die]; I hold your people's breath [I keep the people alive]." "Aha. Who is speaking?" "Something is standing; it is standing on his head. It is a small person." "Oh yes. Poor fellow. His name is quail. They will eat him."

Soon again now they were there. Someone said, "He is to be seen. Were it not for me, they would have starved to death long ago." "Indeed. Who is speaking? What does this one look like?" "Yes. It is small, [but] its head is big." "Oh indeed. He just says so [he claims his own worth, but he is wrong]. He will not be edible. His name is mudfish." "Very well."

Soon then another one said, "He is to be seen. Were it not for me [the people would die]; I hold your people's breath. Long ago they starved to death [except for my aid]." "Who is speaking? What is his appearance?" "Yes. His mouth is small and sharp." "Oh indeed. Well then. Sometimes they will think that they might eat him, but others will not eat him. His name is chub."

Soon then another spoke. "He is to be seen. Were it not for me [the people would die], I hold your people's breath [and save their lives]." "Oh then. What is his appearance?" "Yes. His mouth is rather sharp. He is good-looking." "Why yes indeed [rising then falling tone]. Poor fellow. She is edible. They will boil her soup for a sick person, he will drink it. Her name is trout." "Very well."

Soon then another said, "It is visible. Were it not for us [the people would die]; we hold your people's breath." "Indeed. Who is speaking? What is his appearance?" "Yes. They are tall, sort of blackish persons." "Yes, yes. They will be edible. They will get them; they will roast them on spits beside the fire; they will smoke-dry them; that is what they will eat. Their name is eel."

Soon then another said, "It is visible. Were it not for me [the people would die], I keep your people's breath." "Indeed. Who is speaking? What is his appearance?" "Yes. He is big [and] his body is light in color." "To be sure. Poor fellow. He is edible. They will boil him. And they will also smoke-dry him. That is what they will eat. His name is sturgeon."

Soon then another one, he too said, "He is visible. Were it not for me, I hold their breath." "Indeed. Who speaks?" "Yes. He is a good person. Indeed. Poor fellow. He is edible. They will make all sorts of things with him."

All sorts of things in the water like that, I do not know their names, I do not know what sorts of names [they had]. That is the way they all [all those edible and other water creatures] spoke. I think that I remember only that much of it now.

My mother's mother would say Coyote did [named creatures] like that [not Salmon as indicated] to absolutely everything we eat here. On the other hand my mother-in-law would say, "I do not recall who made the things that were good to eat here." My mother's mother would say, "Coyote did like that to all these things here. He went past all the things that are berries. They [each type of berry] said to him, I am going to pick [stab] you, Coyote!" [Whereupon] he would pull it [off its vine]. "Yes indeed, you are edible! Pretty soon now we [Indians] are coming [into this country]. First the wild strawberries [will ripen about the end of May]. Then also those blackberries, raspberries, small gray huckleberries, mountain huckleberries, serviceberries, crab apples, chokecherries." All those things spoke to him like that, "I am going to stab you, Coyote!"

That is the only way she [my mother's mother] told it [this myth] to me. I do not know whether she told me the [entire] myth, [and in any case] I do not remember it all. When all those berries ripened, then she would tell it to me at that time [saying], "Now Coyote went through [the land and] made all the things that are edible."

While she [my mother-in-law] was telling the myth, now she would say, "They planned [made] all these things that are good, [so that] such things would be our foods. On the other hand these bad things that are inedible, these we do not eat."

Each short episode, and there are over twenty in the narrative, treats of a food. The narrator said that at such and such a season a certain food grows and ripens, if it is a plant, or it comes up the river and becomes edible or obtainable if it is a fish. The food is anthropomorphic. It is a kind of person who speaks with utmost terseness. This food-person addresses both the assembled people and a male deity-like personage, Chinook Salmon in one version, Coyote in another; Mrs. Howard telescoped the two versions which she recalled. The deity-like figure, Salmon or Coyote, is right at hand, listening rather than looking.

The food-being speaks out something as follows, if worded in more acceptable English style. Dear oh dear. It is during the present season that I appear each year. Were it not for me during this season, the people would be unable to keep their breath. That is, I am of decisive importance to the people right now. It is I who in coming days or weeks make it possible for the people to continue to breathe and therefore to live. Long ago before I came, the people used to die of starvation. Or, they nearly starved.

The foregoing is the first stylized item in the recurrent literary form of each of the episodes of the myth.

The second and following item within each episode is a succinct response by Salmon or Coyote, who has been listening. He asks in authoritative manner, Who speaks? That is, Who is this that claims such worth for himself? His reply is as if the wealthy headman of the village were asking his people regarding a visitor or newcomer, Who is this new arrival who claims high station?

The deity-like homologue of a village headman next asks, What is the physical appearance of this claimant?

The third and succeeding item in each episode is a response by the assembled people of the village, a response to their leader's queries. For Salmon or Coyote does not himself yet see, or deports himself as if he has not seen, the food-person who has claimed value. The villagers now inform Salmon or Coyote regarding the overt appearance of the food claimant, but they cite only one or two physical characteristics of that individual. They say briefly and obliquely, She is round-headed—for Camas. Or, He is sort of long—for Wild Carrot. Or, His mouth is rather sharp, and he is handsome—for Trout. As in Pacific Northwest Coast sculpture, the literary artist has the people select for expression only one or two traits of each food-person, and omits all other traits.

Salmon or Coyote at once responds, because he, like a village headman, immediately comprehends what is right and good. He is the one to give utterance to the correct decision, unlike his villagers who can only report what they have seen or heard. But the leader on the one hand, and village members on the other, are inextricable one from another. A village headman or a deity-like figure of an active or otiose kind is unthinkable without his people.

The fourth and last item in each episode is Salmon's or Coyote's quick announcement, I stress announcement not authoritative determination, of the future function and the name of the food claimant. We hear, pontifically enunciated, Yes indeed! Poor, poor person! He—or she—will be edible. The people will boil her with hot pebbles, bake her in an underground oven, and cook her on hot rocks. Her name shall be Camas. Or, for Trout: They will boil her to make soup for sick persons. Her name is to be Trout.

The stylized utterances of deity-like person and food claimant, in each of the four successive items within each episode, are handled somewhat like sequences of minor variations on a single theme in a musical composition.

From the varying manners in which the food-persons express themselves, are spoken to, and are discussed in this myth, as well as from a variety of other evidences in the Clackamas oral literature, I deduce that these Indians regarded their principal foods as persons of a special type. Their view was that these foods wish to attach symbiotically to and be of use and worth to human beings, almost exactly as spirit-powers wish to come to people in order to be accepted, possessed, and used worthily by them. I suggest that the main foods and the spirit-powers constitute conceptual extremes in a continuum of anthropomorphically envisaged spirit entitles which need to relate to people and which are lonesome and unhappy when not related closely to people. The corollary of this formulation is that foods were not regarded as pitiable if and when they were cut up, boiled, mashed, roasted, or smoke-dried, to be used for and by people. All foods were warm, friendly allies and the major foods were a kind of kin to human beings. They saved people's lives, just as kin and spirit-powers saved lives. People, spirit-powers, kin, and many if not all foods were mutually interdependent and interconnected under certain conditions. These three categories of beings needed and wanted each other. They were sad indeed when they were unrelated or unused, that is, when they were alone. Each food, as the myth says, holds the breath, that is, maintains the heart and life, of its people.

Not every anthropomorphically conceived plant in this myth is a food. One is a bitter emetic. Sick persons drank its juice. But the point is that it was a highly regarded because much needed plant. Like the foods and spirit-powers, it saved lives. Therefore it too fitted in the category of animistic entities which related symbiotically with people. All such beings needed and wanted people, as people needed and wanted them.

The emphasis upon each of the foods or food beings which are inventoried in this myth was such that Mrs. Howard's well-informed mother-in-law, whom she quoted, had actually lacked certainty concerning the identity of the deity-like personage, whether Salmon or Coyote, whose judgments and pronouncements constitute the principal portions of the expressive content which receives native verbalization.

The anthropomorphized food beings who follow one another in the episodes of the myth include several kinds of Camas, a bitter emetic root, several Wild Carrots, Bitterroot, Male Grouse, Female Grouse, Quail, Mudfish, Chub, Trout, Eel, Sturgeon, and various berries. Observe that roots, birds, and fish are included, not animals, I believe because other myths resolve problems of the advent, characteristics, and functions of animals that were significant in Clackamas life.

If some of these deductions are correct, the problem arises as to why the Clackamas felt or thought both animistically about foods as anthropomorphic beings, and in terms of their own symbiotic relationship with those beings? In a way the Clackamas played safe in the matter of a degree of realistic response to the external world by locating each personified food in a precultural era, the Myth Age, before things became like the modern world. Presumably a rather hard day by day manipulation of reality, a response which is common human, got in the way of a frank placing of food anthropomorphizations, in the contemporary period. No group of people lives all day long, least of all when they are procuring foods, in a dreamlike trance or communal psychotic disorientation. They do not dig up all the wild carrots and at once talk to them and relate to them as if such roots were persons. A few of the people might do so to a selected few of the carrots, or, a shaman or ritualist might behave in such a fashion during a special seasonal ceremony. But the ideological heritage functions with fewer questionings, if its animistic projections are packaged and relegated, with literary stylization in the narratives of them, to an earlier epoch which leaves only some convincing and tangible evidences.

We know well that animistic notions occur in our culture especially in infancy or early childhood, when things in a youngster's environment are responded to in much the manner in which he responds to his immediate guardians and suppliers of food. The tiny child reacts initially to important things as to important people, that is, as if they were people. He therefore tends to manipulate such things as he manipulates persons. He seeks attention, relationships, and strengths in things much as he finds them and wants them in human beings. Of course I wish to avoid any evolutionist or ethnocentric kind of implication that the Clackamas or any other non-European people had minds which can he equated, in terms of developmental level, with the mind of the child. Nevertheless, we may borrow analogies from our knowledge of processes that are operative in infancy, to see if they operate in another kind of problem. Accordingly, I suggest that in Clackamas culture, the procuring of certain things which were important as well as tasteful and pleasurable, engendered responses of pleasure and security which are somehow comparable to the responses to the granting of relationships and favors by people, whether people as such or humanlike spirit-powers. Needed and wanted things continued to be responded to with a relationship reaction of a sort that appears in early years of life and that is repeated and reinforced in later years. The anticipation, both anxious and pleasurable, that a food of a certain kind would be available during an approaching season, occurred many times each year. The multiplicity of such happy expectations was, of course, great in the nonagricultural groups of the Pacific Northwest—hence the extensive list of foods in this one fragment of a story. Each fresh food had its distinctive and often delicious flavor. Many of the foods that are listed in the myth followed an often long and uncertain winter over which hovered threats of famine. During such a season the various smoke-dried and other stored foods, which must have become progressively more monotonous and flat in taste, had kept the people alive. Now, one fresh thing after another appeared, voluntarily and happily on its part, and was eaten with avidity, delight, and gratitude by its human kin.

The coming of each such food occasioned, I believe, emotional responses similar to those caused by visits of friends and relatives who also remained for only a short while and vanished for another year. Parallel emotional reactions characterized the annual coming of the spirit-powers, in the winter spirit-power dances.

Like all their neighbors, the Clackamas were little if at all given to metaphysical theorization. But their strong responses to each valued food as it appeared, resembled their responses to wanted people and desired spirit-powers who also came seasonally.

Brief and stylized as it is, this myth is therefore not an unimportant, theoryless or stupid story. It expresses, because there is no other way of accounting for the people even telling it, an impressive intensity of feeling regarding relationships with food beings which were qualitatively like those which a person had to kindred and to spirit-powers with whom he was symbiotic.

The role and function of Salmon or Coyote, in this myth, brings up a somewhat different kind of problem of the interpretation of expressive content within a myth. Again, in order to understand such content, deductions which are ventured must also be kept consistent with whatever we know regarding the culture and its oral literature in general. Accordingly, I suggest that Salmon or Coyote amounts to an anthropomorphized representation of the cultural heritage itself, and that this representation is integrated with a precultural symbolization of an idealized village headman that is, a paternal figure. He represents and combines great spirit-power, wealth, beneficence, authority, and a modicum of safety for the residents of his village. It is neither necessary, nor will it ever be possible with the kind of ethnographic and myth evidence which we can hope to glean, to define with precision the relationships between any Chinookan village headman and the people of his town. But I think that there can be little reasonable doubt about the primarily village headmanlike role of interrogation of visitors, decisions, and judgments for the sake of the community, that is played by Salmon or Coyote.

It follows, then, that two distinguishable kinds of symbiotic relationships receive projective expression in the myth. The one has to do with the peculiarly intimate interconnections of foods, kindred, spirit-powers, and people. The other treats of the fatherlike authoritarian who heads the village, and his interconnection with his people. Indeed, foods, kin, and spirit-powers need people and vice versa. A headman, as well as Salmon or Coyote in the precultural era of myths, needs his village people too, and these people depend upon, identify with, and give willingly to their headman.

I have tried to stress a few features of the Clackamas world view which are, I believe, covertly present in this myth. I am confident that they constitute concepts and relationships which were important in Clackamas culture and which alone put life and meaning for us into this seemingly bleak and aridly ritualistic narrative.

Study of this myth suggests and reinforces one further inference about the Clackamas cosmology. Like many other evidences which anthropologists have assembled from the Clackamas and neighboring Indian groups, the myth suggests that all these Indians seem to have been more or less effectively blocked in a direction of achieving any kind of monotheism, whether pure or mixed, because of the manner of functioning of their network of symbiotic relationships and associated concepts which anthropological writers have long referred to under the caption of animism. Whatever the most pressing needs and fears of the Clackamas may have been, their security system appears to have been so well woven in the net of interconnecting and mutually interdependent beings which were all more or less humanlike, that some universal principle, power, force, or deity concept was at the very least difficult for them to comprehend. It, or he, could not easily be introduced or accorded feeling responses that would offer important additional increments of security. We also know that when Christian ideology was introduced among Indians of the Northwest States, it frequently took the initial form of mere supplementation of a few new spirit-power beings, not true deities. The added spirit-powers were for some time regarded as beings who had earlier related exclusively to the Whites and were only now brought into the country with the Whites. Before any Whites entered the Northwest States, the Clackamas and their neighbors seem to have been about as completely non-monotheistic, by any definition of the term monotheism, as a culture could be. The Clackamas oral literature offers manifold support to this deduction.

3

Humor in Clackamas Chinook Oral Literature

Jacobs chided his fellow anthropologists for their lack of scholarly interest in humor. He noted that while they considered social structure, language, and acculturation, for example, to be "important topics to pursue on field expeditions, humor remained unimportant and ignored." Jacobs continued, "There is something almost alarming about such refusal to examine a kind of behavior which is as evident as kinship, cult, or phonemic patterning" (Jacobs 1964, 241). Although this attempt to analyze Clackamas humor leaves much to be desired, at the time it was written it was a ground-breaking effort to demonstrate how a rigorous and systematic approach could be considered. For further thoughts about humor see his chapter on "Humor and Tragedy" (1964, 240-52). The chapter reprinted here was originally published in *The Content and Style of an Oral Literature* (1959b, 178-86). An earlier version appeared in *Culture in History: Essays in Honor of Paul Radin* (Diamond 1960, 181-89).

Clackamas literature generated both laughter and sadness, but smiles are everywhere more easily identifiable than reactions of sorrow. An anthropologist's observations, field notes, and memories allow him to select with much more confidence instances which were funny. Only a few occurrences of a tragic kind of audience sentiment can be identified, and these are only the extremely sorrowful; therefore, an attempt to arrange Clackamas responses on a continuum from laughter to responses of a dolorous nature would probably fail. Nevertheless, I think that an effort to classify humorous responses alone is worthwhile and that the results are helpful for comprehension of the society and its carriers.

In fact, it seems to me that humor is a facet of life which has been almost irresponsibly neglected in anthropological research. It is a part of literatures which folklorists have studied for other components. Its importance for understanding a people and their literature may be no less than the importance of traditionally studied topics such as social structure and religion. At the least, analyses of humor, whether inclosed in an oral literature or expressed in conversation, provide needed corroboration of deductions made from other field data. Possibilities in quantification of humor materials should also be intriguing to workers in the behavioral sciences. I have tried to work out and display a method of analysis which allows a many-sided study of a part of life about which the behavioral sciences know little.

Accordingly, I enumerated 130 instances in the Clackamas collection where I was certain that an audience at a folkloristic recital responded with smiles or laughter. I recognized at least one such reaction in each of thirty myths and three tales. That is, 60 per cent of the myths contained fun, but only 20 per cent of the tales. This difference between myths and tales is significant. A Euro-American might suppose that myths would contain less humor than tales, but the opposite is true.

To Clackamas, myths offered trenchant and unquestioned evidences of prehistory, while tales spoke piquantly and equally validly of recent times. Myths may be regarded as remainders of long periods of village discussions and commentary. Tales were relatively recent acquisitions, not cultural heirlooms like myths. I suppose that the greater elaboration of humor in myths therefore reflects a longer time during which they were possessed, contemplated, theorized upon, and worked over. Their truth was not lessened nor their worth tarnished by embellishments of humor. Absence of a concept of the sacred also made it possible, and even preferable, to treat accounts of the past with a light touch. No community of the Northwest States brooded over narratives of ancient times and people. The long ago and the long since dead were laughed at more comfortably than the present and the recently deceased. The one was far less threatening than the other. Likely reasons for the lower percentage of humorous items in tales are, then, that myths were not so close to the anxieties of today, that most myths were much older than tales, and that myths had therefore received more processing in a culture which did not set fun apart from value ideals.

I took each of the 130 fun situations and attempted to pinpoint each fun-generating factor or stimulus to humor which I believe to have been present in them. I counted 914 such stimuli. Every one of the 130 instances of humor was patently determined by a cluster of stimuli, few or none of which a Clackamas verbalized as such. The average number of stimuli which I identified and estimated in each instance of fun was at least seven. But I am confident that I underestimated, oversimplified, and missed many stimuli which were there. The actual average must have been significantly higher.

I arranged the 914 stimuli in sixteen types, some of which overlap. I feel no vested interest in these types. It would be foolish to claim that they give the best arrangement possible. Indeed, several incongruous polarities which are set apart in the classification might be handled in other ways. Nevertheless, the types which I present have some value: they display differences in the fun-generating factors; for purposes of analysis of humor as a whole, they are to be regarded as meaningful units; they permit the student to avoid oversimplification; and they facilitate studies of humor in its relationship to the society and in other oral literatures of the Northwest, if not elsewhere.

The 914 stimuli include totals from only the first fourteen types because I was unable to conduct arithmetical operations upon types 15 and 16. The tables on the following pages display, with catchwords, the kinds of stimuli which I have assembled to constitute a type. Types 2, 3, and 4 were so varied in content that further subdivisions of each were meaningful and therefore necessary. These subdivisions are presented in Tables 2, 3, and 4, respectively. Type 14 contrasts with types 1 to 13 by being quantitative as well as qualitative.

Instances of type 15, pantomime, mimicry, and vocal mannerisms, were so infrequently noted in field research that they could not be quantified. Occurrences of type 16, which comprises onomatopoetic, diminutive, and augmentative linguistic devices, could be ascertained only following full analysis of the language.

The sixteen categories of fun stimuli, frequencies of items in each of them, and omissions of categories which appear in humor expressed in other societies should receive discussion for whatever light they shed on Clackamas social structure, cultural heritage, and personalities. In the following comments I discuss each type of humor stimulus in the order in which it appears in Table 1.

Type 1, which stresses physical expression, appears to be a common human kind of stimulus to laughter. A notable aspect of fun situations and actors in the literature is that Grizzly people were the prominent ones deliberately and aggressively subjected to slapstick by other actors.

Table 1. Types of Humor Stimulus

Type	Instance	Approx. % of Total
1. Trick, transformation, practical joke, slapstick	94	.10
2. Anatomical reference; regressive behavior (see Table 2)	173	.19
3. Trickiness, cleverness, resourcefulness in relationship (see Table 3)	51	.056
4. Female; older person (see Table 4)	81	.089
5. Pomposity, vanity; foolishness, naïveté, gullibility, stupidity, ignorance, incompetence; childishness, immaturity; lack of skill; timidity; lower class	91	.10
6. Eccentricity; incorrect behavior, the forbidden; incongruity; narcissism, greed, penuriousness	95	.10
7. Insanity due to spirit-power relationship	14	.015
8. Humiliation	58	.06
9. Evildoer comes to grief	59	.06
10. Irony, satire, sarcasm; understatement, exaggeration	41	.04
11. Victory, release from anxiety or tension	44	.05
12. Dishonesty	50	.055
13. Language error, misunderstanding of a verbal form	4	.004
14. Repetition, progression, saturation	59	.06
15. Pantomime, mimicry; vocal mannerism	not noted	
16. Onomatopoeia; diminutive, augmentative verbal form	not noted	
Total	914	app. 1.00

Table 2. References to Anatomy and Regressive Behavior (Type 2)

Subtype	Instances	Approx. % of Total
a. Sex	38	.04
b. Anality	27	.03
c. Mutilation, maiming, physical pathology	32	.03
d. Orality	34	.03
e. Physical unattractiveness	16	.016
f. Becoming unconscious, falling asleep	6	.005
g. Fear of great height	3	not significant
h. Burning	1	not significant
i. Drowning	7	.005
j. Diminutiveness	7	.005
k. Death	2	not significant

Table 3. Resourcefulness in Relationships (Type 3)

Subtype	Instances	Approx. % of Total
a. Men	34	.03
b. Children	16	.016
c. Women	1	not significant

Table 4. Females and Older Persons (Type 4)

Subtype	Instances	Approx. % of Total
a. Females neither children nor aged	56	.058
b. Older women	13	.015
c. Older men	12	.015

For example, a son of Fish Spear Pole Man transformed into a feather (text 31)[1] and floated about in order to tease a Grizzly Woman who tried in vain to catch him. His older brother turned into a snake, and she could not catch him either. Water Bug infuriated and frustrated Grizzly Woman by keeping the fire burning brightly all night long (17).

Coon and Coyote appear to have been the outstanding employers of physical sadism. Coon tortured a succession of Grizzly Men by putting black powder and urine into chisel cuts he made in them (49). Coon teased Coyote with fake magic which seemed to draw food from under a pillow (3). The younger Coyote (9) played tricks on a succession of people, mostly females. Principal cultural factors ensconced in items such as these, and which everyone the world over may find amusing, were the specific kinds of personalities which Grizzly, Coon, and Coyote people stood for. In the literature Grizzlies often represented unlovely older persons, and Coon and the younger Coyote perpetrated deviltries to which many or most pre-adult persons inclined. Besides, slapstick tended to occur at the expense of feminine actors. Along with a deep feeling of incongruity, slapstick appears to substitute for fear of violence and destruction. It replaces fear of real damage to the self with a resolution where no such damage is done or, in oral literature, with hurt to a projection figure who is so poorly regarded that the audience does not identify with him.

The virtual 20 per cent of all stimuli found in type 2 comprised an interplay of two set of factors and an especial importance of one. The common human factor in type 2 consisted of evaluations and therefore learned attitudes, whatever they were in the Northwest, toward anal, oral, and genital behavior and the physical wholeness of the body. Very likely all peoples have laughed at pre-adult physical excesses and at some mutilations suffered by other persons.

The second group of factors in type 2 was much more cultural and local. The collection exhibits laughter at burning once, at seven drownings—a small number for a people who navigated much on waterways—and at two other deaths. The weighty feature about type 2 is its thirty-eight instances of sex stimulus, twenty-seven with an anal reference, thirty-four with an oral stress, and thirty-two captioned as mutilations. The culture was severe in its demands about a premenopausal woman's restricted sphere of activity, the breaking of taboos, children's disobedience, and gentle prolonged sexual foreplay. But it lacked inhibitions about verbal mention of orifice pleasures and showed no evidence of repressing the citation of mutilations. Anal quips connected in some way with the feeling that soiling with excrements was uniquely humiliating. But laughter at urine is never found, and contact with urine was not at all degrading. Probably every house had a wooden urine bowl or box, and people therefore found no more occasion for laughter about it than we do about our bathtubs. Laughter at anal references, in a society which repaired to the brush or woods nearby to defecate, therefore connected with feelings that excrements were debasing. In the same way, sexuality outside the marriage bed was disgraceful. Laughter at sexuality was always, then, at sexual acts committed outside a marital relationship. Laughter at orality appears to have eventuated in another way and to have had a connection with food anxieties in a region where seasonal uncertainties about food production or reserves were substantial.

Type 3 [Trickiness—Eds.] includes pleasurable responses to resourcefulness, skill, and trickiness. Such responses may be universal, but in Clackamas literature only men and children displayed such abilities. Most significantly, the literature presented few female actors who possessed such admired traits after the childhood years. The culture's low regard for the worth of females from puberty to old age is therefore neatly expressed in the figures for humor stimuli of this kind.

Type 4 [Female/old person—Eds.] includes, I think, only regionally circumscribed cultural stimuli. Hostile feelings toward females at and past puberty and toward older men, headmen too, were relieved in laughter at them. Further significance may be found in the fact that of eighty-one stimuli of this type, sixty-nine were leveled at females. People laughed much more frequently at adult females than at men, even headmen. Types 3 and 4 show very well the core of antifeminine sentiment in the Clackamas heritage.

Pleasure at competency, denoted as type 3, is paralleled by relieving laughter at incompetency, which is placed under type 5. The concept of incompetency extended to immaturity of children and to any other childlike or immature behavior. It also covered freemen of poor families. Slaves were not laughed at, at least in the literature, and I do not know why. An interesting spread of the concept of ineptitude was into the area of pretense that was not fully justified. Vanity and pomposity were funny, but evidence is insufficient to demonstrate that a pretentious headman was laughed at. At the same time, headmen were patently subjects of gibes in literature sessions, as is shown by the narrator's handling of upper-class gentry like Coyote. One may find, in a shared feature of types 4 and 5, a decisive process in Chinook humor. It arises in the discomforts and pains felt because of power, controls, and authority possessed by shamans, elders, the rich, and—not least—headmen. Relief is felt when such people are cut down to size, shown to be fallible, or lampooned. Thus the individuals manifestly idealized are rendered bearable by changing them into less than ideal figures. Persons who are incessantly referred to as worthy, good, right, or competent are metamorphosed into actors who are naughty, wrong, prone to error, unreliable, capricious, or enjoying the very satisfactions which they do not permit others to have.

Type 6 [Eccentricity—Eds.] is probably, in its central aspect of incongruity, one of the basic characteristics of many jocund responses the world over. But incongruity differs from culture to culture, and one may make an excellent case for its relativity. In Clackamas literature incongruity applied to greed, penuriousness, extreme self-love, and eccentric ways of the kinds stressed in Northwest societies. In addition, one changes into enjoyment feelings of disappointment, self-pity, fear of self-destruction, or any feelings of unpleasantness or pain. One defends against feelings which are responses to direct contact with unwanted reality by transforming such contact into something which generates a feeling of amusement. Responses to fun include the incongruity of a shift from painful to pleasant feeling, where the former is real and the latter a substitute. There is a contrasting, subliminally, of opposites, at the same time that such opposites are sensed as not opposites but the same. As Martha Wolfenstein has suggested in her *Children's Humor* [1954—Eds.], there seems to be an unconscious fusing of opposites and a concomitant suggestion of the absurdity of such fusing. And there is a postponement or release from feared stress.

Type 7, insanity, probably connected in native feeling with types 3 and 6, that is, with resourcefulness and eccentricity. In any case, it infrequently set off laughter. But insanity, even of kinds which Western culture regards as extreme, may have been thought of, in most communities the world over as in the Northwest, as manifestations of relationship with special supernatural and therefore as relatively "normal" behavior. The few instances of what may be identified as insanity in Clackamas literature accordingly were determined by the manner of their identification by the culture.

Type 8, humiliation, may have been tragic in one setting and comic in another constellation of factors. Humiliation ties in with Northwest aspirations to rise to or maintain social level or acceptance as a worthy person. Constant tension about maintenance of status was drained in laughter at those who demeaned themselves. The literature presented instances which show that the concept of humiliation extended to contact with excrements and relationships with dogs as if they were humans.

Type 9, the evildoer who comes to grief, seems universal and perhaps displays no specific Northwest cultural factors of importance except in the special ways in which a villain was humbled or eliminated.

Type 10—irony, understatement, exaggeration, and the like—which connects especially with the factor of incongruity in type 6, is very likely universal too. These devices were not often employed in Clackamas literature except on a linguistic level. For example, Chinook possessed consonantal shifts which expressed diminutive or augmentative nuances. Occasional employment of such devices for the purpose of incongruous connotations provoked amusement.

Type 11, release from tension, is probably universal and may not contain specific Northwest cultural manifestations except for the devices which alleviated tension.

Type 12, dishonesty, is very likely a product of Northwest values which gave approval to success no matter how trickily or even cruelly attained.

Type 13, language mistakes or misunderstandings, may be common to all human beings. I find nothing distinctively Northwest in hue in this type of stimulus to laughter.

Type 14, repetition, progression, and saturation, must also be universal, although their manifestations in Northwest literatures were in terms of local stylizations. Clackamas used the pattern number five and the "youngest-smartest" motif among specific stimuli of this quantitative kind.

One of the most important and recurrent elements in humor in Western cultures is the factor of surprise, or the sudden and unexpected turn. Clackamas humor in myths and tales lacked such a component, no doubt because the literature was a community possession. Apart from children, auditors were familiar with most or all of the stories of Clackamas provenience and participated actively in year-round discussions of their content.

Another aspect of humor which is found in Western cultures but not in Clackamas is the stylized form which the West calls a "joke." Clackamas probably joked interminably. But they seem to have had no concept of or word for a joke. Their literature displays no evidence of the structured entity which we term "joke" incorporated in stories. They expressed themselves humorously in the day's chitchat and in story recitals. Fun functioned integrally with the rest of conversation and literature; it embellished and lightened all forms of speech even though there was no identifiable joke category. All that we can do, accordingly, is to attempt to spot situations whose components produced a response of the comic. Not a single factor in humor, whether of content or structuring (except for mimicry and vocal mannerisms), was peculiar to fun situations. Only the weight and patterning of several interwoven factors tipped the balance toward laughter.

In order to exemplify the kind of analysis of humor situations which has been suggested, I have selected a portion of the myth of Coon and his father's mother (49) [Jacobs 1959a—Eds.], and a part of the short myth of the married Skunk (19) [Jacobs 1958—Eds.]. Myth 49 commences as follows, in translation:

> They lived there. I do not know how long a time after, he said to her, "Grandma! I am hungry. Grandma! (I am) hungry." "What then will you eat?" She showed him something or other (to eat). "Hm. No!" She showed him something else. "Hm. Oh oh no!" (She showed him) everything (available). She said to him, "What then (do you want)? Go to our storage pit, bring acorns. We shall wash them." "Yes yes grandma! That is what I want." He dashed away, he got to that place, he opened their storage pit (one of the five she had). He ate acorns (and the best ones only). The ones that were wormy he piled elsewhere. He ate them all (only the good ones). He moved on to another one of their storage pits, again he did like that, he piled aside the wormy ones. He ate them (the good ones only) all up (in the second pit). Then he went on again to another of their storage pits. ...

Coon's first words about being hungry are at once funny, I think, because of a complex net of factors which I suggest with appended numbers that refer to stimuli listed in the tables. Coon speaks and acts like a child (5), but he does so because he is really tricky and dishonest (3, 12). He uses his immaturity in order to get the old woman's food (1, 2d). He is a greedy (6) little fellow. Whatever he does to his grandmother is funny because Clackamas laugh at an older woman merely because she is an older woman (4b). An audience probably felt that while Coon might be hungry he was even more motivated to play a mean trick (1) on his grandmother (4b).

Her query, "What then will you eat?" is amusing because the audience knows what the child (5) wants—both food (2d) and an opportunity to be dishonest (12) and to play a mean trick (1, 3) on his grandmother (4b). Her question is also funny because it implies that she is now and always foolishly gullible (5) about the callow youth. "She showed him something or other" continues the stress on an older woman's (4b) naïveté (5).

Coon's reply "Hm. No!" compactly refers, first, to his clever (3) but dishonest (12) initial response of "Hm!" It implies that he is really pondering about her offer of something other than acorns. The audience knows that he wants only those products of her industry. He lets her think that he might accept her offer and at once lets her down with a rebuff expressed in his curt "No!"

The same factors recur (14) in her second offer: "She showed him something else. Further repetition (14) appears in his second reply, "Hm. Oh oh no!" which is funnier than the first because he intensifies his rejection. She is thereby made to appear even more foolish.

Either the storyteller recites four offers by the grandmother and four progressively more definitive rejections (14), or the audience responds as if they were cited, because a Northwest audience always reacts automatically as if there were so many questions and answers.

Upon the fifth offer of acorns Coon "dashed away." The verb "dash" is funny because only a greedy (6) youngster (5) with a hardly repressed oral need (2d) would run rather than walk to the food. Running may also be incongruous (6), for there is no implication that Coon is starving.

In the next sentences Coon rejects edible but wormy acorns and greedily (6) devours (2d) all the good nuts in his grandmother's cache. He really destroys (1) the old woman's (4b) valuable property. He does it without heed (6) for her order to bring the acorns to the house where they can be washed. Without once returning, he ransacks all of her acorn storage pits (14), in each place gorging (2d) on the best nuts.

It is not necessary to continue with the myth to show in greater detail the techniques of repetition and saturation (14). They are pointed at Coon's practical jokes (1), trickiness (3), and orality (2d) at the expense of the gullible (5) old woman (4b), and there is a steady undercurrent of incongruity (6) arising from her loyalty and devotion to a youth who has no generosity toward her. My suggestions of fun stimuli undoubtedly do not include all the factors which render the scene funny to Clackamas. For example, a raconteur doubtless used mimicry and vocal mannerisms (15) and in some instances linguistic devices (16).

Additional exemplification of the complexity of the fabric of factors in a fun situation is provided by a glance at a very different story (text 19) [Jacobs 1958—Eds.], no more than a joke which has been relegated in native theory to a precultural age.

A devoted wife pleads with her husband Skunk, who is in fact a hopelessly incompetent hunter, to go out to the woods and bring home a deer with nice fatty breast meat. When he returns the next day, his face is bandaged. His pack contains not a single slice of meat, only his teeth, which are wrapped in ferns. He has not hunted at all. It turns out that he misunderstood the morpheme for "breast meat" and perceived it as the homonymous morpheme for "tooth." His wife can do no more than throw away his teeth.

Stimuli to laughter in this skit seem to include at least the following: slapstick (1), several anatomical factors such as mutilation (2c) and physical unattractiveness from the loss of teeth (2e), the humiliation a wife suffers because of her ridiculous husband (4a, 8), his incompetence as a hunter and therefore his own humiliating situation (5, 8), the incongruity of going to hunt for good food and returning without it but with one's teeth pulled (6), a verbal misunderstanding (13), and probably pantomime of Skunk's pain and bandaged face (15). These and assuredly other factors which I have failed to perceive apply to the skit as a whole. The phrases and words of the dictation supply a number of additional fun stimuli whose citation would add to the analysis. One might suggest, however, much as in the example above for Coon and his grandmother, that a background of humiliation and pain due to feelings of identification with both the wife and Skunk is so burdensome as to call for relief. An escape from sadness by way of laughter may be an important ingredient of the little play.

Essentially, a response of amusement arises because of the weaving of a special kind of fabric which contains many strands: laughter is consequent upon multiple factors. Some are consciously employed by the narrator and obvious to the audience, but most are subliminal.

Maybe, too, the response is a needed ventilation; one's feeling of identification with the mistreated old woman who is Coon's grandmother might result in sadness and hurt if enough factors that stimulate laughter were not brought in to tip the balance so as to effect an overt response of humor. The extent to which some comedy constitutes for the audience a kind of airing of feeling which offers relief from sadness or pain, owing to identification with a person who is degraded or hurt, has been a moot question among students of humor. Illustrations of humor from the Clackamas collection do not controvert a theory that humor often includes a factor of unpleasantness from which there is need to distract or relieve. Furthermore, the spinning of the web of factors, which balance out to produce smiles or laughter, is not wholly or even largely a matter of sharply conscious manipulation. Most of the components are hidden from both jokester and auditors, and these factors are in large numbers in almost every fun situation. If my attempt to inventory components of Clackamas literary humor is not far off the mark, they rarely number less than six or seven for each such situation. Identification of them, and of a broad factor of relief from dysphoria, must remain hypothetical in instances like those in Clackamas humor because of the passing of native informants. However, in the next years the survivors of adjacent peoples could be employed as partial checks should students wish to engage in such a follow-up.

In summary, central tasks in comprehension of humor in an exotic society include the listing of probable items in an inventory of fun-producing factors, attempts to locate the common human and sociocultural origins of each, and indications of their likely psychological dynamics. Since at present rather little is known about any of these, it seemed useful to commence with definitions of some of the problems, to display a possible methodology of analysis of essential factors in humor situations, and to warn that laughter responses always constitute very complex reactions to many quickly woven-together stimuli, most of which are far below the surface of verbal awareness.

Editors' Notes

1. Text references in parentheses refer to Jacobs 1958 and 1959a.

4

Genres in Northwest States Oral Literatures

Although brief, this previously unpublished paper offers Jacobs's
most complete discussion of Northwest States oral literature genres.
Two additional genres, not considered here, include historical event
narratives (see "An Historical Event Text from a Galice Athabaskan
in Southwestern Oregon" in this volume) and personal experience
narratives (Seaburg 1992). The editors are responsible for all
footnotes. This paper was originally read at the annual meetings of
the American Anthropological Association, Denver, 1965.

I recall no taxonomy of a nonwestern repertoire of myth and tale
types of compositions, each type or genre depicted with many, if
not all, of its sets of features of contrastive content and form, and
each genre and category of items within it presented with their special
connections with other sociocultural items. Characterizations of
folklore genres themselves, such as may be found within a district,
have usually been simplistic or incomplete, or have improperly
emphasized literary features in them rather than their social or
ideological functions. It is right to question whether there are important
operational merits in either a worldwide or regional genre taxonomy
of oral literatures. But at this time a discussion of the contrastive features
present in genres, and their contrasting functions in some one
nonwestern community or district, may serve useful purposes and,
hopefully, lead to discoveries.

Any venture in genre taxonomy will be limited by the quality of the
folkloristic and ethnographic materials for the group or district covered.

In the Pacific Northwest States, the many publications, since the
1880's, which present oral literature data have been somewhat
exceptional in their reliance upon dictations in native languages, with

translations of widely varying precision. The inelegant English of interpreters has granted a smaller number of printings of the region's myths and tales. After virtuous field collection and subsequent publication, most of the linguists and anthropologists who worked in the area, excepting [Franz] Boas, [Gladys A.] Reichard, and [Melville] Jacobs, displayed slight interest in doing anything more with the primary source materials. Specialists in sociocultural anthropology have almost wholly ignored the Northwest States folklores, in spite of their important social and ideological functions, after they were collected and published in a stark form. A very few amateurs and specialists in the humanities have used them for bowdlerized and censored editions designed to sell in elementary schools and in bookstores that offered regional Americana. Guided by the motif, diffusionist, historical and literary concerns of their historico-geographical tradition, professional folklorists have done no more with the Northwest States than to locate presences of tale type and motif content and chart a few distributions.

Long ago, Boas and others pointed to the larger Pacific Northwest's natives' own contrast of myths versus tales. Boas wrote correctly that this larger region's myths comprised recitals of happenings dated in an early era when things were rather different from what they were in the more recent era that was described in tales.[1] Here was a simplistic genre classification. It was the natives' own laconic way of commenting about the two recital forms which they recognized. Boas' taxonomy went no further. Most details which might have characterized the two genres of myths and tales were omitted, and natives themselves rarely identified such details. The social and ideological roles of their literature were hardly indicated. For all Boas' thoroughness in analyses of a number of languages and plastic and graphic arts, he did not set forth, in either details or an orderly way, the significant contrastive traits in folklores which he recorded. Therefore he did not, partly because he could not without such detail, discuss sociocultural connections.

Northwest States Indians perceived, emphasized, and at once phrased contrasts in era, early versus recent times, early for what we call "myths," recent for what we denote as "tales." Indians might also make note of presences in myths, and absences in tales, of leading dramatis personae such as Coyote, Grizzly, Blue Jay, Wild Cat, or Skunk people, supplemented by Indian-like people. Indians quickly verbalized the obvious fact that in myth times such actors were fundamentally people, although some were occasionally garbed like or behaved episodically like animals. Wholly Indian people were also cited as actors in tales, that is, narratives dated as of recent eras. In other words, Indians selected for mention only a few principal expressive components, when they offered a characterization of a genre. They were inattentive to all the other components, although in the intense hours of a recital, both recitalist and audience were acutely alert to exacting expression and treatment of every enjoined feature of content and style, and everyone was then sensitized to every sociocultural connection of expressive content.

If interest is directed to advancement of scientific knowledge of an oral literature, rather than to the geographical distribution and history of just two or three of its parts, it is profitable to look upon it initially as a cultural expression whose complexity and structure resemble a grammar, although it may well be more complex, and display much more of irregularity, than a grammar. Indians themselves perceived only a few structural components which were in direct focus for them.

The entirety of a myth genre, as of a tale genre, includes many things which should be cited and arranged. First, we should look for and, shortly, find structured expressive content, that is, many contrasted sets of expressive units; two, structured style, that is, a few of the same sets of expressive units in their special functions to effect form and frame; three, only a very few sets of linguistic units in the Northwest States, and these sets may function expressively, stylistically, or in both ways. Not least, four, we must probe most carefully and thoroughly for a range of sociocultural functions which attach to the whole genre and to every expressive set within it. Each expressive feature has major and minor relationships to societal groups, play, rites, supernaturalism, child education and imparting of worldview and ethics, and other parts of the sociocultural system. A genre has to be viewed, then, as a special and elaborate net of component structured systems, complex like an exceptionally elaborate language grammar, and classifiable into at least four main kinds of materials. Again, these are expressive content, stylistic features, linguistic features, and all the many sociocultural linkages. When you go beyond laconic citation of the fact of membership in a genre, you proceed to characterize everything that a set of myths or a set of tales exhibits, and in at least these four main types of material. You do not stop with just a label, or mere placement in a remote or recent time-era.

In a short paper, I find no more opportunity to offer detailed characterizations of the Northwest States genre of myths, or its genre of tales, than a grammarian can propose when he notes the fact that a number of very different linguistic structures are found in the region. May I observe, simply, that myths were in large numbers, probably several hundred in each community, and that they exhibited a remarkable variety of what I like to call "dramatic" or "play" structures, some long, some short. These might also be called myth "sub-genres." In my Clackamas Chinook writing I pointed up some contrasts in their structuring.[2] I chose to refer to such structuring in terms of acts and scenes. Like the Clackamas, all groups in the region had one-act, five- or six-scene, and two- to seven or more-act plays, many acts with two or more scenes. I showed that Chinook tales were structurally far simpler in their fewer acts and scenes. I obtained only these two genres, both pre-white, from my Clackamas informant.[3] In pre-white times only these two were also present, I suppose, in other groups of the region.

But in the same region I, and other field workers, have recorded possible examples of at least four additional genres. These were inchoate rather than fully crystallized, but indications point to four or more on the way to community actualization. Let me refer, then, to genres 3, 4, 5, and 6, all post-white. I have no time to offer detailed characterizations of them. Note, and this is of vital importance, that they lacked any linkage to child education, where pre-white myths and tales both functioned. Genre 3, of which we have a few examples from both Sahaptins and Salish in western Washington, employs principally pre-white myth features of content and style. It is a kind of damaged pre-white set of myths, because it adds items of nineteenth-century acculturative content and refashioning, and omits features of content and style, in ways which oldtime Indians would have regarded as in poor taste or improper.[4] Genre 4, which comprises examples which I recorded in several groups in Oregon, is of tales about events which transpired after whites were all about. Stylistically these tales are, I think, just like pre-white tales.[5] For genre 5, I note only one example, recorded by me in a Washington Sahaptin group.[6] It offers a poorly connected series of acts and scenes taken principally from pre-White myths, and a few from Christian beliefs, all presented in pre-white style. The significant thing is what has been done to expressive content. It appears to have been cavalierly mangled by recitalists and discussants who had been severely brainwashed by late nineteenth-century revivalist cults, principally by the region's Shaker religion. My one dictation also displays incongruities, shifts of interest, and other features, which point to confusion about worldview, emotional disturbance, and defective ego integration. I am confident that we may secure additional examples of such a tortured acculturative genre from older Indians who had tried to ingest the supernaturalism which they heard in Shaker meetings and Pentecostal religious services. Obviously, it was woven in with what was still accepted as true history as set forth in pre-white myths. It was an effort to supply a new orientation, a new world view. The sixth and last genre which I cite comprises remodelings of a handful of French Canadian tales which early nineteenth-century Indians originally heard in the medium of the Chinook Jargon used by natives of the province of Quebec who had settled among them. Dr. Leo J. Frachtenberg recorded in Kalapuya a small number of such tales.[7] They showed a remarkably altered set of features of expressive content. But the style in which they were told was almost wholly that of Kalapuya myths. Much of the expressive content that was French had not been perceived at all and was at once translated into Kalapuya kinds of content.[8] Every Indian in the region could identify each member of this acculturative genre as French in origin, because of actors, social relationships, and overt actions that were glaringly non-Indian. The main function of this genre was evidently that of light entertainment.

It is of interest that as long as Indians spoke their language fluently, their genre of pre-white myths survived more or less undamaged in expressive content and stylistic features, all through the destructive six or seven generations from 1810 until the language went extinct. The same observation probably applies to their dance and music repertoires. But the greater the ability to understand English, if not the know-how for functioning in the white man's world, the smaller the repertoire of myths, dances, and songs that was remembered. The repertoire of recitals of other myth-like or tale-like stories, that is, post-white genres 3 to 6, gradually expanded, as the repertoires in the two pre-white genres diminished. The people increasingly amused themselves and their household audiences, especially so after the 1890s, with recitals from the acculturative genres. Nevertheless, in spite of shrinkage in number of myths recalled, the myth genre, that still massive collection of plays of many structures, remained the core and model of the oral literature art. It continued, for older people, as a security prop, a belief system that supplied some certainties in a confusing new world. Mark this as of central interest: it continued to mold recital style in all genres. Acculturation added and altered expressive content, not style, just as almost every language of the region added much vocabulary to take care of new perceptions, but did not alter significantly in grammatical or syntactic structures. Briefly put, acculturation changed expressive content far more than style or structure. Indians supplemented their old repertoires of myths partly because of emotional burdens of maintaining an ancient and patently doomed art whose expressed social relationships, leading actors, values, and humor were lessening in meaning for them. Many younger Indian people did not and could not appreciate most of the myths even though they understood and spoke the language. Some of the new plays were also enjoyed, even by oldtimers, because they tied in with present-day reality and could be laughed at in defensive and relieving sallies.

It is easy to say these and a few other things. But in order to move toward a system of theoretical knowledge about the entirety of a corpus of oral literature, much more is necessary. There should be many examples of each genre, especially the acculturative ones which, so far, are wretchedly represented in Northwest States collections. Above all, each expressive and stylistic feature, after identification, and each social and ideological linkage, requires natives' commentary gained in painstaking question-and-answer sessions. Persistent inquiry, rather than mere verbatim dictation, ought to make up 70 to 90 percent of the time put in with informants by each field worker. Without that kind of field research, little may be deduced and the net return is almost certain to be meager, fragmentary and superficial knowledge. Right now, that is about all we have.

Editors' Notes

1. E.g., Boas (1940, 454ff).
2. Jacobs (1959b, 211-19).
3. Jacobs's Clackamas Chinook consultant, with whom Jacobs worked in 1929 and 1930, was Mrs. Victoria Howard.
4. For an example of this genre, see "Cougar and His Younger Brothers" (Adamson 1934).
5. See "The Sagandahs People," this volume, as an example of Jacobs's genre category 4.
6. See "Coyote's Journey," this volume, for the Upper Cowlitz Sahaptin text to which Jacobs alludes.
7. Frachtenberg's European tales told in Mary's River Kalapuya were published in Jacobs (1945, 275-335) and illustrate Jacobs's genre category 6.
8. See Ramsey (1987) for a discussion of Petit Jean tales in Native American oral traditions. See also Mattina's (1985) The Golden Woman for a discussion of a Colville version of a tale of European origin.

5

Areal Spread of Indian Oral Genre Features in the Northwest States

This important essay represents Jacobs's last and most complete published statement regarding features of expressive style in Northwest Indian folklore. It is a summary presentation of a much larger study, left unfinished at the time of Jacobs's death. An early draft of the essay was read at the annual meeting of the American Folklore Society, November 1970, at Los Angeles and was subsequently edited by Laurence C. Thompson and published in the *Journal of the Folklore Institute* 9.1:10-17 (1972).

In a summary paper of this sort I do not have space to include discussion of descriptive, method, and theory dividends, possible or actualized, from employment of the nineteenth century's spectacular time- and space-oriented comparative method. We all know that method long since became central in folklore researches. We speak of it as historical-geographical folklore. Note the fact that worldwide, continent-wide, region-wide, and district-wide utilizations of this history-oriented method never contributed worthily to substantial or systematic theoretical knowledge. It led to grand maps, catalogues, and orderly accumulations of a few kinds of data. At all times the method produced a special kind of return which was invaluable: it displayed, and it will long continue to expose to view, similarities and contrasts in the overt features with which it operated, motifs and plots principally. The innumerable questions that arise in awarenesses of these and other contrastive features can for some time to come be followed up both in field research and in pursuit of systematic theory about processes. I have used the method here in the form of a quick survey, by no means a full, probing, complete one, of contrastive classes of stylistic features that I have so far perceived in Oregon-Washington-Idaho Indian oral literature genres.

Because this has to be a short paper, I have excluded from consideration every feature of expressive content in the region's genres, where such a feature was not primarily employed for stylistic effect. Nevertheless, superficial examination of the region's features of oral genre style at once generates many exciting questions about folklore feature origins, patternings, processes, motives, feelings, and perceptions. The questions may not all be answerable with fresh probes of the embarrassingly meager inventories in the few collections that we possess. Probably only few questions can be solved. But, most importantly, a science is both a pursuit of systematic theory and a kind of inquiry in which ever more relevant questions are placed about what was and is happening.

There is not space, either, to show how a mere three Northwest states, before 1750, had sixty to seventy Indian languages, two to three thousand bands, hamlets, or villages, and something under, around, or over two hundred thousand people. This hunting-fishing-gathering population could once have yielded a million or more versions of myths, smaller numbers of tales, and no one can estimate how much of other oral genres. The returns in manuscript and print are annoyingly uneven. They range from large numbers of irresponsible, censored, bowdlerized, highly polished and edited, and nearly worthless versions, recorded in native text or colloquial English, to a minute array of precision-dictated and closely translated myth and tale genre texts, with as little English editorial polishing as possible. Myths of most variable merit that have been collected over the region total less than a thousand and will never exceed that number. Tales amount to a few hundred, forever so. The bleak harvest is almost finished. It is maybe one percent of what could have been obtained if the culture-bound, condescending, and racist invaders had the slightest capacity to perceive merit in the heritages of non Europeans. By the time anyone with such capacity went to work, native humiliation and extinction had erased almost everything. Folklore-oriented linguists, and they were the earliest recorders of myths and tales, arrived too late after the pioneers had trampled upon and destroyed the Indians.

Upon a foundation of insufficient sampling in the Northwest States I find at least twenty-one contrastive classes of stylistic features, only a small inventory of features in some classes, great numbers in other classes. That is, I find not just one notable class of style features, usually called 'functions', as in the translation of Vladimir Propp [1958—Eds.]; I find not just one other and a similar notable class of style features, called motifemes, as in Dundes [1964—Eds.], Maranda [(Köngäs and Maranda 1962)—Eds.], and others; I find not just one notable class of style features, called oppositions, polarities, dualities, or dyads, as in Lévi-Strauss [1968—Eds.]. I find these three, to be sure. I also find eighteen others, with very likely more that I have so far missed. I urge that the central classes of features in the large style sector of a Northwest States oral genre in its early morning, winter, and other recitals are to be located not in the three alone, not in the three primarily, but in them and in the others, eighteen or more. I urge, also, that an effort to weigh the relative importance of one class of style features in relation to any others is premature. We have not done enough close analysis of the region's genres to start weighing and assessing.

It is a matter, too, of how you translate 'structural' approach or 'structural mythology', or what you connote by those currently neon-light labels. To me, a small or partial structural analysis is witnessed in Propp's 'functions'; another in Dundes' motifemes; still another in the Hegelian oppositions for which Lévi-Strauss is a protagonist. These three do not expose many of the features of style in the Northwest States' genres. A complete analysis requires identification not of three but of all the contrastive features of style, together with a proper ordering of them in contrastive classes. Since I identify hundreds of style features which drop into twenty-one or more small, medium, and large slots, twenty-one classes, I list them as follows. Each class can be cited only with inadequate brevity in this paper.

1. First is gross architecture of myths and tales in winter evening household recitals. Their architecture may differ in mentions or uses of certain features at other times. I also term this class play structures.

All over the region we find a play structure wherein a succession of scenes sets forth oldest to youngest brother, sister, or friend, each of whom proceeds bullheadedly to certain death. Four do this everywhere except among Tillamook Salish and northwestern Washington State peoples where the number is sometimes three. The youngest and last succeeds, thanks to advice from an encounter supernatural. In another play structure, popular everywhere in the region, we find a long series of equally weighted acts wherein a supernaturally powerful young fellow, one of the Coyote people in a large part of the area, travels and does his thing youthfully, sadistically, and incongruously; in later acts of the long play he behaves maturely and helpfully. A third play structure, widely found too, has a male sibling enduring, in scene after scene, the narcissism, sadism, or violence of his younger sibling. Other play structures are obviously legion. Propp's 'functions' and Dundes' motifemes are to be regarded as alternative but unpreferred ways of citing the scene and act sequences that mark these gross architectural arrangements. Lévi-Strauss' dualities appear to be of negligible consequence in this first class of stylistic features: the four- and five-patterns evidently are many times as important as Hegelian two-patterns in the style class that serves for gross play architecture. Among the innumerable questions that arise from the multiplicity of play structures in each corpus of myths and tales is one that inquires about the quality and nature of perceptions of them by old-time recitalists, pedagogues, discussants, and auditors. This question is going to be more than difficult to answer. Another and related inquiry, also hard to deal with, treats of the ancient flexibility and manipulability of play structures. A third, with causes for the presence of so many short, medium, and long structures. Another, how they appeared in casual speech, in pre-dawn pedagogic sessions, or in other settings.

2. The second class of winter evening recital style features assembles myth and tale introductions.

3. The third class comprises myth epilogues.

4. The fourth class offers stylized ending phrases and words, and a related one, term it a corollary (4a), lists the phrases and words that an evening recitalist had to employ for overnight pauses and resumptions the following night. There is space to remark only that the classes of introductions displayed much greater similarities over the region than the classes of epilogues, endings, and overnight halts and resumptions. I am not sure why.

5. The class of pattern number or rhythm sets forth a dominant five-pattern in almost all peoples of the area, a combination four-for-female and five-for-male class solely among Tillamook Salish, and a four-pattern in northwestern Washington peoples. Every people, however, presented vestigial-like or remnant indications of two- and three-patterns in one percent or less of the instances where enumeration or pattern number was required. Polarities were never items in a pattern number style class. They arose only in social-relationship contexts, frequently indeed, as when an older brother and younger brother, or a man and a woman, were the sole actors or leading actors whose intense relationship points to an especially tender nerve in the society.

6. Style class six sets forth the spare inventory of phrases or words, like *to where the sun rises* or *to the mountains,* that everywhere was the small resource for expression of distance or location. These items were astonishingly similar all over the region. They account for ease and precision of translation from any one to any other wholly unrelated regional language. Borrowing of myths may have been facilitated by them.

7. This seventh class is of the few items that were permissible for expression of time. Regional translatability here was also noteworthy, this in spite of great differences, from language to language, in tense and aspect grammatical devices. Particle or adverbial items like *the next morning, presently,* and *now then* were in all the languages and did not correlate with grammatical features that expressed time or aspect.

8. Historical-geographical scholars' motifs, in the hundreds, assemblages listed fully by Stith Thompson for North American Indians over forty years ago as well as in his later six-volume world coverage motif index classic [(1929, 1955-1958)—Eds.], I prefer to denominate plot expediters. Each was a slice or small stretch of expressive content that functioned primarily in a stylistic way. The region's oral genres' principal expressive content features were not at all located in these Thompson motifs. Expressive content is identifiable, instead, in special features of supernaturalism, kinds of leaders, shamans, wives, heroes, and nuisances, not least in the Northwest States' social relationships that operated most troublesomely, in the principles of ethics that were too often flouted, and in the sociocultural incongruities perceptions of which contributed to entertainment and relieved taut feelings.

When Thompson motifs can be regarded as encapsulated repositories, so to speak, for awarenesses and feelings, there we do find motifs that functioned as expressive content. But, again, the plot expediter and style functions of motifs were vastly more significant than the expressive content functions that they had.

9. The Northwest States' classes of explanatory elements included only a small list in each group. Its list differed markedly from the list in each adjacent group. The little appended explanatory tags did not spread at all. Nor did their manner of utilization except for one feature of style; it was that of the region-wide actor-announcer. Transformers may have been largely projected into the myths by Franz Boas and other earlier anthropological folklorists. Indeed, in the Northwest States' oral genres, transformers may have been absent. On the other

hand, any oral genre actor, major or minor, could step out of character for a moment and announce two or three traits, only that many, of an animal, bird, or natural feature that would appear in later eras.

10. The tenth class treats of linguistic features of style that were peculiar to myth or tale recitals or pre-dawn pedagogic sessions. It is certain that this class was of negligible import, if it was even present, in all Northwest States groups. A well-done structural delineation of all Northwest States classes of style features would exhibit total, or nearly entire, omission of a style class that comprised contrastive linguistic features. Professional linguists seem, today, to be wholly incapable of facing so horrible a fact as a literature style that lacks significant and distinctive linguistic features. They grope for such features like a farmer searching for a diamond in a hay stack.

11. Melody contours and vocal mannerisms of morning pedagogues, year-round discussants, or evening recitalists are unknown except for a random item or two. We can cite Sahaptin monotone declamation of a Coyote person's speech and behavior; falsetto for a Skunk person's words and actions; an octave or two below normal voice for Grizzly actors.

12. The class of permissible references to weather, flowers, grass, mountains, clouds, nature in general, was everywhere minute, indeed virtually nil.

13. The class of references to moods and feelings was also almost nil. Sentiments were deduced from plot action. They were not put into morphemes or words.

14. The class of selected features that described movement and travel was tiny. The style that framed plot action allowed selection of sequences of a very few laconic statements such as *he left, he went a long way, he arrived at a hamlet*. Little more than such short-short utterances was stylistically permissible.

15. The class of references to personality characteristics was also almost a blank, at least so in evening recitals. In them, a headman was never said to be wise, a shaman never powerful, a wife never good, a person never clever or mischievous, except a Wild Cat person in one or two of the region's oral genres. A person's attractiveness and physical beauty required, almost everywhere, one stylized utterance: *he (or she) had long hair*. No other feature or facets of admired anatomy, integrity, or intelligence could be cited. Unadmired items of anatomy that could be selected for expression were few: they included pendulous breasts

and, for men, baldness. Such items were very likely cited in casual speech about myths and tales, maybe too in pre-dawn pedagogy with its myth illustrations.

16. Every community had its manner of required response to each recital utterance, its requisite postures for children and adults at such recitals, and responses and postures which, unfortunately, no one ever inquired about for pre-dawn pedagogy.

17. Songs by myth or tale actors frequently punctuated plot action and functioned for relief, as art, and as entertainment. No style features peculiar to myth or tale singing differentiated it from other singing, as far as is known.

18. The stylistic role of humor was central in evening recitals, probably also in year-round casual conversation about myths and tales. Humor lighted some of the darkest tragic action. Purely humorous myths, short ones, abounded everywhere, in all likelihood. One may wonder how funny the pre-dawn teaching sessions were.

19. All the evidence points to an extreme of laconicism in depiction of action, movement, travel, feelings, relationships, and personalities, with great speed in plot action. Verbigeration and slow action were absent, except for four- and five-pattern scene repetitions. The oral genres therefore attained something approaching a world extreme in laconicism and abstract expression. This was abstract expressionism in the medium of words and verbalizations of relationships and actions.

20. A stylistic class that requires discussion lists features that comprised assertions of improprieties and fears of consequences if proper season of year, time of day, and the like were not adhered to when formally reciting a myth rather than casually talking about parts of it. Indeed, casual discussions of myths were acceptable at all times.

21. The last class identifies and structures the features of what may be called titles. That is, it treats of casual speech references to specific myths and tales. Even in most conversations, references to myths were short, precise, and selected for citation only certain actors and behaviors. In addition, each title system resembled each other title system in the area. Structures of titles were extraordinarily similar in the few language groups, among the sixty or more of the region, where titles were written down by more careful field-workers.

In some districts, metaphor served strikingly. For example, Mrs. Jacobs's remarkable aged Coquille Athabaskan informant punctuated his utterances with *they— the deer—ran, like thunder.* And *they— the deer—came, like the ocean coming.* Metaphor of this kind may be common in the region, but I lack the data to show how common.[1] Other stylistic devices, long familiar in English literature, turn up here and there. But they are only minor embellishments and style supplements, not central features of the oral literatures.

In conclusion, a regional sketch of classes of style features reveals so many nearly identical classes in so many disparate language groups, sociocultural systems, and ideological heritages, some of them four hundred or more miles apart, that it is necessary to ask one decisive question. Long ago, were the closely similar early- morning pedagogic sessions, the similar or identical day- and night-long casual discussions, and the similar winter-recital season model performances principal sociocultural factors, maybe equal ones too, in the unexpectedly wide spreads of stylistic features? It is possible that we can find supports for a theory that features of formal recital style had long since diffused, and were maintained and shared during long eras, to an extent not witnessable for some classes of features of expressive content such as social relationships, world view, plot actions, ethics, incongruities, tragic situations, and actor personalities. In clumsy because simplistic and too general terms, recital features may have been more diffusable and maintainable than recital selections of features of expressive content. Phrased alternatively, many classes of style features may have been more similar over wider diameters than were some of the classes of expressive-content features. Similar functionings of the oral genres, in somewhat different food-gatherer sociocultural systems, account, then, for a hitherto unsuspected contrast between the dynamics of recital style classes and the dynamics of recital expressive-content classes. The supporting or shaping roles of pedagogic sessions and of year-round discussions can only be guessed at. We will never know how much they affected or molded the recitals.

We are especially in the dark about style and content in southwestern Oregon men's sweathouse discussions, pedagogy with youths,[2] recitals, and year-round household and work discussions. The dynamics of oral genre shaping and maintenance in that one smaller region may have been a little different from the rest of the region, possibly only because of the additional variable of a distinctive men's sweathouse way of life in southwestern Oregon.

Editors' Notes

1. The metaphors occur in texts told directly in English. It is not known if they appear in the Native language versions.

2. In southwestern Oregon, where men and boys shared sweathouse sleeping quarters, older boys may have lectured the younger boys about cultural values during early morning pedagogic sessions. Jacobs wondered whether myths and tales told during these pre-dawn sessions may have differed in content and style from those told to mixed audiences during winter evening and other recital times.

Oral Traditional Texts with Interpretations

6

Badger and Coyote Were Neighbors

(Clackamas Chinook)

Victoria Howard dictated this Clackamas Chinook myth to Melville
Jacobs at her home in West Linn, Oregon, in 1929. Mrs. Howard
had heard it from her mother-in-law. This text represents the myth
genre, #1 in Jacobs's taxonomy (see "Genres in Northwest States
Oral Literature," this volume).The text and interpretation reprinted
here are from *The Content and Style of an Oral Literature* (1959b,
27-36). The phonetic text and translation were originally published
in Jacobs 1958, 106-12. See Nichols (1983) for another
interpretation of this text. For ethnographic background on the
Chinookans of the lower Columbia, see Silverstein (1990); also Ruby
and Brown (1976) and Rubin (1999) for more popular treatments.

Coyote and his five children lived there (at an undisclosed
location), four males, one female. Badger was a neighbor
there, he had five children, all males. Each day they (all ten
children) would go here and there. They came back in the evening.
And the next day they would go again. Now that is the way they
were doing. They would go all over, they traveled about.

Now they reached a village, they stayed up above there, they
looked down below at it, they saw where they (the villagers) were
playing ball. And as they stayed there and watched, the people (of
the village beneath) saw them now. They went to the place there
where they played ball. Now they (the villagers) played. When they
threw the ball it (that ball) was just like the sun. Now they stayed
(above) there, they watched them playing. Sometimes it (the ball)
would drop close by them. Now they quit (playing). Then they (the

ten children who were watching) went back home, they went to their houses.

The next day then they did not go anywhere. All day long they chatted about that ball (and schemed about stealing it). They discussed it. Now their father Badger heard them. He said to his sons, "What is it that you are discussing?" So they told their father. "Yes," they said to him, "we got to a village, and they were playing ball. When the ball went it was just like the sun. We thought that we would go get it." Now then he said to his children, "What do you think (about talking this over with Coyote too)?" So then they said to Coyote, "What do you think?" He said, "My children should be the first ones (to run with the ball), if they bring the ball." Badger said, "No. My children should be the first ones to do it (run with the stolen ball)." Coyote said, "No. My children have long bodies, their legs are long. They can run (faster than your children). Your children have short legs." So then he replied to him (to Coyote), "Very well then."

Now the next day they got ready, and they went. They reached there. At that place one of them (the oldest son of Coyote) went immediately to the spot where the ball might drop. He covered (buried) himself at that place (on the playing field). Then another (the next oldest son) buried himself farther on, and another one (the third in age) still farther away. All four (sons of Coyote) covered themselves (with soil on the field). The last one farther on at the end (was) their younger sister. Now the (five) children of Badger merely remained (on the hill above the field), they watched.

Soon afterwards then the people (of that village) came to there, they came to play ball. Now they threw the ball to where it fell close by him (Coyote's oldest son). He seized it. They looked for it, they said, (because they knew that) "Coyote's son is hiding it!" He let it go, and they took it, and they played more. Now it dropped close by him there once again. So then he took it, and he ran. The people turned and looked, they saw him running, he was taking the ball. Now they ran in pursuit, they got close to him, he got close to his younger brother (the second in age), he threw the ball to him. He said to him, "We are dying (going to be killed) because of the ball. Give a large chunk of it to our father." (His pursuers now caught up to and killed him.) Then the other (the second) one took it, and he ran too. The people pursued him, he got close to his young brother

Victoria Howard, Jacobs's Clackamas Chinook consultant.

(Coyote's third son). Now they seized him (the second son), and he threw it to his younger brother. They killed all four of them. Now only their younger sister held the ball, she ran, she ran and ran, she left them quite a distance (behind because she was the fastest runner of them all). She got close to the Badgers. Now as they (the villagers who pursued) seized her she threw the ball to them (to the five Badger children), she said to them, "Give the biggest portion to our father (to Coyote). We have died because of the ball."

The Badgers took the ball. He (the first and oldest Badger child) dropped it when he picked it up. Another (the next to the oldest) took it, he also dropped it when he picked it up. They (the pursuers) got to there, and the people stood there (watching the Badger children fumbling the ball). They said, they told them, "So those are the ones who would be taking away the ball!" They laughed at them (at the seemingly clumsy Badger children). They said, "Let it be a little later before we kill them!" Soon now they (the Badgers) kicked at the ground, and wind blew (and) dust (and) darkness stood there. Dust covered (everything), and the wind blew. Now the Badgers ran, they ran away with the ball. And those people pursued them. They got tired, they got thirsty (from wind and dust), they (the pursuers) turned back to their home.

On the other hand those others (the Badgers) lay down (because of exhaustion) right there when they had gotten close (to their own home). And there they sat (and rested). Now they hallooed, they said to their father, "Badger! we left your children far back there!" Now they hallooed again, they went and told Coyote, "Back yonder we left your children." That is the way they did to them (they first deceived Badger and Coyote). Now Badger went outside, he said to his children, "Now really why did you do like that? You have been teasing and paining him (Coyote)." Then they (the Badger children) went downhill (and entered the village), it was only Badger's children (who returned). They brought the ball with them.

Now Coyote tried in vain to drown himself. He did not die. Then he built a fire, he made a big fire, he leaped into it there. He did not burn, he did not die. He took a rope, he tied it, he tied it on his throat, he pulled himself up, once more he did not die. He took a knife, he cut his throat, (again) he did not die. He did every sort of thing that he intended for killing himself. He gave up. I do not know how many days he was doing like that (trying one or another means of committing suicide). Now he quit it, and he merely wept all the day long. (After a while) he gave that up (too).

Then Badger said to his children, "He has quit (mourning) now. So then cut up the ball for him. Give him half." And they did that for him, they gave him half. He took it, and he went here and there at the place where his children used to play. There he now mashed (into many pieces) that ball, at the place where they used to play. That was where he took it, he mashed it up, the ball was entirely gone (now).

Then they continued to live there, and Coyote was all alone. Now he went to work, he made a loose big pack basket. Then it was getting to be springtime, and when the leaves were coming out, now he got ready, and he went to the place there where they had killed his children. He got to the (grave of the) first one (his oldest son). He picked ferns, he lined his pack basket with them. He got to the place where they had killed the first of his sons, he collected his bones, he put them into it (into the basket), he laid them in it neatly. Then he got more ferns, he picked the leaves, he covered (the bones of) his son. Now he went a little farther, and he again got to bones (of his second son). Then he also put them into it (into the basket), and that is the way he did again. He collected the bones of all five of his children.

Now he went on, he proceeded very very slowly, he went only a short distance. Then he camped overnight. The next day he proceeded again, also very slowly like that. On the fifth day, then he heard them (talking to one another in the basket). They said, "You are lying upon me. Move a little." Then he went along all the more slowly. Now he kept going, he went just a short distance, and then he picked more leaves, he covered it all (with utmost care and constant replenishing with fresh leaves). And that is the way he did as he went along.

She (perhaps a centipede) would run across his path, she would say to him, "Sniff sniff sniff! (because of the bad odor of decaying flesh) Coyote is taking dead persons along!" He paid no heed to her. Now she ran repeatedly and all the more in front of him, again she would speak like that to him, "Sniff! Coyote is carrying dead persons along!" He laid his basket down very very slowly (with utmost care), he got a stick, he ran after her. I do not know where she went and hid.

Then he packed his carrying basket on his back again, and now he went very very slowly, and he heard his children. Now they were chatting, they were saying, "Move around slowly and carefully! we are making our father tired." Then he was glad, and he went along even more slowly and cautiously. (He walked so very slowly that) he saw his (previous night's) campfire, and then he again camped overnight.

He went on again the next morning, and then that thing (the bug) ran back and forth across his path right there by his feet. Now he became angry. He placed his basket down, and again he chased it. I do not know where it hid.

On the fifth day then he heard them laughing. So he went along even more painstakingly. Now that thing went still more back and forth in front of him by his feet. He forgot (in his great irritation and tension), he (much too abruptly) loosened and let go his pack basket. "Oh oh oh" his children sounded (and at once died from the shock of the sudden movement of the basket). All done, he finished, and he again put back his basket on himself. When he went along now he did not hear them talking at all. He went along then. They were dead now when he uncovered his basket. Only bones were inside it. He reached his house. The following day then they buried them. He finished (with that effort). He wept for five days.

Then he said, "Indeed I myself did like that (and lost my children because of my doing). The people (who will populate this country) are coming and close by now. Only in that one manner shall it be, when persons die. In that one way had I brought my children back, then the people would be like that (in later eras). When they died in summertime wintertime or toward springtime, after the leaves (came on the trees) they (all the dead) would have come back to life, and such persons would have revived on the fifth day (following a ritual like the one I attempted). But now his (any mourner's) sorrow departs from him after ten days (of formal mourning). Then he can go to anywhere where something (entertaining) is happening or they are gambling (and) he may (then shed his mourning and) watch on at it."

Let us examine this plot and its form in detail. The narrator did not say which one of the Myth Age men who were named Coyote has four sons and a youngest and favorite child who is a female, nor did she indicate the names of the sons. Older storytellers would have recalled and noted both. However, Mrs. Howard did give the daughter's name, literally translated as "good runner" or "fast runner." This daughter has a spirit-power for foot-racing, somewhat as in another myth (*Clackamas Chinook Texts*, 7 [(Jacobs 1958)—Eds.]) where a Coyote's daughter, also a favorite child, has a spirit-power —this time for fatty foods.

The fact that the fifth, youngest, and most fleet-footed of Coyote's children is a daughter is not central to this myth, although it serves to identify the Coyote actor who is the tragic parent of the drama. The daughter's presence also reminded an audience about the exceptional regard in which several Coyotes held their feminine offspring. Such affection is of interest in a social system where females occupied a lower status and where projections of females in the Myth Age were often unflattering. Since the literature also presents the younger child as the smartest, the play barely hints at an Oedipal theme: it is really ignored in the plot and is not evinced again even at a deeper level of awareness.

The Coyote of this myth is to a degree consistent with the familiar Columbia River Valley composite of a more or less entertaining narcissist (this aspect of him usually placed in the earlier portion of the play) and an adult, mature, and deity-like man. Usually the second part of the composite completes the myth. The structuring of such a personality in a plot which also has two parts—the first Id-dominated, the second reality-oriented—connects with the native conceptualization of genetic developments in the personality of a man.

Actually, the myth provides no significant increment to the inventory of Myth Age personalities or to knowledge of Clackamas concepts of personality characterization. Since Badger is a plot expediter—he stands for any father who has a number of sons—and his children represent any village youngsters who are sensible because they are well reared, a recitalist suppresses citation of other traits of their personalities.

When Coyote's five children and his neighbor Badger's five are at play, they wander about, like any Northwest States group of children. They emerge from the woods and see a nearby village where people are playing a game with a marvelous ball. "It shines like the sun" is a literal translation of words which are very likely a poetic way of indicating that the ball is a remarkably good one and that the visiting children would like to have it. Unfortunately, the ball suggests something about which ethnographic and myth materials offer no really satisfactory clues. Perhaps the ball is just a shinny ball of wood (Indians of western Oregon played this game). Perhaps the myth implies, instead, something which is admirable and therefore referred to metaphorically as an object as bright as—that is, as impressive or excellent as—the sun. The logical ethnographic deduction would seem to be that youngsters of one hamlet might roam to another hamlet and conduct a raid to obtain valuables from it. It would appear that danger accompanied such excursions and that there was tension between children as well as adults of different settlements.

The next day the ten children, who continually play together, devise a scheme to steal the ball. Badger's children tell him about the plan. He suggests that they discuss it with Coyote, and they do so, perhaps in the spirit in which children shared desires and plans with respected elders of the household and with the village headman. Coyote persuades Badger that his own Coyote children should take the ball first because they have longer legs and bodies than the Badger children. This passage is primarily a petty item of naturalist biology which accounts for the anatomy of badgers, but it may also imply that Coyote is expressing pride, as a Northwest Coast man might, in his children. He is therefore also speaking, in characteristic Northwest Coast temper, with hurtful detraction of his friend's children. Since Coyotes are headmen, it is fitting that he speak as such worthies would have spoken.

So on the next day, the Coyote children steal the ball. The feature of style which I call "youngest-smartest" requires that the oldest carry the ball first. He sprints with it to the next in age, and so on to the fifth, who is the speediest although she is female. She passes the ball to the Badger children. By the time they have acquired it the villagers have pursued and killed all five of Coyote's children. The Badger children are smarter than the reckless Coyotes. The Badgers stand and pick up and drop the ball as if they were fumbling it, and the pursuing villagers pause to ridicule the seemingly clumsy Badgers. When the villagers are all around, the Badgers kick at the soil, a wind comes up, and the place becomes dusty and dark. The villagers cannot peer through the dust to see what the Badgers are doing. Now they are free to run away at their own moderate speed with less danger of capture and death. The intelligent subterfuge of the children who know their limitation allows them to escape with their lives and with the ball.

When the Badger children near their home, they at once try an extremely cruel deception on their father. They call to him as if they were the young Coyotes returning. They tell him that his children have been killed. When Mrs. Howard was translating, she added the comment that Coyote then tells Badger that the Badger children "could not do anything," which is hardly a sympathetic way of addressing a parent thrown into sudden shock and grief. Coyote is thereby portrayed as lacking in warmth of feeling for his friend. The storyteller does not resort to a verb or statement which offers a single lineament of Badger's feelings. The raconteur presents solely some facts of external behavior— the return of the Badger children, their misrepresentation of themselves, and Coyote's disparaging observation about Badger's children. These are the two or three cues which the audience receives. Individuals might respond according to the identification which each has for children, Coyote, or the shocked Badger father, and in terms of a Northwest Indian's perception of such a situation and the relationships in it.

I think that Badger's response, whatever it is or whatever each member of the audience feels empathically for him, is not necessarily the principal expressive feature of this scene. The sentiments of the grieved and tricked parent would perhaps be thought central by a Euro-American raconteur because of his concern for control of children by a father and because of a Euro-American father's feelings about his progeny. Speculation about audience identification with the shocked Badger should not be burdened by the typical Euro-American manner of involvement in the needs of a father. I believe that Clackamas witnessed as much if not more of identification with the children who so mercilessly deceived their parent, and with Coyote, who in typical Northwest Coast fashion decries the young Badgers although he supposes that they have just died. I have no doubt that his ungracious observation was amusing to Clackamas. He was more interested in cutting down to size the young Badgers, even after their death, than he was concerned about being supportive to their anguished sire, his neighbor and friend.

Some members of the audience may have identified with the bereaved father, others with the sadistic actors. But the point is that stimulation of audience response to the scene is unguided—the raconteur did nothing to structure audience reaction. She presented only an outline of a situation, and her sketchy depiction left each person free to respond according to his leanings. The audience knew that Badger would quickly feel better because it was Coyote who would shortly learn about the fate of his own children. Therefore the audience need not long identify with Badger, if it did so at all. In Western literatures a reader does not know what is going to happen. Since most of the oral literature audience already know, their response of identification with one or another actor is determined by foreknowledge.

Now the Badger children come closer, speak to Coyote, and reveal the truth about his frightful loss. When they near their father and Coyote they can no longer maintain the imposture. Coyote is obviously overwhelmed, although the storyteller does not employ such a descriptive verb. Mrs. Howard subsequently informed me, and a more practiced narrator probably said, that Coyote falls down, rolls on the ground in agony, and cries out in the intensity of his dismay and grief. Badger's behavior is limned with similar brevity and externality. It is clear that he has more kindliness than Coyote because he scolds his children for their deception which fooled both him and Coyote and which only augments Coyote's tragedy.

Over a period of days the sorrowing father attempts to commit suicide. He tries to drown himself, but he cannot. He tries to leap into a big fire, to hang himself, and to cut his throat—perhaps he tries other devices, too. But he lives. One wonders whether his ineptitude or his strength of will to remain alive are greater than his wish to destroy himself. At last Coyote gives up the abortive efforts at self-destruction; then he weeps for some days. Finally he returns to normal behavior and manner of living.

Badger, who is consistently benevolent, has his children cut the ball and give half of it to Coyote, because of the equal share in it that the five Coyote children established with their five Badger colleagues in thievery. The division of spoils probably reflects native custom wherein plunder is shared within the raiding party. (It is also of interest, apropos of native evaluations, that the two parents never advised their children against undertaking the foray.) Now Coyote takes his half of the ball, chops it into small pieces, and leaves them at the playground where his deceased children lie. To all appearances he does not want to see or possess the reminder of his children's sad fate and his loss; perhaps, too, his action parallels the customary burying or disposing of a deceased individual's personal effects so that they are not close to his home.

So far the plot centers upon a tragedy wherein a parent is so crushed by the death of his children that he strives, at least consciously, to destroy himself. The grieving parent's attempts fail for reasons which the raconteur neither reveals nor needs to divulge but which can be deduced from our knowledge of the personality of a Coyote and from general knowledge of causes of failure at suicide. Presumably everybody, in every society, has mixed feelings about his extinction. Coyote's inability to succeed in self-destruction is also consistent with the literature's delineation of a Coyote: whenever that actor responds to a wholly internal stimulus or need, he is a bungler. When something entirely outside himself challenges, something much more important than himself, his responses are powerful, adult, even deity-like. In the first part of this myth, Coyote is perhaps felt to be the trickster who is so absorbed in himself—and his children are an extension of himself—that he has only a modicum of hostility toward the outside world. The energy in his hostility is feeble, and he directs it, in the form of a slight antagonism, against Badger. His urge to kill himself is not reinforced by a need to strike at Badger or anyone else. Clackamas probably laughed at his successive ventures at suicide and commented about his ineptitude. They also laughed, I think, because they identified with him and were relieved when he remained alive. Of course, since they recalled the story, they knew that he would not kill himself, and so they were released to laugh at fumblings at the same time that they felt pity for him.

However, we should not read in too much about the psychology of suicide among Clackamas. Nowhere else is suicide noted in their myths, and the region's ethnographic notations of instances of suicide are virtually nil. Stylized procedures for suicide must have been present, but evidences of them, except for this myth, are lacking. Field data which can be utilized for formulations concerning social relationships and central features of personality are so fragmentary that we must be especially cautious in inferences about the causation or manifestations of any infrequent or pathological behavior like suicide.

During the following winter Coyote, who now lives by himself, is obviously continuing to think of his children. He therefore makes a loose pack basket, with a singular purpose in mind. In the springtime he goes to the playground where his children lie buried in shallow graves dug by their executioners. He lines his pack basket with fresh ferns, carefully lays the bones of his children in it, and cushions each skeleton with fronds. Since he appropriates nothing which really belongs to the village, the removal of bones from the graves causes no opposition in the residents.

Now Coyote proceeds homeward with the precious pack on his back. He walks with extreme slowness and caution so as to avoid jarring the bones and "killing" the children for all time. Although the walk from his home to the graves near the other village takes only some hours, the return requires five days because of his measured steps. He must never jar the bones. It is very likely on the fourth day, when he is close to home, that he hears or believes that he hears the children talking in the basket behind his head. At once he walks still more slowly and carefully. He constantly adds fresh fronds to the basket, perhaps in the belief that they will help in curing the children. There is drama and pathos in this adding of curative greens, in this at once hopeful and sad experiment designed to change decomposing flesh into healthy living matter.

Now a horrible centipede-like bug crosses back and forth in front of him, calling to him, "Coyote is carrying dead people!" and sniffing in a manner which indicates that the contents of the basket smell like decomposing corpses. Coyote is annoyed. He lays down the basket with utmost care and he pursues the bug with a stick. But she is so fast that he cannot find her (a prefixed morpheme for gender notes her sex). When he resumes his slow walk, the children in the pack talk again. Or he supposes that they are talking. Then the bug reappears and distracts him again; he chases it as before but cannot kill it. While he walks along, he senses that the children are shifting positions in the basket in order to make each other more comfortable. That is, he feels that they are alive or virtually alive. Now his hope mounts to its highest pitch, and the audience can identify with the parent who feels that lost ones are about to be delivered living and well.

The next and last day, when Coyote is proceeding at a pace no faster than creeping and home is in sight, the bug once again runs back and forth in front of him. It annoys him to a point where he lets down his basket abruptly, and the children die immediately because of the suddenness of his movement. He realizes what he has done to his children when he no longer feels or hears them as he walks, but he does not examine the contents of the basket until he reaches home. Then he finds only lifeless bones.

The drama says simply that Badger and Coyote give the remains a final burial, in a manner which may have reminded Clackamas of neighboring peoples, such as Tillamooks, who practiced ceremonial reburial. When the story succinctly adds that Coyote weeps again for five days, it implies that now his grief is under control and that he mourns in a stylized manner. Again, canons of literary form bar any mention of feelings. The storyteller remarks solely about facts of the burial and Coyote's subsequent five days of weeping. Selection of these two items provides the stimuli to spur the audience' reaction. It is as if, in terms of current communication theory, an elaborate body of information was transmitted in two neatly coded signals. Every member of the audience would automatically decode and comprehend. Today, because of the deaths of employable native informants, a scholar can only speculate about the details of such comprehension.

In the scene which follows, Coyote assumes his role of announcer of things to come. He says humbly that if he had done otherwise, all dead persons would be revived in springtime after the first fresh leaves were opened. But, he proclaims, people will henceforth die and remain dead, even as his children have died; furthermore, a male mourner's formal expression of sorrow, even a parent's, will last no more than ten days. The myth ignores mention of the much longer period of mourning that was assigned to females.

The principal stress in this drama is patently upon the problem of death, but it is not wholly of the kind that folklorists caption "The

Origin of Death." Its theme is not so much causation of death as the tragedy and sorrow of a bereaved father. Although a mother's experience of such sorrow is not suggested, one wonders whether women responded to the drama much as men, and therefore whether omission of a mother is stylistic parsimony rather than a meaningful feature of expressive content. Although the words of the play deal with fathers, their children, and death, it may not be a man's rather than a woman's story, because it really treats of broad problems of death, immortality, and the feelings of any grieved parent. Parents may be symbolized, with characteristic Northwest Coast antifeminism, by fathers.

Audience identification with Coyote flows partly from the deep wishes in everyone to circumvent the outrage and horror of decomposition and permanent death for kin and for one's self. Coyote's nearly successful rescue of his beloved children and his almost triumphant resuscitation of them are imaginative projections of a wish that people might return unscathed from a terrible death, perhaps long after burial and decay. The play is by the same token a projection of a wish that one's deceased children might return to life and that one might be indestructible himself!

This is not all. Latent features of the myth, that is, audience responses at deeper levels of awareness, are perhaps not so few or simple; yet further speculation about them may be worth venturing. The recitalist portrays Coyote as a father who almost manages to do the impossible for his children (it was at least possible in the remote era of myths), and Coyote appears to be succeeding because he hears the children speaking, and he feels their movements. Success is almost achieved when at the crucial moment he no longer can control the fury, the outrage, stirred in him by a tormentor who is overtly only a nasty bug but who covertly may represent feelings that are much more basic than those initiated by a mere bug.

The centipede mocks Coyote until his poise and his care in walking disintegrate. Who could remain well coordinated in the decisive moments before one's five children escape from everlasting death into eternal life? The fast-moving bug's reiterated taunts unnerve Coyote in the infinitely anxious and ultimate minutes of the victory which he feels is virtually his. The creature's sniffs tell him that the children are more than dead: they are putrid, even as he shall be some day. An unbearably tragic reality confronts Coyote in spite of his wishes. And there is a sound dramatic touch as well as psychological insight in the selection of a centipede as the symbol of nagging reality. It is a hideous bug who says to Coyote, in effect, that he is deceiving himself in supposing that any dead and disgustingly putrescent person can be revived. The bug develops in Coyote both frenzy and a flickering attention to reality; his anger grows with increasing fear and doubt that movements he feels and voices he hears in the pack basket are really the living children. He is in mounting terror that they may remain bones and decaying flesh in spite of his supernatural power and his care. And so in his final agony of uncertainty and frustration, he strikes out at that which symbolizes reality.

Finally he has to look at the lifeless bones and flesh which, with the bug, constitute another facet of this drama's symbolization of reality. Coyote must accept reality even though it is extreme tragedy for him. Reality is corpses. It is only when Coyote achieves final acceptance that he announces the manner in which reality will operate for future people, as for himself. No one will ever be able to return from death or to effect the return of others.

When Coyote fails, it is as if he suddenly matures—in a manner which Northwest Indians point up by his transition to a godlike enunciator of the future. As with us, a person who suffers deeply and is humiliated by his error may thereupon urge others not to act as ill-advisedly. Still more, acceptance of a cruel reality is mature and wise. Now Coyote reacts not as a mere human being who is unable to succeed and who lashes about in frenzy. He becomes the herald of the future, a role which ordinary human beings never play, and he no longer seeks suicide. Now he and all other males will mourn only during a ritually limited period of five or ten days. The death of loved kin will be resolved not in a self-destructive response or in irate striking-out but in the culture's formalized manner and time for expression of grief. After the tenth day, people will cease overt and stylized expressions of sorrow. Social participations, even gambling, may follow.

The myth which deals in this dramatic manner with the universal challenge of death also appears, as do a number of other myths, to put deities in their place in this culture which never accorded omnipotence or omniscience to a projection figure. The myth appears to say that even the most deity-like personage was circumscribed in what he could do. He was unable to defeat decomposition, that is, an inevitable and eternal death. There is a reality which the most potent of persons cannot control, and a more specialized group in a wealthier society than the Clackamas might have formulated in words the fact of such a reality.

Nor did Coyote's inability to conquer death arise solely from the nature of living things; it came also from a human failure to control his aggressive impulses. It would therefore appear that here, as elsewhere, Clackamas hardly ventured upon a distinction between nature and man. To Clackamas, that which is tragic is consequent upon man's nature, and his capacities and qualities are due to the nature of his human-like predecessors in the Myth Age. Coyote lacked self-control—anger rose in him to such a pitch that it shattered him. Again, the drama documents the conviction that there has never been a perfect or godlike person, one who could handle with poise every situation, no matter how grim. No one, certainly not Coyote, has ever been all-wise, all-powerful, or perfect. That is why no person of the modern period may live forever.

A philosophically more sophisticated recitalist might have said, "That which our predecessors in this Clackamas land experienced because of their human limitations correlates as cause of our happinesses and tragedies." No god intervenes in the destiny of human beings, and there never was a god. Only the human-like actors of the myths played a role in fashioning the world. Thus the myth offers important evidence of the Clackamas world view. Coyote puts in words that which must be for all time regarding death.

7

The Old Man and His Daughter-in-law.
Her Fingers Stuck Together

(Clackamas Chinook)

Victoria Howard dictated this myth text to Jacobs at her home in
West Linn, Oregon in 1930. She had learned it from her mother-in-
law. The English translation of this text is reprinted from *Clackamas
Chinook Texts,* Part 2 (1959a, 310-12); Jacobs's interpretation is
from *The People Are Coming Soon* (1960a, 202-5). Silverstein
(1990) provides an ethnographic sketch of the Chinookans of the
lower Columbia; see also Ruby and Brown (1976) and Rubin (1999)
for more popular treatments.

When my mother-in-law ate something, and her fingers
became sticky, she would twiddle her fingers, she would
say, "That is the way that the woman became in the
myth." She said, "Oh dear me. Tomorrow it will be stuck together.
My fingers will be sticky."

An old man, his son, (and) his wife were living there. They had
quantities of food. At a distance from there (in another village were)
her parents (and) her younger sisters. They prepared quantities of
various things, they stored them for the winter. Now I do not know
what year it was, and then it became cold. They could do nothing.
They ran out of all their food. As for those others (the old man, his
son, and his daughter-in-law) they ran short of food too. The old
man would go down to the river, he would get some (a very few
poor fish), I do not know what he would take back with him, he
would bring it back home. That is what they would eat. When they
finished eating, he would gather up the bones, he would take them
and put them into the river there. He wished that they (the fish

bones) would become fish. They would (indeed) become old ones (old and poor fish), and so the following day those were what he would go fetch. All that winter and I do not know for how long a time that was all that they ate.

Now she (his daughter-in-law) got tired of it (of eating poor and old fish every day). She thought, "Oh dear me. My parents have quantities of all sorts of things to eat at their place. They have fixed it, they have stored it. While I here day after day have my fingers stuck together (from these wretched old fish), day after day they are stuck together." Her father-in-law knew about it (her resentful attitude). She thought, "I shall go back home. I shall go get all sorts of food of ours (in my parents' village). Now I am hungry." Her father-in-law knew what she was thinking.

So the following day she made preparations (to leave). He (her father-in-law) never asked her where she was going. Now she went away. She was going along, I do not know at what place, her father knew (that she was coming). He said to his daughters (her four younger and unmarried sisters), "Your older sister is on the way here. What is there for her to eat? Perhaps you might kill her dog. Boil it for her." She was going along. She got to there. Her father said to her, "Why have you come? Now we have nothing to eat. Here is your dog, your younger sisters boiled it for you." She remained at the place there, she ate her dog. She thought, "Indeed. Really it was only we (at my husband's home) who had something (because old fish is far better than dog) to eat. I shall go back tomorrow." She went the following day then, she went back.

As she was going along, presently then he said to his son, "Your wife is coming, she is coming back to here." He replied to him, "No. She will not get here. Make snow!" He (the father) said to him, "Oh let it be. Let her come." "No. I do not want to see her (ever again)." After some time he (the father reluctantly) went to the river, he got cottonwood bark, he brought it back. He burned it, it all burned. He gathered up the ashes, he took them, he went outside, he blew them up toward the sky. He blew and blew them all. He went inside, he sat down. Pretty soon afterward then snow sat (fell), it came down.

Now that woman herself was coming along, the snow fell on her, she became cold. Somewhere or other there she went underneath (to get under cover), she thought, "The snow will stop pretty soon, before I proceed." The snow came down, she got covered over, she died at that place, before it ceased (snowing) there.

The two of them yonder lived on there. They were not hungry. The following day in the morning there was no snow whatever. Those parents of hers over there, I do not know what they did. Now so far for that.

Story story.

The precultural actors of this short drama are neither named nor identified with animal-like spirit-powers. During an especially cold winter, famine conditions arise as they may have in Clackamas districts. A wife ostensibly tires of old fish, produced from fish bones, that her husband's father is able to make with his spirit-power in order to keep the family from starvation. A related concept—that fish bones which are thrown into streams mutate into fish—is present in a wide area of the Northwest States. Old rather than fresh fish express the straits to which the starving villagers have been reduced. The wife complains to herself that her fingers are sticking together from the old fish which she must eat in order to live. She is really fretting about dietary monotony and, therefore, about the poverty which her sticky fingers represent. At another level, she is angry because her food and prestige needs are not being met in a home which obviously is of poor persons. She therefore departs and, in effect, deserts her husband and his people to return to her father's household. She supposes that he has more and better food. The narrator gives no suggestion about her manner of travel, whether by canoe or afoot. Nor does he verbalize her feelings.

When her father learns that she is coming, he is angry because he is equally deprived, if not worse off. He tells four unmarried daughters, who are still living with him, to kill and boil her dog for her to eat when she arrives. Of course, she is more than chagrined to have to eat her dog. She then realizes that her husband's home is actually in a lesser plight. Her husband is not as poor as her parent. She therefore returns, but now her husband demands that his father kill her by causing a snowstorm while she is *en route*. Her father-in-law prefers forgiveness, but her husband insists upon an irretrievable action. Reluctantly the father-in-law burns cottonwood bark, blows the ashes to the sky, and produces a snowstorm. The wife then freezes to death on the trail. One other myth, "They Deserted the Mean Boy" (text 47) [Jacobs

1959a—Eds.], contains the same theater device of a snowstorm caused by ashes of cottonwood bark.

The myth is manifestly a morality play, one of several in the collection, at the same time that it is a drama of family and in-law relationships. The leading actor is a bad wife. The resolution describes her dire punishment. She is bad because she undervalues husband and in-laws who are symbolized in one man, the kindly, forgiving, or judicious father of her husband. She overvalues her own family and depreciates her husband's. In time of famine she not only deserts her husband and in-laws, she descends upon her natal family, becomes an intolerable additional burden, and shames them.

Like three Transitional Era tales (texts 55, 56, 57-58) [Jacobs 1959a—Eds.], the myth highlights fear of wintertime famines. It also expresses feelings about one kind of unacceptable behavior concentrated in the person of a married woman who becomes panicky when starvation threatens. Food anxiety is present but is not a principal expressive feature. To Clackamas the myth was essentially a drama of family life, and its stress was upon the ethics of intrafamilial relationships. It asserts that a married woman should accept with unquestioning loyalty inconveniences and crises for which her husband and in-laws are not responsible.

Her husband's demand that she die expresses the people's harsh ethical standards. The society rightly punishes her, because she lacks loyalty to the husband and family who have purchased her, and because she abandons them in their time of need. Her action also amounts to humiliation of her husband and his kin, because it implies that they lack as much ability to resolve a crisis as her own family. She shames her husband, above all.

Her father equally gives voice to standards when he responds with anger. Although a father does not kill his daughter, he subjects her to the greatest humiliation by killing her dog and having his younger daughters serve it to her. He does this in a region where no provocation, not even starvation, justified eating a creature which is "worthless." A dog eats feces. The father's punishment for her desertion and shaming of the family that has bought her approaches in severity her punishment of death by exposure. The horrible meal of dog is very likely worse than if her father serves her no food whatever.

Her father-in-law's reluctance to make the snowstorm and so cause her death may be an oblique way of saying that he is older and more tempered in judgment than his inflexible son. The older man may fear that her death caused by his spirit-power will result in vengeance by her relatives. The play does not conclude with a notation that her father takes vengeance. His judgment of the justice of his daughter's last punishment is not mentioned. Presumably, he agrees with the verdict of her husband, and so a feud between in-law groups is not provoked.

The actors in this family drama and dour morality play lack specific delineation. Each represents a type: first and foremost, the wife who suffers the appropriate penalty for criminal rejection and humiliation of husband and in-law family; the severely just husband; the equally Draconian father of the woman; and her cautious father-in-law.

The paucity of ethnographic information about Clackamas and neighboring peoples is such that we cannot deduce that a wife who rejected in-laws during a famine would have met death. Probably the tragedy went beyond action that would have been taken by Clackamas in-laws. Modern people would have been fearful of a vengeance feud; they would have reacted somewhat like the precultural father-in-law before his son pressured him to kill the erring wife. However, the myth supplied strong sanctioning of ideals about the social responsibility of a wife. She must never express herself in a manner that indicated underestimation of the worth of her husband and his relatives.

Mark the understanding which is implicit regarding the wife's failure to resolve her Oedipal relationship, that is, the feeling that no man can be quite as protective and resourceful as her father. To be sure, he also stands for his family and household. But in any society a girl may feel that her father, or some paternal figure, is the most powerful and security-giving of men. One among several deficiencies in the wife of the myth is her failure to mature to a point where she feels that another man may have as much virtue and capacity as her father. Her behavior is bad because it is both immature and humiliating to her affinal kin. Her father seems able to remain related to four younger daughters who are still living with him because they have not yet been purchased in marriage. His oldest daughter, who has been bought and who should have substituted her husband in her father's stead, shames her sire when she retreats to her childhood household. Her father had accepted money and valuables for a defective feminine commodity. If Clackamas had an economic system like that of early twentieth-century Euro-Americans, it might be said that he felt like the merchant who was publicly disgraced because of his sale of shoddy merchandise. Only some of his anger is caused by the exposure and is directed at its cause.

He is also angry at the returned girl who wants to partake of his scanty fare and at the shame of her immaturity and disregard for the worth of her husband and in-laws. Her father-in-law may also be angry at her—the play does not say so explicitly—but initially he is unwilling to punish her by death because as a father he would have especial feeling for a loved daughter who behaved badly but wanted to return to him. Her husband would not feel like that because he does not yet have a daughter, as far as we know.

A word of inquiry may be added about the thought that in a Northwest States Indian society people also had to make resolutions which were Oedipal-like about their natal kin and co-villagers in addition to their parents. For the custodians of security and the representatives of right behavior were not largely the parents, as in Western civilization. A Northwest States Oedipal pattern of relationships and feelings comprised parents, parents' kin, and parents' village populace. When a woman pulled up childhood anchors and departed to reside in her husband's village, she was engaging in one of the most feared and wanted moves. Suffering befell those who could not make the change with mature responses.

The absence of a word of mention of the mother of the girl is significant. Since the girl's mother, if she has one, can have no public voice in decisions about the fate of her daughter, reference to a mother is omitted. Stylistically the drama remains focused upon essential actors. It retains unity and simplicity. Expressively it exhibits west-of-Cascades depreciation of females, in addition to its other themes and functions.

8

She Deceived Herself with Milt

(Clackamas Chinook)

"She Deceived Herself with Milt" was dictated by Jacobs's Clackamas Chinook consultant, Victoria Howard, in 1930. Mrs. Howard had heard this myth from both her grandmother and her mother-in-law. The English translation of this text is reprinted from *Clackamas Chinook Texts, Part 2* (1959a, 348-50); Jacobs's interpretation is from *The People Are Coming Soon* (1960a, 243-47). He saw the story as a commentary on polygamy. For a different interpretation of this narrative see Jarold Ramsey's essay, "Genderic and Racial Appropriation in Victoria Howard's 'The Honorable Milt'," in *Oral Tradition* 10.2:263-81 (1995).

People were living there. They were continually smoke-drying salmon and various things. There was one widow. They (fishermen) would come, they would come ashore there. Now she would be going about at that place. Right after they threw them (their catch of fish) ashore, she would get one or two to take with her. She smoke-dried them. (In consequence) her house was full of food. In the winter they (other villagers) would get hungry, and then they would buy various things from her. That is how she had many valuables.

I do not know how long a time, and then she got one (large and fat) salmon, she butchered it well, she took out its milt. She thought, "Dear oh dear. It is nice. I shall not eat it." She wished, "Oh that you become a person." I do not know where she put it.

I do not know how long a time afterwards, and then some person was sleeping beside her. She thought, "Oh my! I wonder where the person came from to me! She lay there for a while. Then she thought, "Perhaps he is not from here. Perhaps the person got to here from a long distance away." Presently as she was thinking about it, he then said to her, "What is your heart making you know (what are you thinking about)? You yourself said to me, I wish that you would become a person." She reflected. "Oh yes," she thought. "It just has to be that milt." She looked at him in the morning. "Goodness. A fine-looking man, he is light of skin." Now they remained there, I do not know how long a time they lived there.

Then some other woman began to steal him from her. After quite some time then she (the other woman) took him away from her. She continued to live there. When she (the other woman) saw her, she would say, she would tell him, "Oh dear me. Your poor poor (former) wife! Look at her!" He would reply to her, "Leave her alone!" After quite some time then she laughed at her all the more. They (villagers) said to her (the deserted wife), "Dear oh dear. Why does your co-wife laugh at and mock you all the time?" She said, "Oh let it be!"

Now time after time when they (the married couple) were sitting there, she (the deserted first wife) passed by them (two), she (the second wife) nudged her husband, she said to him, "Look at your (former) wife! Oh dear! the poor poor woman." He replied to her, "Leave her alone!" She laughed at her all the more. She (the deserted first wife) went along, she went back to them (the married couple), and now she danced in front of them. She said (in the words of her song),

"She deceived herself with milt."

She (the second wife) nudged him (and again mocked his first wife by saying), "Oh dear oh dear! that poor poor wife of yours." He continued to say, "Do leave her alone." The fifth time (when she had sung the song five times), she extended her spirit-power regalia (toward the couple). The woman (the second wife) turned and looked, only milt lay beside her. She (the second wife) arose, she went away. That first woman took the milt, she threw it at her (at the second woman). She (the deserted first wife) said to her, "You are leaving your husband!" But that other woman went away. She pursued her. Again she took the milt, she threw it at her, (saying) "This thing here is your husband!" She (the second wife) went back home, she reached her house, and there she remained, she stayed there. And that is what she continued to do.

Now I recall only that much of it.

An unnamed widow who lives alone is industrious and has quantities of smoke-dried fish which she sells in late winter to people who have run short of food. Therefore she has many valuables. One day she wishes that a milt which she removes from an especially good salmon would transform into a person. She does not eat this milt, but she puts it somewhere. Some time afterward a man is sleeping beside her. He is attractive, it is said, because his complexion is light. He reveals that he is Milt. They are now husband and wife.

The wish by the lonely person for a companion expresses the same process which received discussion in the myths of Awl (text 27) and Stick Drum Gambler (text 29) [(Jacobs 1958)—Eds.]. The first scene repeats the idea of those plays. A person who very much wants that which is important to her, such as salmon, may be joined by it in a kin relationship. Like all Clackamas, the woman of this myth's first scene knows that a spirit-power also wants to relate as kin to a person who wishes it. One feature renders the relationship depicted in the scene distinct from the relationships of Awl and Stick Gambler to the men who acquire them as anthropomorphized supernaturals. The widow here does not desire merely that the vital food, salmon, become a person. She pointedly wishes for just the male constituent or essence of it to become her husband. She also wants it to be her spirit-power.[1] She marries her male fantasy.

A Clackamas recitalist usually found no need to affirm how long the couple remain husband and wife. It is sufficient to report that later another woman has an affair with him. Although he continues to be the spirit-power of the first woman, he leaves to become the husband of the second. When the second wife mocks Milt's first wife, he admonishes her not to do so, perhaps because a slanderous expression might eventuate in serious tensions. Furthermore, theological considerations are involved in his protest. He does not like depreciatory observations about his former wife, because he really belongs to her. It was her wish which mutated him from mere milt into the semblance of a human being. It brought him to a community of human beings. All spirit-powers want to come to people and to relate like kin to them. His first wife is, therefore, still his kin although they are not living as man and wife. He is no longer relating intimately to her, but that may be because people have difficulties with spirit-power relatives exactly as people get into troublesome relationships with kin.

The first wife only appears to be unperturbed at the jeering. After a while she sings and dances in front of the couple. The words of her song are, "She deceived herself with milt." She repeats the song five times in stylistically correct form. Then she extends her spirit-power regalia, whatever they are, toward the couple, whereupon Milt disappears and only a salmon milt is lying beside the second wife. Although the raconteur would have no occasion in the presence of a native audience to describe the regalia, it is likely that whatever it is it has to do with the Milt spirit-power of the deserted woman. Therefore she is able once again to alter the physical manifestation of her supernatural and at the point where her need to do so becomes great. She does not act against Milt who is really hers at the time when he separates to live with the other woman. Probably she allows him to be taken by the second woman because he is, after all, not a real person. She does act against both him and his second wife when the latter uses him to shame her. Now he suffers complete rejection and severance from his first wife. He becomes just a milt again. When his present wife walks away from the milt on the ground, the former wife throws it at her and calls out mockingly and with great anger, "You are deserting your husband!"

Mrs. Howard laughed heartily when she dictated that Milt was light of skin. In an aside she added that he must have been a half-breed! Much hilarity was provoked during recitals by incongruous extrapolations of items that could be only of recent decades and subsequent to the advent of Caucasians. My impression is that among modern Indians of the Northwest States, this type of imaginative humor was a constant resort. Laughter at the expense of the invaders relieved the unpleasantness, even the bitterness, of what was strange, sordid, or humiliating in the environment of acculturation.

Mrs. Howard also gave text and translation of a brief ethnographic item (text 136) [(Jacobs 1959a)—Eds.] which should be noted here because it gives additional exemplification of humor of this kind. "Our house (when I lived with my then mother-in-law Mrs. Watcheeno) was close to the road. When a person (a Caucasian) passed by, she (Mrs. Watcheeno) would look at him, and she would laugh and say, 'Oh dear. That is a light person. Maybe it is Milt' Then she would sing, and this is what she would say (in the song words), 'She deceived herself with Milt.'"

Bitterness toward Caucasians was expressed by projecting onto the pathetic second woman of the myth who deceives herself by indulging in an ephemeral relationship. Caucasians are like her husband who is only a milt, and both are intemperate providers of nothing more than seminal fluid. The connection of Milt with Caucasians was especially appropriate and obvious to Clackamas because of Milt's light complexion. Every Indian informant I have worked with in Oregon and Washington, from Washington Sahaptins south to the Athabaskans of the Rogue River of southwestern Oregon, also assured me that lighter skins had been preferred in pre-Caucasian times. Clackamas preferred light hair color too. In the remarkable Oedipal myth of a polygamous headman (text 38) [(Jacobs 1959a)—Eds.], his favorite wife, Long Brownish Hair, is beautiful because her hair is long and lighter than the usual jet black. Utilization of urine for hair shampoos may connect with preference for hair that is somewhat bleached. That is, hair that is free of vermin and immaculate has been shampooed with urine. Preference for lighter skin is harder to explain. Connection with Caucasians and their dislike of darker skins is, I think, improbable.

The first wife, who initially acquired Milt as supernatural and husband, knows that she has gotten something of no permanent value as a husband. After enduring a saturation of ridicule from the woman who has taken the husband constituent of her supernatural, she dances and sings in front of the couple, in effect saying to the second wife, "All you got from me was something that is worthless, anyway!" In other words, she is less humiliated by loss of her husband who lacks kin—except for herself—than she is shamed by being mocked as a poor thing when she does not feel that she is to be pitied. For is she not industrious and well off, with her house and its bales of smoke-dried salmon and pouches of valuables?

The ethnographic notes do not include sufficient materials, on the question of rejection and discarding of spirit-powers, for theorization regarding the first wife's nullification of the relationship with Milt as a spirit-power. It seems likely that she repudiates that relationship, and the myth does not suggest a consequence, if any, of such dissociation. In other Northwest States communities a person who got rid, if he could, of a spirit-power suffered illness at the least. More often death was the penalty.

A question remains as to whether the first wife rejects the whole supernatural or only the segment which is her husband. She appears to change him back into the form which is properly his, and we are left to speculate concerning her subsequent career. Maybe she can continue as a well-to-do person because her milt spirit power, whether retained or surrendered, may have nothing to do with her industry and her efficient collecting of salmon that are left for her by fishermen. A milt was very likely an unimportant part of a salmon from the point of view of Chinooks, and therefore a milt supernatural may have been of minor worth. Only the widow's loneliness and need for a husband are responsible for her making so inconsequential a substance into a man.

In spite of the first wife's feeling of security and willingness to tolerate a loss of that which provided only an ephemeral sexual affair, the suggestion by the second woman that the first wife has lost a real husband is indeed humiliating. The first wife resents the intimation that her husband deserted her because of her inadequacy.

Clackamas undoubtedly expressed in everyday discussions and in this myth an anxiety about a woman "stealing" a man from another woman. The play acts out and relieves such concern by means of ridicule of the man who is "stolen." It equates him with milt which does not last long and which also lacks a kin group. In addition, the myth belittles the woman who steals him, by the implication that all she really acquires in him is the milt of sexual intercourse. She does not gain a relationship with new in-law kin, which is greatly desired in marriage. Community ethics regarding rigorous maintenance both of the nuclear family and of the relationship between two lineages that are knit together by a marriage is in this way bolstered by holding up to scorn those who venture upon impermanent liaisons and "stealing" of husbands.

In Clackamas mythology theft of wives is nowhere a theme except for Coyote and for the headman's son in the principal Oedipal myth (text 38) [(Jacobs 1959a)—Eds.]. Women equated with money in a special way. Theft of valued female property, although such larceny certainly occurred, may have been too charged with disapproval, and with dangers of expense and murders in feuds, to receive frequent handling in the oral literature. Or, the society's machinery for resolving such trouble situations worked smoothly. Village headmen and maybe shamans, who could afford the tremendous risk in such affairs, had the compensation in money beads that would make the thing right with the unhappy cuckold and his lineage.

The meagre ethnographic notations contain no evidence that rich Clackamas interested themselves sexually in other men's wives. All we are told, in effect, is that well-to-do men purchased virgins, and that they used female slaves for sexual purposes.

The myth also describes a man who performs solely a sexual function. That is, he is like a milt, not a person. At least he is not portrayed as doing anything except functioning sexually and attempting to quiet his second wife when she jeers at his first. He seems essentially passive. The core of this myth is, therefore, not supernaturalism but a contest between two women. Assuredly it was a woman's, not a man's, drama.

The manner in which the first wife throws milt at the second is psychologically sound. The first wife is no longer interested in her former husband although she might have done something to get him back. In the throwing, the first wife reveals that she no longer wants the useless creature in any form, although she craves revenge and relief from humiliating gibes. She gets revenge because her supernaturally potent dance-song and the correlated regalia turn the ineffectual man from what he appears to be into what he really is. The telling is subtle. It says that at that moment the second wife looks and sees only milt beside her. This is as if she looks and it is revealed to her that she has stolen something that is ephemeral and valueless. At last this woman perceives reality.

The recital develops no distinctive personalities. It is a drama of morals in a triangle of role-players: a husband, his first wife, and his second. It offers a lesson that relationship, not sex, is decisive for marital permanence.

The myth may reflect that portion of cultural ethics which frowned upon women who quarreled, especially co-wives in polygamous families. Men did not want their wives to wrangle. They tended to urge women to get along with one another.

Perhaps too, Clackamas felt that the relationships in the triangle of actors symbolize a small polygamous household where co-wives successively enjoy a man sexually but lack deep, genuine, or long-enduring emotional relationship with him. The myth may accordingly, and in a hidden way, express distaste for polygamy, and specifically the sometimes fevered competitiveness of co-wives. It points frankly to the ease with which a woman can divest herself of positive feelings for a husband who lacks capacity to stand firm in his marital relationship to her. The myth utilizes two types of disapproved persons: an ineffectual and disloyal husband, and his jealous second wife. The latter remains anxious about his relationship with his former wife, and foolishly subjects her to humiliation.

Editors' Note

1. Jacobs does not explain how he determines that the woman wants Milt as a spirit power.

9

Wildcat

(Klikitat Sahaptin)

"Wildcat" was dictated by Joe Hunt to Melville Jacobs in December 1928 at Husum, Washington. It was translated into English by Sam N. Eyley Jr., at Morton in December 1931. The phonetic text and its translation were published in Jacobs (1937, 23-26; 1934, 27-30). The interpretation and revised translation are from a previously unpublished manuscript (Jacobs 1959d). Jacobs's new translation differs from the 1934 publication in only minor details. Brief biographical notes on Hunt and Eyley and the circumstances of Jacobs's Sahaptin fieldwork can be found in Jacobs (1929, v, 241-44; 1934, ix-xi, 3, 102). For an extended discussion of Northwest Coast cognate and related texts, see Randall (1949). Lévi-Strauss (1995) has published a structuralist analysis of this regionally widespread plot. The Sahaptin Indians lived along the Columbia River and its tributaries to the east of the Chinookan peoples. Although they made extensive use of salmon and other anadromous fish from the Columbia, they lived in the arid lands of the Plateau that would not support the dense populations of the lower Columbia, nor did they enjoy the trading opportunities that enriched the Chinookans closer to the mouth of the river. As Jacobs notes, Sahaptin society was more egalitarian and lacked true class distinctions. See Hunn (1990) for a full historical and ethnographic treatment of the Sahaptin peoples.

This myth is a translation of a dictation by the Klikitat Sahaptin shaman, Joe Hunt, who offered it to me in December 1928 during my third visit to him.
The myth text follows.

There were a great many people. There was the headman. He announced, "There will be spirit-power singing." The people sang spirit-power songs, the followers of the headman sang. "The spirit-power singing will be for five nights." They sang spirit-power songs, and when it was not yet the fifth night (the following occurred).

The headman had an unmarried daughter. She was one of those who sang her spirit-power song. Wildcat was there himself, he was ugly to look at. The one who was that unmarried girl said, "There is no one who could possess (marry) me." He (Wildcat) went (to the dance). When they were singing their spirit-power songs, Wildcat thought, "I shall go myself and see how they are singing the spirit-power songs." Wildcat knew (what his supernatural would allow him to achieve). He went, he climbed on top of the (headman's) house, from up above he looked in through the smoke hole, when he looked he saw the unmarried girl singing her spirit-power song, she was standing and singing (and dancing). Wildcat reflected, "I will spit down into the unmarried girl." The unmarried girl was singing her spirit-power song, the unmarried girl sang looking above, Wildcat spit right into the unmarried girl's mouth, he spit into the unmarried girl. Then Wildcat went, he went back to his own house.

They sang spirit-power songs for five nights. In that duration of time the unmarried girl became with child, in her abdomen. When they quit on the fifth night, the unmarried girl had become with child, in her abdomen. The unmarried girl realized then, "How is it that I have become with child? No man ever slept with me." That is what the unmarried girl thought, the unmarried girl was exceedingly ashamed. When the infant in her abdomen became large, the unmarried girl gave birth to the child.

The people learned, "The unmarried girl gave birth to an infant! Who could have taken her secretly?" So the people spoke. When she had given birth to the infant, the baby cried continually, nothing could stop the baby's crying. The headman said, "You are to gather together, all my people!" That is what they (the men of the band) did. When they had assembled, the headman said, "If you hold it, and the infant becomes quiet, and it does not cry, it will be yours then, and the woman (my daughter, too)." That is what the headman said. And then all the people (the men) did it (one after another man held the baby), but no, the baby continued to cry. All of them as many kinds of people as there were, they could not do it (could not stop the infant's crying).

They found out that Wildcat himself was the only remaining one. He considered, "It must be my own child indeed." That is what Wildcat thought. "Well, I will go myself and see what has occurred at that meeting of theirs." Wildcat went, he entered the place there, he saw, "There are a great many people." That baby was crying, all sorts of persons (men) were holding it in vain, they failed, they passed the baby around. As many people as there were, but in vain. There old man Wildcat himself sat down. The headman said, "How about Wildcat himself holding it like that?" The unmarried young woman thought, "Wildcat could never have done it to me. By his appearance Wildcat is an ugly old man. He is not for me." So thought the unmarried woman. They were passing the child around. One after another held it, but the infant continued to cry. "Now let Wildcat himself hold it!" "Ah. Poor wretched me hold the child in my ugly hands!" "Take it anyway!" They gave it to him. "Very well. I'll take it." They gave him the infant. The moment Wildcat took it, the infant became silent from its crying.

A great number of the people (the headman's kin) were abashed. The people (said), "Oh dear! He has taken (had sexual relations with) our woman." The woman was very much ashamed. "That obviously hideous old man, scarred all over, did not do it to me anywhere, and I could never have had his child!" That is what the woman thought. The headman was exceedingly ashamed. The headman said then, "All my people make preparations. We are going to desert them. I do not want my child (daughter) and the ugly old man." That man (the headman) went out. "Away with them now!" Wildcat thought nothing of it. He said to the woman, "Do not ever feel badly about it. Never mind now! when they desert us. Never mind!" That is how he spoke to the woman. All the people left them. They were left, they were alone now.

He said to the woman, "I am going to make a sweathouse, I will sweat (upon occasion during) five days." That is what he said to the woman. That is how Wildcat made the sweathouse, and he sweated

Joe Hunt, Jacobs's Klikitat Sahaptin consultant.

(a number of times during the) five days. There had been three (days), on the fourth day the woman saw, "Oh dear! What a very fine man is coming out of the sweathouse! According to appearances the man's hair is fine, to appearances he is clean (his complexion is good now)." The woman thought, "It must be that another and different man has come to me from some place." So thought the woman. When it was the fifth day, then, "I will cease sweating now." He came out, he shook the dust from his garments, he hung up his wildcat clothes, he hung them up, he shook and shook them. The woman saw, "Goodness! he has a number of (fine and valuable) garments." The man took them, he went back to the house, he took the (fine) clothes inside. He said to her, "Here you are! Do not ever feel badly about it." That is how he spoke to the woman.

They slept through one night. Wildcat went away to hunt. He shot and killed a deer, he brought it back. "Oh! quantities of food!" There was a great amount of food. The boy became tall. The boy played. (They had) a great amount of food and meat.

All those people (the headman's kin and band) were poor and wretched now. They were starving, there was no kind of food, they became poor. Wildcat knew it. He thought, "All the people of the headman have become poor."

I do not know what Buzzard himself thought. He went to see, and I do not know how he found it out, but when he arrived back, "Yes, yes. The boy is already tall. They have quantities of food. It is no longer that poor Wildcat, to appearances it is a strong and active man, and no longer that Wildcat." The woman said to Buzzard, "I will share our food with you." She gave him a small amount of food. He took it home, he informed them, "Oh those people live very nicely, those whom we deserted. They have quantities of food." And all the people of the headman were starving.

The headman said, "You yourself, Little Weasel, are to go to see your older brother." Little Weasel went, he went to see Wildcat, he arrived. "Oh. They have quantities of food." He (Wildcat) said to him, "How are you getting along in your wanderings, my younger brother?" He replied to him, "The headman told me, 'Go visit him!' and so I have come to see you there." Then, "Yes. I am well off now. There is nothing the matter with me." He gave him food. Little Weasel carried that back home to the headman's place, and he related all to the headman. "That is how he is."

The headman said to him, "You will go now, (to find out) how he will speak (about us and about his plans). If he tells me (affirmatively), then I will return home directly." Weasel went, he reached Wildcat's place, he said to him, "That is how the headman has sent me as messenger. If you say that the headman may come back home, he will bring home all the people." He said to him, "If he himself decides, 'I will go home now,' he may come home." That is how the older brother spoke to him. And then that is what he told the headman. "That is how he spoke."

That is what they did then. He brought all the people back home. Wildcat prepared as many houses as there were, full of food for them. The people reached that place, (there was) a great amount of food, they lived well on the quantities of Wildcat's food. The headman became well again. That one was not (the ugly) Wildcat. Wildcat was a better one now.

Observe the first phrase: "There were a great many people." This is a stylized introductory sentence which, in Sahaptin and some other Northwest States myths, may replace or precede the stylized sentence which cites or names the first two or three actors of the first scene. When a recitalist commences by saying that there were many people he may do this also, partly, because the first scene treats of a settlement of his people, a meeting of the adult men, or a dance where many persons are present. He never describes particulars of such a location or occasion. The bare statement is filled in with the full understanding which auditors had. Next, the first actor to speak is cited but not by name, because his name is not meaningful in the plot which is about a loathsome old man named Wildcat. In other Northwest States literatures the plot's scabby individual is a youth.[1] I suggest below why an older man appears here.

A leading man of a Sahaptin band, or in coastal villages a well-to-do head of a household, calls out to the people that there will be spirit-power singing and dancing. Again, particulars of such winter seances are not usually phrased in myth recitals. Auditors comprehend that a series of five nights of singing and dancing of people's own spirit-power songs-and-dances will ensue, with a fifth night which keeps up into especially late hours, perhaps till dawn, at which time the family of the man who gives the five sessions supplies food, gifts too, to all who are then present. They depart after the serving of food and the presenting of gifts.

In this myth the headman's unmarried daughter, ipso facto a young person who is desirable in marriage, asserts that "no one could possess me." The narrator does not need to inform auditors that the girl says this privately or in public. The significant thing to Klikitat or other Sahaptins is that the girl's words represent the fact that she, maybe because of her tie to her father, refuses to marry at this time. Everyone in the band and visitors at the spirit-power seances know it and regard her willfulness as improper. Auditors are not told that she is immature, snobbish, frightened, still loves her father so much that she is appalled at the prospect of leaving his domicile, or any other reason—all bad ones—for her choice to stay single for a while longer. Narrators almost never pause to register motives. A public declamation by the raconteur focuses on the plot's high points to Sahaptins, not the many matters about which Euro-Americans might also be curious and which their literatures permissibly select for expression. A stark announcement that "no one can possess me" is sufficient and correct. It allows auditors to amplify imaginatively with responses which Sahaptin society and culture generate. The girl's utterance is a stylized way of saying that all the people, band members and others, know that she is not presently going to marry although she ought to. Such knowledge is placed laconically in her words of direct discourse.

The recital turns to the ugly old man whose name is Wildcat. One word is enough to say, with utmost compactness, "He knew." This word means to a Sahaptin audience, with its foreknowledge of plot and its unquestioning acceptance of a religious ideology and correlated biological premises, that Wildcat is perfectly acquainted with the abilities of his supernatural kin. It or they accord him the somewhat unusual capacity to impregnate with spittle. Accordingly, on the first or second night of the five nights of spirit-power dancing, Wildcat does not remain with the others inside the headman's abode where the seances are going on. He steals outside to the roof and peers down through the smoke vent while the unmarried girl is performing her spirit-power song-dance. At the most opportune moment he expectorates so that his spittle drops neatly into her open mouth as she sings. Then he departs for his own house. He has no further motive to stay. His feelings about what he has done are such that he wants no part of what goes on.

Things sometimes happen with miraculous rapidity in a myth era. That is why the hapless girl discovers, on the fifth and last night, that she is pregnant. The speed intensifies the disgrace. Although she knows that she has been a virgin and therefore a proper young lady, her pregnancy is almost at once obvious to her. An unmarried pregnant girl felt deeply ashamed, as did her close kin when they found out. In other Northwest States groups she would not show herself outside the house in daylight. The recital progresses with the greatest celerity. The narrator at once announces that the girl gives birth. Events of the intervening days or months are ignored, as are everyone's feelings. The significant thing is the parturition and it alone receives even a terse mention. Neither plot nor style requires indication of the infant's sex or of the customary presence of a female relative to assist at the birth. Illegitimacy and shame are the essentials. The style requires suppression of everything which does not point them up. Only an illegitimate newborn infant is referred to and there is plenty of time to mention that the baby is a boy. Much later in his version the recitalist does so, perhaps unnecessarily. Sahaptin oral-literature style, in this and other examples by Joe Hunt, is remarkable, to Euro-Americans, in its omission and avoidance of items other than those few which trigger the audience's responses for vitalizing details which they project into the plot. To be sure, a raconteur of a coastal Washington society which knew a cognate version might now make mention of the sex of higher status, but in districts in or east of the mountains the status of females was little if at all inferior. So then, just an infant is born, and we are not told how or where because such information is irritating irrelevance.

Next, the narrator mentions that the people discuss the paternity of the baby, who cries without let-up. As a result, the headman summons "my people," that is, the adult males of his band. He promises that the man who is able to pacify the infant may have his daughter and her baby. In fact, the man who can quiet the baby must be its father and must have impregnated the girl. The attractiveness of the headman's offer is illumined by understanding of the premarital and in-law gift exchanges which will be bypassed by the male who acquires a wife and baby so inexpensively. If an already-married gentleman is revealed as the baby's father, the headman's daughter has to reconcile herself to the role of second or third wife in a polygamous household. When only the ugliest of the community's men, Wildcat, is left to be tested by his holding the infant, he protests modestly. But he does it when the others' insistence cannot be resisted. No Northwest States Indian long countered demands, maybe because of the regionwide terror lest there be hurt feelings and because of a conviction that the others might be humiliated. The moment Wildcat holds the noisy baby it ceases crying. Biological paternity is proven instantaneously. In terms of the social background the interesting thing here is the new shame which the headman, his daughter, and their kin and fellow members of the band feel. The humiliation about the disgusting older man whom the child unmistakably identifies as its father is such that the community desert the couple and the baby.

At once Wildcat graciously tells his bride not to feel badly about their pariah-like situation. The recitalist says nothing about her fear, ignominy, and loneliness. An audience understands how inexpressibly frightful her feelings are.

When the couple are alone Wildcat takes the stylistically requisite number of five successive steamings, doubtless on five successive days, in his small beehive-shaped sweathouse close by the river. Ethnographers are well acquainted with physical appurtenances of the region's sweat-bath custom, if not with its much more significant social, religious, and psychological functions. Sweat baths were resorted to by both sexes for various sicknesses and aches which did not seem to call for the services of a shaman; he administered to persons whose ailments were severe or maybe lethal. Wildcat's sores and scabs, as translators word it, justify only sweat baths. The fourth day, his wife observes that he is different upon his emergence from the steaming hut, when he dashes into the stream before returning to his residence. He has become nice-looking. Her words phrase only two aspects of his appearance, his cleanness and the quality and length of his head hair. One of the selected items is worthy of remark. Euro-Americans place value upon cleanliness, and so we need not make a point of discussing that. But long hair of both sexes affected all Northwest States Indians, as far as I know, with feelings at least as ardent as those stirred in Euro-American men by bosoms which represent the anatomical values of the hour. One wonders if the region's unanimity about the beauty in long hair connects with childhood conditioning about the care of hair: west of the mountains and in all communities where urine was collected in wooden buckets, people used it as the efficient means which they had to control head lice. It might be used on the skin too. After an application of urine a person washed himself off with water or plunged into the always nearby stream. Parents removed head-hair vermin from their children and mates did it for each other, biting the lice to crack the shells. Urine stirred no laughter in the region, but fecal references and head lice did. The defenses in responses of amusement to anality and head lice suggest special areas of tension. The values about cleanliness included anal neatness and immaculate long head hair. It is an unhappy commentary on the field researches of anthropologists of recent decades that the reports on Indians both east and west of the Cascades Mountains lack meaningful items which explain why the natives felt as they obviously did about matters which were as important to their self-regard as those which connected with urination, defecation, head hair, and maybe other portions of the body.

After the fifth sweat bath and plunge Wildcat hangs up his wild-cat fur. The recitalist cites only the sweat bath because from his point of view it is much more significant: a person sang certain spirit-power songs during his twenty to twenty-five minutes within the sweat hut; as far as we know there was no singing during the minute or two in the water. Beneath the wild-cat fur the unprepossessing old man had been, all along, an engaging young man. The next day—a new action always occurs "the next day" in Northwest States folklores—Wildcat hunts successfully, of course. He is quite a man, in fact the finest of men. That is why the couple now acquire unexampled surpluses of smoke-dried deer and elk meat. The words say, too, that their boy grows tall. Only at this late moment in the drama, does the recitalist specify that the child is a male. I think that the verbal revelation is promoted in this scene because the storyteller must now suggest that the family becomes outstandingly well-to-do through the fine hunter, his excellent son, and his wife's industry and skill in preparation of smoke-dried foods and tanned hides. Furthermore, the scene serves to contrast an almost heroic household, its stores of meat for the winter and its other valuable possessions, with the poverty, hunger, and wretchedness of those who had deserted their kin and fellow member of the band. There was justice in the desertion of those who had disgraced the community, but there was justice in the subsequent reckonings. Patently the Indians were mixed in their feelings about the values in a situation such as this myth presents. Illegitimacy bothers every society which strongly rewards legitimacy. That must be one of the reasons why cognates of the Klikitat version are found widely over the Northwest States.

In a Clackamas Chinook version, from a large group only a few score miles to the southwest of the Klikitats, two older Crow women, poor people of the village, return to discover the affluent household; they are warned to keep secret what they have seen.[2] In the Klikitat version one man, Buzzard, finds out about Wildcat and his family. Wildcat's wife tells Buzzard that she will share her stores of food with the starving people who had deserted her when she was most in need. The Clackamas version, from a sharply stratified village society, reflects anger and lethal hostility to the well-to-do who had departed; there is friendship only to the poor, represented by the Crow women. The Klikitat version, from a barely if at all stratified band community, reflects only kindness to the unfortunate and starving, even if they did desert and humiliate Wildcat and his family. I am confident that different emphases, tensions, and values marked the two social systems, Clackamas and Klikitat, although they were geographically close to each other. The Clackamas group seems more hypersensitive, angry, suspicious, and unwilling to forgive. Feelings which arose in tensions created by the respective social systems were projected into the behavior of the myth actors and were cardinal factors shaping the myth plots. The obvious common origin of the Clackamas and Klikitat versions hardly accounts for differences which appear in the actors, plots, stresses, and motivations. It is just as important to explain details of difference as to account for gross similarity, although a century and more of folklore studies has done little to advance knowledge about the causes of differences in cognate versions.

Additional disparities in the two peoples' development of the plot might be noted. But I want to highlight only the fact that over much of the Northwest States, certainly in both the Sahaptin and Chinook groups, there was worry lest a maritally eligible daughter be desired by an older man, especially by a shaman whose spirit-powers might be used murderously in reprisal against the girl and her close kin if she were not given to him in marriage. When he offered the right amount of gifts or money her family did not dare to turn him down. When the girl in the Klikitat plot says that she will marry no man she is really saying, in the plot's context, that she will reject an older suitor. In its Klikitat expressive content the plot definitely represents any feared and unattractive older man whose supernaturals can force a girl's father, out of extreme apprehension, to hand her over in a marriage which she and her kin abhor. They are terrified. Of course, the plot goes further and can do so if it is put into a myth-age setting. Wildcat is so irresistibly powerful that, in spite of the girl's announcement that she will not marry, he can engage in long-distance impregnation in order to acquire what he truly wants: a return to youthful desirability and self-regard. Since he is an older man his sexual capacity may be less. The Klikitat myth in effect says that that is so. My suggestion is that old Wildcat's spittle has increased in potency in inverse proportion to his semen, which has diminished. And at a deep psychological level semen equals spittle. If I am right about this equation it is of psychological interest although not much need be made of it for comprehension of the myth.

The salient and indisputable component of the act is the cultural feeling about repellant and supernaturally threatening older men. That sentiment has some roots in older men's lesser economic role. But it arises mainly in the circumstances that such men engage in more household participation than younger men do. Older persons assume responsibilities as disciplinarians and pedagogues to the household's pre-adolescents while parents are busy with basic production. Although informed elders are respected, even venerated, for the handicrafts, artistry, and security which they grant everyone, the oral literatures express principally the hostility which is generated by elders' disciplinary, watch-dog, and judgmental activities. Elders want to and frequently manage to secure additional spirit-powers as defenses, one might suppose, against community ambivalence toward them, waning attractiveness, and approaching extinction of the self. When late-acquired spirit-powers include shamanistic ones, as they often do, that is, they accord capacity to determine life and death for other people, the mixed feelings about elders are more than reinforced. These attitudes become an ever more complex tangle of components in a range from affection and respect to terror and hatred.

Wildcat assuredly represents a repulsive extreme. He is eliminated by the wish, which actualizes, for the attractive young husband. He transforms into his unthreatening opposite with the lovely long hair.

I find it of interest that Klikitats use a regionally widespread plot, one which is motivated in alternative ways elsewhere, to ventilate their feeling about unpleasant older men, men of shamanistic capacity, whose spirit-powers are such that they can intimidate people and terrorize girls into marrying them. Neither the unstratified Klikitat bands nor the much wealthier villages of the lower Columbia River and the coast can resolve peoples' conflicting feelings about older men.

After Buzzard's return to the starving band, with supplies which one man is able to carry, the headman dispatches Weasel, who would be especially well-received by his "brother" Wildcat in an anxiety-laden situation, to be the emissary to the fortunate family. Weasel also receives Wildcat's gifts of much-needed food and he carries them back to his people's deplorable camp. The headman then sends Weasel to find out if Wildcat will allow his former leader to return with all the people. Again, Klikitat values in the direction of leniency and mercy are expressed in Wildcat's permission to the headman and the band members to return. The version adds that Wildcat prepares the houses and places quantities of food in them.

Among its several themes the version contains one of clemency, forbearance, and generosity, even to those who wrongly desert a degraded couple. This theme is peculiarly Sahaptin and east-of-mountains, for it does not appear in versions from the wealthier societies which lie to the west of the divide.[3]

Another theme is widespread. It expresses an aspect of the region's romantic theory about biological heredity: an orphaned infant who cannot speak will automatically signal its recognition of its parent, and only that parent can silence its shrieks. Northwest Indians had many parental surrogates who entered the picture after the infant was weaned and when it walked and spoke. These surrogates continued to function in European parental ways for over a decade of the child's life. It was a nursing, preverbal, and pre-toddling youngster who needed its biological parents and who, at least in western Oregon Indian villages, would up and return to the land of babies, wherever that was, if it sensed the slightest rejection by its new parents.

Psychiatrists might choose to note a food-anxiety theme in this myth and, of course, it is there and in a great many other myths throughout the area. Most Northwest States natives were aware of the possibilities of famine, especially around February and March. It would be curious if recurring horrors like famine were not reflected in myths.

Significant, indeed, is the regionwide theme of shame, felt by parent and hitherto unmarried female alike, when she becomes pregnant. The myth, with its cognate versions in other groups, offers a wish-fulfilling resolution of such debasement: a wonderful hunter is the husband, not a hideous person whom she is obliged to accept in her first marriage.

Wildcat more than makes up for his brash method of impregnating his wife, that is, of raping her. Who would not prefer that the old rapist, whom one is required to marry, metamorphose into an outstandingly fine provider and gracious young gentleman with most romantic tonsure?

Still another theme, also shared in the area, expresses natives' acceptance of and respect for the decisions of youngsters. Here it is an almost newborn baby who makes the choice which determines everyone's destiny.

Not least in the inventory of themes, regionwide plots express anxiety about the interest which supernaturally powerful and uncomely older men have in taking well-favored damsels to their bosoms.

Characteristics of style which this myth displays include its stark presentation of only those few descriptive items which are needed to carry the plot and to trigger auditors' responses, and its enclosed five-patterns. Mr. Hunt did not often dictate the formal introductory and closing words. I think that he omitted them principally because the audience included only Mrs. Hunt and me. The number and posture of the auditors probably did not feel right to him. In addition, the stylized phrases which he evidently omitted were standard for his entire repertoire of myths and he knew that I was aware of the places where they ought to be inserted in my notes. It is of interest that the time when this one myth was dictated to me was in December and therefore a proper period of the year for a stylistically right recital. Apart from the omissions, I think that the version is a fine example of one of the commonest types of short play in a pre-white genre.

Editors' Notes

1. But see the Upper Skagit story from Puget Sound collected by Leon Metcalf and translated and published by Violet Hilbert (Hilbert 1995: 159-82), "Nobility at Utsalady," with a plot very close to Wildcat. The hero, "Bobcat," is also afflicted with a loathsome skin disease. Although he is not portrayed as old, he is clearly an adult, not a child.
2. See *Clackamas Chinook Texts,* 47, "They Deserted the Mean Boy" (Jacobs 1959a, 409-17). An interpretation of this text appears in Jacobs (1960a, 308-12).
3. It also appears in the Puget Sound version cited above. But the Upper Skagit, living in small egalitarian communities along the upper reaches of the Skagit River, resembled the east of the mountains Sahaptins more closely in this respect than their close neighbors in the wealthy saltwater villages of Puget Sound.

10

Sun and His Daughter

(Klikitat Sahaptin)

The myth text, "Sun and His Daughter," was dictated by Joe Hunt to Melville Jacobs in October 1928 at Husum, Washington. It was translated into English by J.J. Spencer. Like the preceding selection, "Wildcat," the phonetic text and translation were published in Jacobs (1937, 28-34; 1934, 33-39). The interpretation and revised translation are also from the unpublished manuscript (Jacobs 1959d). Similarly, the new translation differs little from the 1934 translation. Brief biographical notes on Hunt and Spenser, and the circumstances of Jacobs's Sahaptin fieldwork, appear in Jacobs (1929, v, 241-44; 1934, ix-xi, 3). See Hunn (1990) for historical and ethnographic information about the Sahaptin Indians.

This example of the pre-white myths, dictated in 1928 by my Klikitat Sahaptin informant, Mr. Hunt, contains an explanatory addition of so unexpected and modern a kind for that gentleman that at first I considered it better to sample elsewhere the extensive collection of myths with purely Indian expressive content which he recounted to me. The myth is pre-white in content and style except for its one adaptation. That novel component is instructive. It shows how smoothly and quickly new emphases and content may be woven, maybe by discussants, maybe by recitalists, into an oral literature from a food-gathering people which did not have a group of specialists in the fabrication and transmission of myths. To be sure, Klikitats of 1928 had been enveloped by whites for about a century, but Mr. Hunt was one of the very few who remained comparatively steadfast in dedication to pre-white values and orientations.

The text follows.

There were many people. There were two brothers. There was a chief. He had many people. I suppose it was in this river (the Columbia) that there was an island, at that place was a woman. All the men failed to approach her, she did not want any of the people, nor did she desire people of foreign origin (such as Chinooks). Two of them were brothers. The older brother said to him, "I am going to go to the woman myself." The younger brother said to him, "Very well. Go now." When it became dark the man went. He crossed over to the island by canoe. That was the place where the woman was.

He went ashore to the house, he knocked, the woman arose, she opened the door for him. The man entered through the door, in the rear of the room the man was already sitting! The woman looked for him but she could not see him. She turned, she saw the man coolly sitting there. She said to him, "Why have you come to me in this manner?" The man replied, "Indeed. I have not come without reason. I have been wanting you to be my wife." That is how the man spoke to the woman. The woman remained silent. She said to him, "Come back again after a while. Then I will tell you how (yes or no). Return home now!"

The man went away, he returned home. He stayed two nights. He told his younger brother, "That is how the woman spoke to me. I am going again." The man went away. In the very same manner he arrived at the house. He knocked at the door, the woman arose and opened the door for him. Nothing there! She shut it. The woman turned. Unconcerned, the man was seated there, to all appearances he had come inside some time before. She said to him, "How do you happen to be here?" "Why indeed! You told me, 'Return today.' And so I have come here to you."

The man's hair was long. The woman said to him, "Give me that hair of yours. Cut your own hair and give it to me. Then we shall be two (husband and wife)." The man replied, "Why indeed should I give it to you? I want what I have. I do not have my hair in order to cut it. I want it myself. Why should I give it to you?" The woman said to him, "Since you want it, then indeed I do not desire you at all." The man remained silent, he said nothing. Then he said, "Since you speak the truth, I will give it to you. You will cut it for me yourself." That is how he spoke to the woman. The woman said, "Very well." She took his hair, she cut his long (hair), she took it to the side of the house, she laid it away. She said to him, "Return home, and come here tomorrow." That is how the woman spoke to him. "At that time you are to come to my place."

The man went home. He reached his younger brother's and he told him, "That is how the woman spoke to me. She took my hair." That is how he told his younger brother. "Tomorrow I shall go to the woman's place." Next day he went away.

He reached the woman's place. He knocked at the door, the woman opened it. The man had already entered. Unconcernedly he was sitting there. The woman did not see him. She turned, she saw him sitting there unconcernedly. She spoke to him. She took the hair, and she said to him, "I suppose you want to take this? Well, I am returning it to you. Take it home with you! You would not give it to me anyway, so that we might become two (man and wife). Take it home! I suppose you came to get it. Take it home!" The man was exceedingly ashamed. He took it, he went out, he took it home, he brought it back to his younger brother's place. Not a thing did he say to his younger brother. He lay down, he went to sleep, during five days he did not get up. Then he woke up. He went down to the water, he swam in the water. His hair was long now. He went ashore.

He told his younger brother about it. "That is how the woman treated me." The people had no knowledge at all of what had been happening. He said to his younger brother, "You must help me. We will make arrows." The younger brother said to him, "Very well." He made arrows, he cut many of them. Two arrows he set upright. Where the two were he piled them (many other arrows) up full (between the two upright arrows). He wrapped them (with fastening of hazel sprouts) in five bundles. He said to his younger brother, "I am going to leave you now. I am going to go far away to where the sun rises, that is where I shall go. As for this feather which I am setting up here, you will watch this feather. If it should fall you will think, 'Surely my older brother has died somewhere.' That is how you will think. But if during five years it does not fall, I shall be coming home. I shall see you then, my younger brother." That is how he spoke to his younger brother. But he did not speak to his people, he said nothing.

He went to a country far away, he went eastward. He would go so far along, then he would stick one arrow into the ground, so far along he would go, and he would place another arrow in the ground, until all those five arrow bundles were gone.

He went on. He went on and came to where a certain place was. He knew exactly where to go. He knew where it was he had arrived. There was a house, and he went to there, to the house. The woman went out to him at once. She said to him, "How is it that you have come, my husband? Hurry! Come! Come inside into the house. Do not stand so long there." The man went, he entered the woman's house. She said to him, "My father is a dangerous being. (He is Sun, and his younger brother is Moon.) Watch yourself carefully. I know the land from which you have come." That is how the woman spoke to him. She said to him, "I will keep you in hiding. My father will be coming home pretty soon. He might kill you and then he would eat you. See! That is his house. The bones of persons are piled up there." That is how the woman spoke to the man. "I will hide you." The woman hid the man.

When it became dark he (Sun) would arrive. After, when it became daylight, he would go as far as the land lies. He would always go over it there. That was how he had his work. At some place on his way along he would kill a person, he would bring him back. "My father is a dangerous being." That is how she spoke to him. "Do not worry." That is how the woman spoke to the man. "Later on you will see, but not just now." He remained until daylight.

He (Sun) arrived. He said to her, "Do not say, 'No!' Say 'Yes' to me! 'A person came here. It is he I am hiding.' That is the way you will speak to me!" His daughter said to him, "Yes. Now I am constantly telling you, your querying makes me tired. But I will tell you. A man came indeed and I want him to be mine." That is how the woman spoke to her father. He said to her, "Well, I will look at him before I go. Then I will soon be off." That is how the father spoke to the woman. The woman pondered, "Perhaps he may kill my (husband). Maybe he is lying to me." That is how she feared her father. But he said to her, "I will not do anything to your (husband). Since you desire your (husband), I would never kill your (husband)." That is how the father spoke to the woman. She brought the man out into view. Sun saw him. "Clearly he must have

come here from a long distance, from as far as the land lies.
Certainly that is where he came from." That is what Sun supposed.
He said to her, "Very well. He is yours. I shall not do anything to
your (husband), my child." He left them. Sun came this way, he
came toward the earth.

The woman said to the man, "You must not eat what my father
has for food. That is what my father eats (he is a cannibal)." So she
told the man. "I will make you a spear. You will go down to the
water in this river, you will see there are fish in the river here. You
will spear one of them, you will bring it back home, and we two will
eat it. That is (proper) food." The man felt as she did about it. The
woman made a spear for him. He went down to the river, he saw
there were Chinook salmon in the water. He speared one and he
brought it back to the woman's place. He said to her, "See! This is
food. Persons will not be (eaten)." He and his wife ate. They hid all
of it. "My father might see it. He would not like it of us." So the
woman thought.

She said to him, "You must go again. I will make an arrow for
you. You will ascend this mountain, you will see there are deer, you
will shoot one, you will bring back the meat, you will eat it." "Yes,"
replied the man. The woman made an arrow for him. She said to
him, "You will ascend at this place." At that place the man went and
climbed to the top and he saw, "There are deer." Sure enough he
killed one. He took the meat, he brought it home to the woman's
place. He ate the meat. This is how the woman spoke to him. "This
will be food in this country, as far as the land lies. This will be food.
If I do not get rid of that (human) food of my father's, my father
and I will have to quarrel about it." So she spoke to the man.

Sure enough, Sun returned home. He said to her, "Ah my child!
What has an odor in your house?" She said to him, "Yes. I now have
this for my food. I tell you, in no long time the land will be
changed. People will be there. That is where you will do work for
the people. Nevermore will you eat people. Your idea is thoroughly
wrong. That is how (the people coming to) the land speak (think).
Wherever you have been going you must now quit such (cannibal)
food. They (the foods themselves) will be your own children in the
future when the land has been changed." That is how his child
spoke to Sun. He argued with her a long while but her father could
not get the better of her (in the discussion). She won over him.

She told him (Sun), "From now on eat this food. Nothing will happen to you. This is fish. This is deer. This is what will be food now when the land has been changed. There will be people for all time on your road, as far as the land lies." So she and her father argued. Sun ate the fish and deer. He said, "Very well. You speak truly, my child. If I do right I shall never become lost. Everything will be completed now. I agree with you, my child." That is how he spoke to her.

They had a boy child and they had a girl child. Sun was exceedingly glad about it (and proud to have these grandchildren). "Now I hold my girl child in respect. It will be an important law when the land will have changed itself. There will be different people. The land will be illuminated with my child." That is how Sun thought.

His child knew his thoughts. "My father is thinking rightly now. He has no longer brought his (cannibal) food. He eats salmon and meat now." She told him, "That is how it will be, when the children (the roots, berries, fish, deer, etc.) of this land grow up. This is the food a man will eat. Deer and fish will be older brother to them. Fruits, berries, and roots will be their older sisters as far as the land lies. In future, people will grow because of them." That is how the woman spoke.

"I am going to go now." She said to the man, "Let us return to where you came from. Your younger brother is waiting for you. Let us go home now." So she spoke to the man. He replied to her, "Very well." She said to her father, "I shall go by water. Make a canoe for me. That is what I shall go with." Her father said to her, "Very well." He made a canoe for her. Her father gave her a little something, he made a pack for her.

"I shall tell how you are to go, here where the land is. This land is surrounded by water. You will go around this land in the water from the place where I always complete my journey. That is where you will enter this little stream." That is how he spoke to her. He whose name is Moon spoke. "I will take them myself. I will watch them on their way. Nothing will happen to them." That is how Moon spoke. "You (Moon) will go in the night. All day long I myself will take them." And, to be sure, he (Moon) did take them as if they were his own children. The older brother of Moon was Sun. He would go about in the night and Sun in the daytime. He slept all night. Moon went all through the night. That is how the two brothers worked.

They came there. The man and his wife came around to there by canoe. As they went along the canoe grew, it became large. They came to where this stream empties. There they set up a large pole. A great and important law she made (for Sun to set there in future). "This is as far as my father will go. He will never cross over this land. Similarly Sun will come so far, from the east. And again, he will travel above through the sky to where I, his child, will be." That is how she set this great law at that place. They (the husband and wife and their children) entered this stream. They came to where his people and his younger brother were, the place from which he had gone.

His younger brother learned, "My older brother has come." He did not inform the people about it. They arrived. When it dawned the man knew. "My older brother has arrived." He went down to the water. He saw him. The man went out. He said to him, "Come aboard, my younger brother!" He laid a plank over to the shore for him. He went on it to his older brother. His two children were there. He said to him, "I have come back home, my younger brother. You must tell all our people now. You will bring them down to the water tomorrow. And how is that woman?" (the woman who had wanted to cut his hair.) He replied to him, "Why yes. She is all right." He said to him, "As many relatives as there are of the woman, indeed they are not to come. Leave all the relatives of the woman. Not until after all our own relatives (have arrived), then later the woman may bring her own relatives." That is how he spoke to his younger brother. "Very well."

He said to his people, "That one who has come is no dangerous being. It is my older brother returning. All of you will come down to the water. I will take you to the water." That is how he spoke to his people. They said to him, "Very well."

There was also a person who dwelt here, who was a headman. The headman said, "You may go down to the water." All the people went down to the water. And then the woman came out, the children, and the man. He gave all his people little things (that is, appropriate gifts). He told them, "As many as there are of those relatives of the woman (who has never married), let her bring them afterwards, herself." That woman was quite anxious to see him. She did not think, "That man who has returned is the one." The woman was very anxious to see him. They told her people and they took her to that place. The man came out. He said to them, "Come! Walk upon this (plank) to the canoe. You have been wanting to see me for a long time." The woman thought directly, "I do want to see him." The canoe became a little farther away. He said to her, "Come aboard now." The woman walked aboard, she had gone half way when the canoe moved and then the woman fell into the water.

He said to her, "You treated me exceedingly badly. I suppose you have been thinking, 'I shall never have a man, I shall be without a man now.' But the land will become different. There will be different people. Everything is ready. It will be named so, here. That is the law I bring from the east. You caused me to go find it, and I have found it is wonderful, when it will have become a different land with different kinds of peoples. They will name you 'black dress.' That is what your heart and life will be. You will never accept a man but you will also be strong in power." That is the way he spoke to all her people. As many as there were of them, he gave them nothing, he turned them away (without gifts). "You will be different from these people. These many are my own people now. Never at any time will the moon, sun, or stars weaken, the land will have life because of them, it will lie there for the people."

That is all now.

Like all recitalists of his people and region, Mr. Hunt commences a myth with citations of the leading actors of the play's first scene. Not one of these actors receives a name, because the most important and idiosyncratic personalities among the actors do not appear until later scenes. As a matter of fact the two brothers are important. But their behavior does not hinge upon distinctive traits of personality, which would result in associating them with types of persons such as Coyotes, Bears, Grizzlies, or Deer, among other myth-age people. The theme, which at once develops treats of a marriageable female who lives unlike other unmarried girls: she is wholly alone in her house on an island in the Columbia River. She refuses all suitor offers. Both traits, an unmarried girl living alone and her rejection of all suitors, are out of line with Northwest States Indians' customs. If a girl chose such behavior no one could force her to do their bidding. Her actions very likely represent the wishes of many girls and the fears of their kin. That is why the myth screen pictures such a girl.

One of two brothers, who are from another band, has remarkable supernatural power. At the moment when he enters the woman's house he surprises her by appearing seated in the rear of the dwelling. He asks her to marry him. She tells him to come back another time for her answer. After two nights he reappears and is seated inside with the same phenomenal speed. I cannot find meaning in his lightning entries beyond the deductions that they point to his most unusual supernatural, to his strong wish for her, possibly also to his especial virility. Maybe, too, it is dramatically necessary to testify, in some such way, to his unexampled spirit-power in order to render plausible his subsequent journey to Sun and Sun's daughter.

Upon his second remarkable visit the maiden offers to bargain. She asks him to cut his long hair and to give it to her before she will agree to become his wife. To a Euro-American a request such as this might appear to constitute a kind of native literal-minded logic because we find at the end of the drama that the recitalist represents this woman as a Catholic nun. Why should she not therefore wish her mate to be closely shorn, too? However, I prefer the hypothesis that European notions are not yet affecting Mr. Hunt's manipulation of the plot, that the scene is still of wholly Indian source, and that the request for the remarkable man's long hair is a clear-cut Indian expression of a female's hostility to any man who would come to marry her. When the suitor insists and comes a second time, she can counter the reiteration of his request with difficulty because repeated urging is invariably effective among Northwest States Indians. Now she can handle his insistence only by asking for a sacrifice which she supposes no person would make because long hair is the most important of all anatomical features in determining attractiveness and beauty. It is the most important secondary sexual character. A person who lacks long hair suffers from a self-image like that of the individual who in western civilization is badly maimed or crippled. From the point of view of a Freudian-oriented theory in psychiatry, the requirement that the suitor surrender his long hair amounts to a proposal that he castrate or most severely mutilate himself. The demand is only less hostile than an injunction that he kill himself. The man's response is measured. Presently he gives in. He tells her that she can have him if she will cut his hair. I think that the frightfulness of doing it to himself would be manifest to Indians. But when she obtains his tresses she does the unexpected. She tells him to leave and come back the next day. Her order is the first indication that in general she is more than anti-husband.

For the first time she appears to be dishonest, too. At least she postpones her marriage without a prior suggestion that she might delay.

The next day when he reappears she tells him to take back his cut hair because he had not wanted to give it to her in the first place. Now it is clear that she is more than dishonest. She is intolerably aggressive and humiliating. She has deceived him so successfully, rejected him so completely, and he is still so lacking in a person's most treasured body feature, that he is profoundly ashamed. He goes to his home and says nothing, not even to his younger brother with whom he has been living. He does not arise from his bed for five days—a duration framed mechanically by the pattern number, five. The words of the version do not say so but doubtless he eats nothing. His is the familiar stylized behavior, which I term stylized depression or withdrawal, the culturally-shaped form of acting-out which most Northwest States Indians, young and old, resorted to when their humiliation, hurt, and anger were too great to be handled in the course of daily relationships and labor. An individual withdrew to his bed, face turned away from people. He let others do the work and the worrying, let others offer solutions, and he allowed his kinfolk to provide the comfort, understanding, and sustenance which he craved, as if he were an infant again. He was really asking for attention and for narcissistic supplies. His regression to baby-like action forced the people to grant exactly what he wanted. The five-day withdrawal pattern removed potentially violent persons from public places, even from ordinary household relationships, until they had time to work through their wounded feelings, with the supportive attentions, which alone made such a cure possible. Everyone respected the privacy of a person who was trying to manage tumultuous feelings by means of a stylized depression. It functioned, no doubt, to blow off steam quietly and safely where explosions, maybe feuds, might otherwise occur. It generated such concern, among everyone who lived around the angry person, that the people discussed what needed to be done and thereby moved toward a pacific resolution of the impasse, if resolution were possible without humiliation.

The myth proceeds to recount that the withdrawn brother's hair grows back to its former length after the five days and a swim. Since this is a pre-modern era, supernaturals effect wonders which their kind have not been able to achieve since the mythic epoch.

Now the older brother tells his sibling about the wretched affair with the hostile young lady. But they are not of a mind to confront her. Their plans are directed elsewhere. They make a vast number of arrows, wrapping them in the stylized number of five bundles, for the older brother to take along on his forthcoming travels. The great distance over which he proposes to journey is symbolized by the number of arrows in each of five bundles. At his house he sets up a feather, which will function, as it does in the myths of other Northwest States peoples, as a signal, which reveals whether its owner is dead or alive. If the feather falls it means that he is dead. But he does not suppose that he will die and so he promises to return, if he lives, after five years. When the recitalist says that he departs without speaking to anyone else, we are being told that the journey is like a quest for supernaturals. The suppliant says nothing to his band members about his intent although he might remark briefly about his purpose to a brother, parent, or grandparent. Our actor now leaves and as he proceeds he places the arrows in the ground at intervals.

At long last he reaches a house where a woman, the daughter of Sun, calls him "husband." She hides him lest her father kill and eat him. This is a scene of cannibal horror, triggered by a single sentence, which refers to a pile of human skeletons nearby. Terror is the greater because cannibalism is absent in Sahaptin and neighboring societies. However, Northwest States myth dramas contain numbers of projection figures who eat humans. Sun is a cannibal who, of course, departs at dawn. He returns at dusk with a person he has killed along the way. When Sun arrives he knows, so great is his supernatural power and maybe the acuity of his olfactory sense, that a living human being is there. The daughter, who fears her redoubtable father, does not deny the presence of a human. She expostulates that she wants the man. Presently Sun calms her by telling her that he will not kill her husband. Unlike Clackamas Chinook myth cannibals, whose omnivorousness is unquenchable, the Klikitat Sun draws the line at his daughter's human mate and spares him. I think that his permission to his daughter to have the man of her choice reflects that trait in east-of-Cascades social systems.

The next act presents Sun's daughter as a kind of teacher and an announcer of the ways human beings will live in future times. The plot utilizes her husband as the representative of all the people of eras to come. She tells him that human beings will never be eaten. She makes a fish spear for him as if it were the first fish spear in world history. She informs him that the Chinook salmon, which he spears, is food. The expressive content of the scene really is saying that henceforth salmon is to be the most valued of all provender. In the following scene she is teaching all the people, through him, that the next most esteemed of all comestibles will be venison. The words say, in the characteristic style where one item represents all the items of a class, that she makes an arrow for him, just as earlier she had made one fish spear for him. Again he follows her instructions and he kills a deer. She summarizes her food-production precepts and her distaste for her father's procurement of human flesh by indicating that salmon and deer will be foods and that she may have to "quarrel" with her father about his cannibal fare. The word she employs signifies only a stylized verbal contest between myth-era disputants, one of whom shortly wins the argument, whereupon a portion of the future is settled upon. When Sun returns he smells new victuals, non-cannibal kinds, in the house. She responds by telling him that he is never to eat people again. And in a most significant passage she says that the people's foods will be Sun's "own children." She wins the wrangle, which centers upon the future kinds of subsistence for people. Salmon and deer alone are specified but, as everywhere else, one or two items symbolize an entire class of items. In another important passage Sun, who at length capitulates to his daughter, says that "everything will be completed now." That is, he assents to the fact that he had been living in an incomplete world. It was an era in which pre-human and cruel things were done. He is actually agreeing that the many unfinished features of the myth period will give way to the "completed" ways, which the modern Indian peoples enjoy. Notations of specific mechanisms of the changes from imperfection and deficiency to completedness do not appear in a Northwest States oral literature. We find principally announcements, by almost any myth actors, of such changes. This myth, therefore, is one among a great many which depict an inchoate precultural world and the assertions, by even an unnamed actor like Sun's daughter, which parallel the changes that transpired for the sake of later peoples' comforts and security. Such portrayal presents important components of the people's worldview. And the public and reiterated pronouncement of portions of the worldview is one of the many vital functions, a validating one here, of myths. A discussion between disputants is often the plot-expediting device which offers the "history" of a specific kind of metamorphosis from myth-era immaturity, incompleteness, and insecurity, to completion, proper cultural ways, and safety for the Indians who are later to enter and populate the land.

In still another trenchant passage Sun's daughter says even more to her august father, as if she were addressing all the people of their era. She asserts that deer and salmon will be "older brothers" to the people and that fruits, berries, and roots will be "older sisters." These older siblings will "make the people grow." In interpretations of Clackamas Chinook myths I deduced that the major foods were a special kind of kin, according to the Clackamas world view.[1] In this Klikitat myth, Sun's daughter offers an explicit phrasing of the same concept, with a few additions. The foods are not merely like relatives. They are Sun's own children and they are also the older siblings of the people. Foods are special kinds of relatives and, like relatives, they help people to grow and to live. However, I have not yet come upon an explicit phrasing of the notion that Klikitat Sahaptins regarded Sun as their father, although he is certainly the father of their food-siblings. Another and maybe similar father-of-the-foods concept has turned up in Coos myth texts from the central Oregon coast, about two-hundred or more miles to the southwest.[2]

Now Sun's daughter tells her husband that they will go back to his home. Such a visit or return by a married couple is, of course, regionwide custom. Again, according to custom, she requests that her father provide the canoe for the trip, and he offers directions for it. He also prepares gifts, which will be placed in the craft—more reflection of custom. Sun's younger brother who is revealed, at this point, as Moon—an interesting feature of Klikitat cosmology because Moon is often a female in other mythologies of the region—offers to go along as the nighttime guide on the journey. Sun proposes to show the way for the young couple in daytime. The two guides express only some naturalistic astronomy here. The recitalist says, maybe significantly so as an item of interest in comprehension of familiar and broader social relationships, that Moon guides the couple "as if they were his own children." A father's brother presumably related in this way, whatever its details were, to his niece and her husband.

Presently, at a distant point during the trip, the daughter announces the place where Sun is to set in the future and she speaks of the direction of his daily movement. Such announcing is not only some more naturalist astronomy. It is typical stylization. Whatever is to be is put in words by any actor who is present in the current scene of the drama. Nothing more causal, mechanically so, is likely to be said. We hear principally laconic announcements of features of the world and way of life to be.

Presumably five years go by. When the couple reach the man's native village he asks his younger brother about the first woman, the one who had so deeply hurt him and because of whom he had proceeded on his successful five-year venture to find and incorporate powerful new supernaturals. He tells his younger brother that the woman's relatives are not to come with her to his boat until his own relatives have arrived to welcome him and his wife.

An intriguing passage is in the younger brother's soothing report to the people: the man who has just come is no "dangerous being," that is, he is not a person who comes from an alien settlement and has supernaturals, which might endanger the community. A brother was not likely to remain absent five years. Kin visited one another often, maybe annually to once every two years, on the average. Therefore a person, even one whom everyone recognized as kin, who returned after a long stretch of years was, like members of a distant community, an individual who might have introjected supernaturals against which the local populace lacked defenses—defenses built into their shamans or into other repositories of non-material kin who could protect them. In short, the younger brother's words express the nature of the region's prevailing misgivings about strangers: they may be entering and visiting with their spirit-powers which we cannot counter or neutralize. We may become sick. We may die. A new disease which no one can handle may be introduced into our midst, perhaps with secret intent by the visitor. But it is not the younger brother who has the last word. Although he gives reassurance it is the band's headman who tells the people that it is right for them to welcome the long-absent brother who, with his new family, is still in the canoe which carried them from afar. The returned gentleman down at the beach of course distributes gifts right there. The words say "little things" but the presents may be far more valuable than their modest and mannered characterization suggests.

Then the still unmarried woman who long before had sadistically cut the worthy gentleman's hair arrives and walks, too, upon a plank to the canoe. Everyone comes to greet the distinguished traveler lest there be bad feelings. At this point the dictation's utterances are not wholly clear to me, but I suggest that one of the gentleman's supernaturals makes his canoe edge away from the beach so that the unmarried lady tumbles into the river. The recitalist does not say that she swims or clambers safely back to dry ground, or that she drowns. Her physical fate is a minor matter. What is essential is not the vengeance but the announcement-epilogue to which the returned brother alone gives voice. It is unusually wordy. Above all, it is a modernly appended concept. It names women who refuse men in marriage "black dress." This appellation must have become the nineteenth-century Klikitat denotation for a nun. The dictation also says that such women will be strong in supernatural power. I regard this segment of the epilogue as a nice illustration of the way in which Klikitat discussants, maybe other Sahaptins too, had projected their notions and feelings about nuns into the most suitable or relevant scene of a myth without really changing the play's principal emphases, personalities, relationships, or expressions of value ideals. I propose that in this scene we have an early stage of change in a myth's expressive content, wherein an addition of descriptive material, maybe also an ancillary bit of new explanatory content, takes care of the Indians' mordant curiosity and concern about the supernaturally powerful, unmarried, shorn, and black-garbed females who had come to their land. These are the facets of such females, which the raconteur selects for phrasing. It is of further interest that "black dress" and her kin receive no gifts from the returned traveler. He rejects the woman and her lineage. He does not grant them even the customary modest gifts which temporary visitors from far-off communities, visitors also resident at the village, would have received from a returned traveler. I can only guess that the dismissal of "black dress" and her relatives reflects nineteenth-century rejection of the whites in gift-giving situations or, more likely, a special hostility, rooted in pre-white values, to any person who had subjected one to extreme humiliation. One would not offer even minute tokens to such a person or to her kin.

The only one of the myth's personalities who is distinctive is the unmarried woman. All the other actors are stereotypes of persons or person-like spirit-powers.

There is a romantic central theme. It deals with any person who, when humbled, departs to "find" a supernatural who may relate to him and presently help him resolve his frustration and recover from his social inadequacy. The encounter with a supernatural and the welding of kin-like ties with it are as profoundly romantic as anything can be. Sex, marriage, and love are Europeans' romantic themes. A Northwest States romantic theme offers a relationship with a special sort of newly-encountered person who has some idiosyncratic kind of strength and who wishes to be bonded to a human suppliant.

The principal actor in the drama is, then, a deeply troubled man who travels in order to mend his feelings, to reinvigorate his self-regard, and to ripen into a new maturity. The plot turns upon the romantic quality of his success, romantic because it deals with the relationship which he achieves with a supernatural, a relationship desired just as intensely by that spirit. No Klikitat could hope to marry Sun's daughter. However, the myth projection of a supernatural and her family who are beyond the reach of modern mortals functions as the most sentimental and ecstatic of all possible wish-fulfillments.

Another vital aspect of the drama, important primarily from the point of view of an alien's curiosity concerning Northwest States Indians, appears in the handling of feminine actors. To be sure, the first woman of the play is bad because she rejects all men in marriage. Nevertheless she has strong spirit-powers! The role played by the other woman, Sun's daughter, who functions two-facetedly as the traveler's excellent wife and as the good supernatural whom he "finds" far to the east, is one which hardly appears for female myth actors in the wealthier communities of Chinooks along the Columbia River and in societies along the Pacific coast. For the Klikitat Sun's daughter is quite a lady. She stands up to and disputes vital matters with her father, one of the greatest of the supernaturals, and she wins hands down. I think that this component of plot action connects with a fact of a social system: Klikitat and other Sahaptin women suffered little if at all from a Chinook and coastal ideal of second-class citizenship for females. Sun's daughter even tells her father what to eat and where he may travel for all future time, rather fundamental matters for him. Of course, like a proper wife she accompanies her new husband, whom she accepts without waiting for her father's approval, on the trip back to the mate's home community. Her stature is in no wise diminished by patrilocal residence custom.

Maybe the Klikitats theorized that a supernatural's union with a human being is so fine a thing that it augments her power. Therefore she becomes stronger than her aging progenitor. The scene may constitute a projection of community approval of a very young woman who, by her marriage, has entered upon maturity and is strengthened by her new bonds with her husband and his kin.

I therefore offer the thought that this myth expresses—it is especially evident to Euro-Americans—the high station and much respected decisions of Sahaptin females, by contrast with their status of less than parity in groups to the west of the Klikitats.

However, the myth is not a woman's story, and I think it is also not a man's story. It is centrally a spirit-power quest-and-success drama which accordingly partakes of a supremely romantic quality. The principal reason for giving a man the role of leading actor is to permit an unprecedentedly distant and long journey. Men traveled much farther than women.

The style and structure of the recital include the usual interspersed five-patterns, and a journey-in-several-acts genre or form which characterizes many Northwest States myths.

Editors' Notes

1. See "A Few Observations on the World View of the Clackamas Chinook Indians," this volume; also Jacobs 1960a, 58-64.
2. See Jacobs 1940, 243 for references to Coos Father-of-the-Foods texts.

11

Coyote's Journey

(Upper Cowlitz Sahaptin)

This is a syncretic mixture of aboriginal and Christian mythic elements, an example of Jacobs's genre 5 (in "Genres in Northwest States Oral Literatures," in this volume). Lewy Costima dictated this Upper Cowlitz Sahaptin text to Melville Jacobs "during a day's visit to Costima's farm at Bremer, near Morton, Washington, in August 1927; [Sam N.] Eyley Jr. translated a few days later" (Jacobs 1934, 238). The phonetic text and translation were subsequently published in Jacobs 1937, 205-11; 1934, 238-46. The interpretation and revised translation, published here for the first time, are from an unpublished manuscript (Jacobs 1959d). Jacobs's new translation differs from the 1934 translation in only minor details. Brief biographical notes on Costima and Eyley and the circumstances of Jacobs's Sahaptin fieldwork can be found in Jacobs (1929, v, 241-44) and Jacobs (1934, ix-xi, 102, 238). See Hunn (1990) for historical and ethnographic information about the Sahaptin Indians and Barnett (1957), Amoss (1990), and Ruby and Brown (1996) for the Indian Shaker Church.

The dictation which follows is a rare example of a lately developed Washington State oral-literature genre. I doubt that the recital of Mr. Lewy Costima, an Upper Cowlitz Sahaptin who helped me record it in the summer of 1927, would be regarded by any Native as an artistically worthy effort. Many raconteurs and discussants, over a period of maybe some decades more, would be required to hammer out and temper this kind of product before its content and form could be judged as meritorious as pre-white myths. I doubt that we will ever be able to suggest a precise date for the beginnings of Mr. Costima's type of recital, although it may go as far back as the 1870s or 1880s, that is, the period two or three generations after entry of whites into the most isolated valleys of Washington west of the mountains. A small percentage of the state's Salish and Sahaptin Indians participated in nurturing the genre, and they did it when they felt strongly that the white man's world was all around them and irretrievably so. Anthropologists have failed to record many examples of this recital form because of their feeling of need to write everything they could obtain which was evidently pre-white and, in some instances, because of a disinterest in the ideology and functioning of the Indian Shakers. For Mr. Costima was an enthusiastic adherent of the Indian Shaker religion. He volunteered the text. Like many Shakers, he did not seem to wish to give dictations of pre-Shaker materials. The contents of his text are nevertheless a remarkable mixture of pre-white myth components and borrowings from nineteenth-century western Washington Indians' inconsiderable understanding of the Christians' ideological heritage. The dictation's characteristics of style are easily traceable to the pre-white myth genre and to the early nineteenth century expanded, annotated, or descriptively developed genre exemplified, for example, in Sophie Smith's dictation "Cougar and His Younger Brother" (Adamson 1934, 202-9). Although the Costima text rambles and is probably not a good example of an art form in the earliest stage of its development, I think that it is valuable for folklore theory because of the clarity with which it displays processes of borrowing, innovation, and amalgamation of features of oral literature in a period of unusually rapid and thoroughgoing change. Gaucheries and incongruities in the text may amuse us because of our culture-bound responses to and feeble capacity to identify with a small group of food-gathering people who reacted in a special way to envelopment, rejection, and crushing humiliation by the whites.

Dots are in places where Mr. Costima used a Native word whose sounds in most instances can be represented only by special transcriptional symbols.

The text follows.

The chief (Jesus) sent Coyote from above to this land. He had sent Crow first, he had him come to see how the people were, (how) they were then. When that Crow arrived, he saw people lying about, dead. He went and ate their eyes and then he went on, and he went above again toward home, to the place of the chief (Jesus). He (Jesus) asked him, "How did it appear to you?" It seemed to him to be pretty good. But he said to him, "Why, no! You have been eating their eyes. Very evidently you have been doing ill. You are finished, that is as much work as you will obtain." Then he ceased right there. The chief let him go, he became a crow. He became a black crow.

The chief (Jesus) above spoke, "I will take another one, and I will send him to go and see." Coyote said, "Let me be the one!" And so Coyote came, he arrived here. He (Jesus) had told him, "That is how you are to be, exactly like myself." And so Coyote became exactly like the chief above. He took (a staff of) wood. In that manner he turned into a fish. The chief had said, "I would have you do to everything exactly as I do it." That is how Coyote did, he appeared in this land, (functioning as) the chief he took care of this land, he made everything, he made the streams, he indicated whatever names there were to be.

He named the … (Cowlitz River). Coyote came this way from … (Kelso, Washington), as he came he named rivers and creeks. As he came (upriver) he named one of them … (Toutle River), he named another … (a creek opposite Castle Rock, Washington), he named another … (Olequa River), still another he named … (Salmon Creek, which is below Toledo, Washington), another he named. … As he came he named … ("strawberry place", a site below Salkum), he named … ("white fir") creek, he named another … (Salkum), he named … (Winston Creek, which is below Mayfield). At that place he made a place to catch fish, he made a seat from which to spear fish, he made it for spearing better, so that one could tug strong and not fall into the water. There in the river he made a place where it boils and bubbles, there fish come out on the surface, right there he speared them.

Coyote came on upstream, as he came he named that river … , he came on from there and here he made … (Silver Creek) creek. He came on from there, he made … (Klikitat Creek), he came from there to where another stream flows out named … (Tilton Creek, at Morton, Washington). At that place he came out from the river to a prairie, there he placed roots, camas, he put strawberries, he put … roots, he made these foods for the people, and he made … roots. Coyote sat there, sitting there he said, "I have been making all sorts of things. Now that the people coming are already near, I will prepare all sorts of food for them, so that they will not starve. When they come, they will obtain them and eat them." And he spoke thus, "I will make timber so that they may burn wood and keep themselves good and warm, they will not be cold, they will keep warm."

When the people came, they arrived there, and two of them sat there, one woman, and one man, eyeless, mouthless. He said, "I will come to you, and I will complete you." Then the chief went, he spoke in this manner, "Do not call out to anything. A dangerous being may call to you, but you are never to call in reply." They spoke in this manner, "Yes." They stayed there perhaps one turn around (one hour), when it called out to them. The woman said, "A headman is calling out in this direction. The person who has been completing our eyes and mouth must be coming." The man said, "No. It must be from the bad one (the Devil)." The woman said, "No." He of the bad one called out and came along, he sat there, and he spoke in that manner. At that place he opened both their eyes, and they saw, far off they saw. "Do you see well?" They spoke thus, "I do, very well." He opened their mouths, and at once they said, "I do, very well." "Are you all right with that?" "Yes." He told the man, "I can see well with my eyes, you have opened my eyes well." He spoke to him in this manner, "If my younger sister will be first to have her eyes opened, then I will have my own opened." He went to them and opened all these eyes of theirs, and the man's mouth (too).

Then the chief above (Jesus) arrived. "Who opened your eyes?" "Oh!" he said, "The one from the bad one (the Devil) must have deceived me." The chief (Jesus) said, "He has beaten me now. I suppose I will make life short." Coyote made it short (for them), the chief above (Jesus) made it short (then) for Coyote. "You are to give them all sorts of things. You will give them prayers, you will give them to the people. When the time comes when they die, it will be all right with prayers. They are not to tell his, (lest) their life become short, the life of the people will become short. When they die they will come quickly, directly to up above, prayer will bring them if they have always prayed, if they have believed in the chief above (Jesus). Good will come, the land will be short-lived, it will be made over again. When the land becomes old, I will make it over again at that time."

Coyote went on then from that place, he went on from … (Mossy Rock prairie), he made a fishing place at which to catch salmon trout, he named it … ("nose," at the upper end of the Cowlitz River canyon), a place where many fine fish could be caught. "The people are traveling toward here, and they are close by now. This is a place where they will be. Now I shall make it, so that from now on there will be light. I shall make stars so that the land may be light. I shall make the moon so that it may be light. I shall make the sun that it may be light. When they sleep it will be warm. The people will go here and there feeling good and warm. Because they are coming close to here now on their journey."

When he went on he came upon, "People have already begun to be here. Apparently they reached here some time ago, and there is no fire whatever. They obtain fish but they merely pierce them, roast them, and cook them (by dancing around them). When they dance they become done, they dance and they are done, entirely without fire." Coyote came along, he reached there. "What are you doing?" "We dance and it is cooked and can be eaten. Whoever dances hardest is the quickest to eat." Coyote said, "Make a fire quickly!" They prepared firewood. Coyote took out his fire (implements), he browned fine dry cedar bark shavings, he applied his fire (implements) to it, this is how he did it, he twirled it till it was hot, and then fire came out of it, he took it, he placed it in those dry cedar bark shavings, he blew on the fire, it burned. "Come here! Take the fire!" They made two fires there yonder, and at that place they roasted salmon, it became well cooked. "Because I am hungry I shall go and eat." Coyote made a long knife to cut with, he made an axe to chop with, he made all sorts of things. Coyote finished everything there. "I'll be going on." He went away, he cried out (in the flush of achievement), "Waaaaaaaa!"

When he went on he saw on the opposite side of the river that they were making a fish dam with persons, people made it, they cut open persons, they cut them open with knives. "What can they be doing? They form a fish dam in order to catch salmon." There were a number of babies crying, they were cold. He was angry. "Ah! Why do you cause the babies to be cold?" He made the people come out of the water, and Coyote told them (how to make a dam without using humans' bodies). He chopped wood, he made a fish dam. Then the people went, they chopped wood. When Coyote made the fish dam he fastened it with hazel rope, he completed it. He took soft maple and willows and made dip nets with which to catch salmon. Coyote ran along, he fished with a dip net, he caught salmon, he hauled up three of them, he brought them to shore. "Prepare the food! I am hungry. I want to go and eat." He made a shallow water trap with sticks, he laid it in the water of a small creek, and he caught salmon. He said, "That is how you will be. That is what you will make for your future food as long as you are here." Coyote made a basket trap for them in Tilton Creek here. "There will always be a basket trap there. In summer, in the dry season when the river goes dry, there will always be fish there. Graylings, salmon trout, silverside, Chinook salmon, steelhead will go into it."

Coyote came on, as he came he named a brook ... (near Mossy Rock). He came on and again he gave the name ... (a site one mile west of Riffe). Again as he came he named a salmon trout site... , many salmon trout (are there). As he came along he named ... ("penis place," a point of land in the Cowlitz River a mile east of Riffe), on the opposite side he named it. ... As he came along he again gave the name ... ("thicket of young firs" several miles east of Riffe), he named ..., on the opposite side he named it ... ("being packed along"). He came on and named a high mountain ... (a hill southwest of Nesika), he came along and named ... (a weed, in quantities near the Kiona family homestead at Nesika), he named ..., he named ... ("ashwood place," a creek near the Iley farm at Nesika and also named ..., "muskrat place"), the next one yonder ... ("steelhead place," which is Landers Creek at Nesika), on the opposite side ... ("sucker place," a creek opposite Nesika). At one place, ..., there are snags in the river (three to four miles above Nesika in the Cowlitz River). (There is) ... (a treeless area below Cosmos), ... (a hill a mile or two miles below Cosmos).

A fine brave man, a fine chief, Coyote. He made all the different kinds of foods for the people so that they could dwell here and always be supplied with food. (There is) ... mouth (Rainy Creek), the river makes a bend (at) ... (another treeless area), ... (a rocky narrows four miles above Cosmos) is a good place to catch food (fish), a great quantity of food is taken (there), at the whirlpool at ... there is always food to be caught. "There will be many people there. In future they will have a good big time, they will always catch food (there). It is a fine place. Above there at ... ("muskrat") they will catch trout and salmon trout, at that ... ("muskrat") they will make trout hooks, there they will get food with long ropes, they will haul them out of the water, early in the morning they will see a great many fish, trout, salmon trout, Dolly Varden, graylings, suckers." (There are) ... ("leaves place," a mountain about ten miles south of Cosmos), ... (a creek below Cowlitz Falls), ... (Goat Creek, below Cowlitz Falls).

At ... ("sweathouse," a rock at Cowlitz Falls) Coyote sat down, he planned what to make (and then he borrowed Wren's prodigious penis in order to extend it to a female on the opposite bank). He thought that he would make ... (Mt. Rainier), that he would make ... (Mt. Adams), that he would make ... ("the person from whom smoke comes," Mt. St. Helens). He thought where. He thought that he would make falls at which to catch fish, in future time a great many people would be there on opposite sides. "Wren will be there, in time to come he will dwell there. They (the Indians) are coming now. On the other side (of the Cowlitz River) many people will be at ... (a site with the name of an edible plant found in quantity near Cowlitz Falls). Blue Jays, pheasants, ... birds will be there in time to come near the falls, they will live there, at that place great numbers of persons, women and men, will be in future times. At the place where Chinook salmon, silversides, steelheads and Jack salmon rest on their way upstream, at ... (a site near Cowlitz Falls), there will be a place to spear fish, to catch fish with pole and spear point, at that place they will be speared with them. They will take fish out of the water for food."

The great man Coyote completed it. "They (the Indians) will be coming now." A number of people lived there. They gathered food, they did it well, the women felt proud. They went down to the water because it was a warm day, the sun was shining, they went to the water, the five unmarried girls went into the water for a swim. Coyote himself traveled along in that direction, as he was going along he saw the women in swimming, from the opposite side. He stepped upon and made a hole in a large rock. He thrust (his penis) across the stream toward the women but it was too short, not long enough, he was unable to do it, he gave it up.

He went on, he went and saw Wren, he reached him. Wren (said), "How are you, younger brother? What are you doing? What do you want?" "No. I (want to) borrow a soft basket (which has your enormously long penis in it) from you. I would like to take it here and there today." Wren said, "No. You would make mine (my organ) hungry." "Oh no. I would give it food." Wren said, "Very well then." And he gave it to Coyote, he loaned it to him.

The brave Coyote carried it away. He reached the place. "The unmarried girls are bathing there now." He sat down, he thrust it across the stream there to the oldest of the women. He did it, now that was how it became tight in her. When she took it the woman said, "Oh it's nice in the water now." But after one hour she became tired and cold. The people told her to cut it off. (Someone) went, obtained a knife, cut at it, it was a bad knife, it did not cut through at all. Some bird flew by and it told them to cut it off with … grass (which is sharp-edged). Then (someone) went and cut it through with … grass. Part of it shrank back toward Coyote, part of it in this direction. The woman pulled it out of the water, she carried it toward home.

Coyote himself went on, he returned it to Wren's soft basket. Wren said, "This thing of mine has become hungry." Wren went, he took an axe, he chipped off small pieces of the bark of medium-sized firs, he fed them to it but it would not eat. He said, "The rascal, Coyote! He has killed my penis!" He looked at it, he examined it closely, it had been cut through, it was dead.

Coyote went on, he took snakes and frogs, he placed them here on his hat, he placed feathers around it, and then he went upriver as a shaman, (he pretended that he was) a powerful shaman. They saw, "There is a shaman traveling by on the other side of the river." They shouted, "Are you a shaman?" He did not call over at all. Coyote kept traveling on in the same direction paying no heed. After some time he called out, "I am a shaman! I am a powerful shaman! When I cure sicknesses they become well." "Call to him! (Tell the) shaman (that someone) has become ill." Then Coyote said, "I'll come." He reached the river, he made a small thing on which to walk, he walked on it (maybe a foot-log bridge), he crossed the river, he proceeded to the sick person.

When he arrived he said, "Who is to do the singing? and five or six to drum for me? Then I'll doctor." Coyote (presently) doctored, he went, he sang (his doctoring song, over the sick woman who was suffering from the tip of the organ which she could not take out). Then he said, "It's bad. Where is the sweathouse? I'll doctor her there." The people said, "A sweathouse is there down below (near the water)." Coyote said, "Very good. You carry her away (to the sweathouse)." They lifted her, they put her inside when they had taken her to the sweathouse, they placed the woman inside the sweathouse. Coyote doctored, they went away, they went back home while Coyote himself was all alone with that woman. He joined (his stump of an organ) to the (tip of) the penis in her there. That woman squealed, she cried out, "Coyote is killing me!" They, Blue Jay, ... bird, ... bird, and ... bird ran to the sweathouse, they reached it club in hand to strike Coyote, but when they got to the door of the sweathouse Coyote emerged, they missed him, he got out, "Aha!" he ran away, none of them could strike him.

The woman no longer had anything down here (inside her), she arose well (cured), she ran on, when she peeped out she told her younger sisters, "Speak well and with gratitude to the shaman. He cured me. I am well now." She spoke loudly and angrily to her younger sisters. The younger sisters said to her, "You yourself said, 'He's killing me!' (But) you became well immediately after."

Coyote went on upriver. He named ... ("it curves"), he named ... ("junction," at the mouth of the Cispus River), he named ... ("pointed," near Cowlitz Falls). He went over a rise and named a creek there ... ("trout place"). He named ... ("little babies' place," about a mile above ...), ... ("... fern root place," four to five miles west of Randle), ..., ... (Kiona Creek), ... (Silver Creek), ... ("scratch," near Randle), ... (a fishing site), ... (a site at Randle), ... ("snipe place," a treeless site near Randle). He went farther, he named a stream ... (Silver Creek), it is a bad creek there, steelhead are there. At the large falls above, it gives signs to people, it kills them. When Coyote reached there he made it cease, he took it by the tail, he pulled it out, he killed it, he threw it entirely away to the Devil, and then he went away.

He went on upstream, he emerged into an open place, a trail went along, and above there a woman lay on her back, she called out to everyone, they would ascend toward her, the Soft Basket Person would bite and kill men. Coyote knew that the Soft Basket Person was killing a great many people. "Now then I'll kill the darn woman!"

When he came out of the woods and he was going along the trail she shouted to him, "May you not be having an erection?" He never even paid attention. Five times the woman called, five times, and then Coyote listened and said, "Yes! I have a mighty erection. I want to have a woman very, very much." The woman said, "I have an erection myself." Then Coyote went on, he climbed up toward the woman's place. He sat down and reflected. He made a hot penis of stone. Then he went on, he climbed up above, there the dangerous Soft Basket Person lay on her back. When Coyote reached there he said, "Ah yes! my deceased relative's wife! I do have a mighty erection." "Dear, oh dear!" "I'll do it to you now with your eyes shut. You must not look. I may hurt you when I insert it. Keep yourself from suffering from the pain of it, my in-law! Mine is very strong." The woman said, "All right." She shut her eyes and then Coyote took out the (hot stone) penis, he inserted it, he thrust it in, and his deceased relative's wife squealed. "Harder! It will be all right after a while!" He thrust it inside, ... (a sound like a rush of water), the woman exploded, ... (sound of an explosion) the evil Soft Basket Person (exploded). He said, "There are many people now on the way here (that is, the modern Indians are coming into the land). A woman will never kill people. When persons copulate they will be making babies." Coyote went on.

He named a stream ... (eight to ten miles above Randle), another (he named) ... (Skate Creek, at Lewis), another ... (a mountain near Lewis), another ... ("person who bubbles," a creek above Lewis), another ..., another ... ("steelhead place," a creek), another ..., a place for Chinook salmon. Another he named ... (Clear Fork), another he named ... (Muddy Fork).

He ate camas there and then he became hungry. Coyote went down toward the river, he went along there, he broke off a stick, and this is what he did to his feet. He stepped in the water of the ... (Clear Fork), he did it in this manner, he scraped with the sharp stick, out came salmon, graylings, a great many of them. He caught them, he did it to the graylings in this manner with his hands, he threw them ashore, he took them, he made a fire, he roasted them, he ate them.

He said, "At this place will be salmon, Chinook salmon, steelhead, silverside, grayling, Dolly Vardens, a great many large Dolly Vardens. They will not go farther up the stream, none will be above Ohanepecash, no people will ever dwell above there, there will be a great deal of snow in the winter (there). The people will always be (below) at this place here, at this place they will have salmon for food."

The very first utterance in this text gives evidence that at least one adherent of the Shaker Indian religion, Mr. Costima, identified the whites' supernatural, Jesus, as a person whose powers exceeded those of Coyote, the Upper Cowlitz Indians' supernaturally best-equipped actor of the myth era. Jesus is like a western Washington headman: he sends emissaries to other communities. And he lives in the sky country, not on the earth below. He had initially dispatched a Crow man to report how the people were living down on the earth. A male Crow is unusual in Northwest States dramatis personae to the south of the Cowlitz River, where myths frequently include poor older Crow women. It seems that since a headman never sends a woman messenger or scout, and the plot requires a person who harms the people, a scavenger, a male Crow actor, is projected. I cannot determine why the first scene tells about a land below where the people have already died. Crow has nothing much to do down on the land but to pause, before he returns, to eat the eyes of corpses. The scene seems to serve the function of pointing up how unsatisfactory things are in the land of this time. Corpses are mutilated by scavengers because the people do not bury their dead in the proper Indian manner, in shallow graves. Jesus is displeased with Crow's report that things are good below. How can they be satisfactory when a bad person can eat the eyes of dead people? The lines do not say that Jesus punishes Crow or changes his scout into a mere bird. In typical Northwest States fashion the recitalist merely announces that Crow metamorphoses into a bird, a change which need not imply that female Crows at just that time became birds, too. I think that the intent is to announce that presently all Crow people transform into dirty scavenger birds. Like all the literatures of the region, the representative of a group or class makes the decisive change and everyone understands, without question, that all others of the type undergo the same change at about the same time.

In words put in Jesus' mouth, the recitalist has said only that Crows will no longer receive work assignments which require responsibility. Now a Coyote man, supernaturally the most powerful of the Coyote people, volunteers for the mission to report on conditions in the land below. Jesus tells Coyote that "You are to be exactly like me." The blending of the two myth-era personages, Coyote and Jesus, is of exceeding interest. The repute and powers of the leading Coyote actor were such that a century of surrounding by whites, missionaries, and others who persistently claimed the greatest powers for Jesus has resulted in a conviction that Coyote acted in Jesus' stead in western Washington. Unlike some other Northwest States Indians of the early twentieth century Mr. Costima did not assert that Coyote and Jesus were one and the same person. But he and others felt that Coyote did Northwest work which was similar to Jesus' contributions to the people of other lands.

The identification is effected with one Christian-like descriptive item for Coyote: Mr. Costima gives him a staff of wood. The limitation to a single delineative item is Indian literary style. The recitalist often omits such an item or he selects one or two features which are sufficient for depiction of the actor.

Next, Mr. Costima announces the things Coyote does. The words and phrases are wholly Indian in style: "he made everything." That is, Coyote does a number of important things for the Indians who will presently enter the land. "Everything" is a word which must not be translated in terms of a Euro-American concept. In the context of the recital the word means only "a number of important things." "He made the streams" also signifies far less than its literal translation into a European language. It implies a few riffles and cascades where the people would construct fish dams, place fish traps, and the like. On the other hand, Coyote's naming of sites, the inventory of which occupies a major portion of the recital, is literally just that. One might deduce facets of the Cowlitz world view by means of a simple classification of sites whose names are presented and by notation of their economic or other functions. A cursory glance at the site names suggests that fishing and food-procuring locales are a central interest. The recitalist has up to this point noted and named eleven tributaries of the Cowlitz River; each either has its Salish-speaking village, usually at its entry into the Cowlitz at a place where salmon are gotten in quantities, or it is at a site where berries or roots are obtained. A twelfth tributary, at Morton, Washington, is in Upper Cowlitz Sahaptin-speaking country. The remainder of the dictation applies to that territory. The recitalist says in stylized pre-white myth form, "The people coming are already near." He adds that Coyote "prepares," that is he locates sites where major food production will occur. A rather unusual item is the one about "making timber" so that the people will have bark for fuel. It is necessary to note that bark rather than wood is the principal fuel. I do not recall an announcement of just this kind about bark in other Northwest States myths. I suggest that it may be a Shaker or other modern addition which rounds out the delineation of the work which Coyote does for the Indian people who are later to enter the land.

The next scene is unclear in spots but is obviously a creative adaptation of a scene from a pre-white Coyote myth. Its overt content is predominantly Christian. Coyote tells a couple who lack mouths and eyes that they must not reply if a dangerous supernatural calls out to them. One of the concepts here is the Indian notion of myth-era persons who are incomplete and who do not do things well. In spite of Coyote's warning, a supernatural who is neither named nor described comes to the pair and opens their eyes and mouths. Then Jesus arrives and infers that a bad supernatural, whom Mr. Costima probably equated with the Christians' devil, has "completed" the two. I do not understand why Jesus is represented as dissatisfied about what had been done to the handicapped persons, but it may be that he is concerned because the devil rather than his own emissary had done the good work. Jesus then makes life short (that is, not everlasting) for Coyote and for all people, after which he announces that people will pray. Upon their death those who have prayed and believed in Jesus will come quickly to the sky country. And when the land "becomes old, I will make it over again." The concept of the land becoming old and being made young again is obscure to me, but I believe that it is an Indian notion rather than a misinterpretation of Christian cosmology, and that we lack supporting details revealing just what it means. I am quite sure that it contains no concept of reincarnation.

In the next scene, which is in Upper Cowlitz Sahaptin-speaking districts, Coyote makes a fishing place and then, in a remarkable passage which I think goes beyond pre-white ideas about a Coyote's capacities, he makes the stars, moon, and sun for the sake of the Indians who are, he says, traveling toward the Cowlitz country. No recitalist ever suggests how long it may be before the permanent Indian residents arrive. The core of the scene is, first, its pre-white concept of a world which is unsatisfactory because it and its residents are incomplete, and secondly, its pre-white-like employment, in the person of Coyote, of a supernaturally powerfully adult, the surrogate of a settlement's security-giving and fatherlike headman, who does the most vital things for the sake of the people who will be making their living there. I do not recall that Coyote is able to create the stars, sun, and moon in wholly pre-white myths anywhere in the region. Such creativity for Coyote may be a development of the middle nineteenth-century Christian period, especially that of the early 1880s which also marked the beginnings of the Shaker Indian religion, when Indians ventured anew to account for what had been done in their homeland during myth times. Many Indians' acceptance of Christian ideas about the Holy Trinity functioned principally to reinforce old beliefs about supernaturally pre-eminent myth actors, now equated with the Christians' leading supernaturals and therefore credited with fresh achievements. An interesting codicil to the new world view is a conviction that the Christians' spirit-powers, God, Jesus, and the Holy Ghost, were supernaturally creative or transformers in lands far to the east of Washington State. Washington Indians retained Coyote for the basic tasks of creation which were executed in their own countryside. In Mr. Costima's myth Coyote is reported as receiving a generalized order from Jesus to do the work and, of course, Coyote pays special attention to Mr. Costima's Cowlitz River valley and its environs.

In the following scene Coyote reaches people who lack fire. They cook the most important food, fish, by dancing around them. The more energetic the dancing the quicker the roast is done. Coyote teaches these pathetic people how to make fire, knives, and axes. The scene is thoroughly pre-white in content. Even in style it has mainly Indian forms, for example, the phrase "Coyote finished everything there" is typical of Coyote myths and signifies, to be sure, that that lordly gentleman only completes the work he set for himself or decided to do at that one settlement. Of course when he gives fire-making and cutting tools to a few persons at one site he is really bestowing superior techniques upon the people in the many settlements all over the land. No myth explains how the techniques, newly acquired through Coyote's demonstrations at a single village, manage to spread to all the other villages. The anthropologists' notion about cultural diffusion is not an Indian idea. Nor is there, apparently, the least need felt by raconteurs, audiences, and community discussants to explain more than Coyote's initial and altruistic granting of technological know-how.

The scene which follows presents Coyote arriving at a Cowlitz River settlement where a fish dam is constructed of the bodies of live human beings. Coyote cuts wood and shows how the dam should be of that impersonal material. He makes a dip net and demonstrates its use. He makes a trap for employment where the water is shallow. He tells the people to prepare the salmon he has caught in the new ways—he is hungry, as always, and he wants a meal. The frequency with which the gentleman goes about getting himself fed contrasts impressively with the lesser involvement in satisfaction of oral needs among Old World deities. Coyote announces that people will obtain salmon in the manner which he has exemplified. He speaks specifically of a creek at Morton, Washington, which he says will always have fish, obtained by a basket trap. The scene is pre-white in content and very much so in style.

The next portion of the myth offers names and functions of places along the upper reaches of the Cowlitz River valley; Coyote announces as he journeys along it. In the course of these namings and announcements Mr. Costima introduces a ritual-like utterance typical for a myth of a Coyote journey up an important river valley. "A fine brave man, a fine headman, Coyote. He made all the different kinds of foods for the people, so that they could dwell here and always be supplied with food." The emphasis in this recurrent anthem-like refrain are, as always, on the security-granting leader who takes care of his people, and on the food supply.

It is extremely significant for purposes of analysis of processes of creative remodeling of myth materials that Mr. Costima does not omit, at its usual place at Cowlitz Falls, the far-flung comedy of Coyote's borrowing of Wren's gigantic penis and the subsequent scene of its amazing extension across the stream into the girl bathing there. Maybe Mr. Costima was much too buoyant, loquacious, and Indian, in spite of his professed Shaker orthodoxy, to bypass, when he arrives at the right geographical location, an entertaining act which deals with sex in the most important myth. And so, at or near Cowlitz Falls Coyote observes five unmarried girls in the water on the other side. For a moment, naming, announcing, and exhibitions of desirable implements go by the boards. Coyote is a sexual dynamo for a while. He extends his penis, in a transparently wish-fulfilling venture, to ascertain if it is long enough to reach the desirable young things across from him. It is too short. He goes on and comes to a Wren man. He asks to borrow that actor's penis, which is long enough, patently so because it is curled within a large soft basket which presumably it fills right to the top, although an Indian recitalist never pauses to supply such a depiction of its impressiveness. I do not know enough about the region's ideological associations around Wren actors to deduce why the man with the enormously provocative penis is identified with an actor who later becomes a tiny bird. About a hundred miles south of Cowlitz Falls the Clackamas Chinook Wren actor is an immature youth whose lecherous grandmother instructs him in sex.[1] We do not hear that there is anything special about his organ except that, to an older woman, any youth's is satisfactory. For some unascertained reason Wren actors may be especially involved in sexual divertissement. The adult Wren of the Upper Cowlitz myth capitulates to Coyote's pleas to borrow the unique organ. Coyote offers to feed it—later in the play it is revealed that Wren nourishes it with chips of fir bark. And to the south, along the Columbia, it bites its unnamed owner's legs if it is not fed constantly.[2] Insistent oral hunger seems to be equated with the male organ's need which also must not be long denied. Wren's granting of Coyote's request for a loan of the ever-ravenous instrument is consistent with the inability, throughout the Northwest States, of any actor to remain adamant when another actor repeatedly requests something. The relatedness of people is such that even a stranger who is encountered along the trail will lend if not give away his prized member if the suppliant continues to plead for it! Or, steadfast refusal of a plea may generate a feeling of shame, with possible bloody and therefore fearful consequences. Again, whatever the motivation, myth actors do not long say "no." I suspect that the ease with which they are persuaded carries only a little further one of the facts of social relationships, but its frequent citation in myths suggests that people were ambivalent about the generosity and compliance which the peace and common safety dictated.

Coyote extends his borrowed organ across the river into the oldest of the five women. She says, "Oh it has become nice in the water." She does not dare say why it is nice, lest she be humiliated. The quip is humorous because of its several components which include incongruity, deceit, sex in itself, and laughter at the expense of females. The joke exposes Native cynicism about the ethics of an unmarried girl. She will take some sex if no one finds out. A large payment in marriage will be made for her, her social status will be high, and her family will not be disgraced if she is ostensibly a virgin. I find no built-in superego which makes her feel guilty about enjoying extramarital sexual intercourse if she can get away with it furtively.

Mr. Costima's citing of penetration of the oldest girl is of interest. Chinooks to the south and other Sahaptins east of the mountains represent the deflorated girl as the youngest of the five, that is, the girl who is of greatest value in marriage, the one whose loss of virginity would be most damaging to the self-respect and status of her family, and the one whose violation would please Coyote most. Mr. Costima's employment of the oldest rather than the youngest of the five girls may be a mistake. On the other hand, he may have chosen her because of pressure from the "oldest dumbest" motif which may extend south to the Cowlitz valley and which, according to Sally Snyder, is found among Puget Sound Salish peoples a hundred or more miles to the north.[3] The oldest girl might be represented as acceding to the rape and feeling less guilt because she is not as bright or principled as her sisters.

The recitalist adds an extra portion of sadism to the scene when the regionwide use of a sharp-edged grass to cut off the tip of Coyote's organ is preceded by the failure of a dull stone knife to sever the organ. When Coyote returns the member to Wren and he rolls it up in its soft basket it will not eat its usual pieces of fir bark. Wren exclaims that Coyote "has killed my penis." The organ is referred to as if it were a person.

Since the plot action centers Coyote, the recitalist drops the question, if it was a question to Indians, about Wren's feelings and of the destiny of his badly mutilated and therefore defunct organ. In good literary style Wren is not mentioned again. The action proceeds with Coyote who places snakes, frogs and feathers on his headband or cap and so masquerades as a shaman. The accoutrements are incongruous because snake and frog spirit-powers are worthless—they would not cure a sneeze. The deceit is funny because Coyote does not have spirit-powers to cure a sexual ailment. The anticipation of sadistic behavior is amusing. Action at the expense of females is intrinsically entertaining, too, in the area. Auditors know that the girl is ill because the penis tip cannot be extracted and that Coyote is planning to do it in the course of delighting himself with a second rape.

Also diverting is Coyote's refusal to heed the shouted question, "Are you a shaman?" He poses as a shaman by pretending the kind of introverted, inner-directed behavior which the people associate with some shamans. Actually, a Coyote's personality—and a principal reason why various myth actors are accorded a Coyote designation—is outer-directed, immediately responsive to basic drives, and inclined to mischief. Here the Coyote actor is the young fellow on a journey of adventure, out to see the world.

When he first doctors the girl in a house, with everyone present, he is in line with customary therapeutic procedure, which means that the assembled folk join him in singing his curing songs as he labors over the patient in order to remove the disease cause. Nothing is more incongruous and preposterously funny than to tell the helpers and onlookers to carry the girl to a sweathouse where he can work over her without others present and singing with them. Only a myth-age shaman could get away with such trickery.

Observe the aberrant pattern number four, which occurs a few scores of miles to the north on Puget Sound, for the bird people who hear the girl shrieking. When the girl comes out and informs everyone that the shaman cured her, the repartee is amusing.

The next scene is a series of grantings of names to sites, with one curious item: at a stream now named Silver Creek Coyote takes a supernatural which has been killing people and he "throws it away to the devil." The addition of the concept of the devil is, again, evidence of the surface fusion of native and European notions in Mr. Costima's world view.

The next scene is a familiar Sahaptin play within a play. A supernaturally powerful and murderous woman, whom I dub for purposes of quick reference the Soft Basket Woman, is lying on her back above a trail. She induces men who pass by to have intercourse with her. She is, indeed, a myth-age representative of the modern female of easy favors and at deeper psychological levels she expresses Native feelings about women who control men's lives. In the myth her toothed vagina severs men's organs and so they die. I suggest an equation of forbidden extramarital sex and punishment by mutilation of the genitals, as an extension of the Freudian concept of castration as the punishment for incest. Each equation has its cultural causes.

When Coyote passes the place the woman calls to him five times—pattern number again—before he replies. His seeming woolgathering or inattention is deliberate and sadistic. Therefore it is funny, the more so because sex is offered by a woman. Who ever heard of a man who failed to heed so delightful a bidding? When he agrees to have intercourse he brags about the size of his organ and he tells the woman to shut her eyes. When she explodes, one wonders if the detonation and the torrent are not symbolic components, rather obvious ones to Indians, of an ejaculatory climax. When it is all over and the woman, or what is left of her, is lying there dead, Coyote announces in the typical fashion of the literary style, that is, with one auditor or none at all, that a woman will never again kill men during copulation. Might we not add, cynically, that this society, which was only slightly tilted in the direction of regarding the masculine sex more favorably, continued to allow men to enjoy, even as Coyote did, the luxury of killing women during the sexual embrace. The converse was inadmissible.

The final scene is again principally place-naming and it lacks other significance.

In summary, the dictation appears to be a somewhat spontaneous and idiosyncratic piecing together of scenes from the long pre-white myth of the journey of the Sahaptins' leading Coyote actor, coupled with citations of many place names and including a few other matters which are mostly technology of food procurement. There are also some tacked-on items of world view which are traceable to regionally characteristic misunderstandings of Christian ideology.[4] The short plays or scenes within the dictation are close to pre-white myth content and style. The particular sequence of scenes is very likely fabricated by Mr. Costima. In all likelihood the dictation is an example of innumerable ventures, by late nineteenth-century Indians, to weave into a whole cloth their pre-white myth content and the shreds which they had gleaned of the Christian world view. The genre is patently inchoate. What we have in it are, I think, numbers of individual trial balloons, among which this dictation is the only one which I was able to record in a form and translation sufficiently intelligible to warrant publication. I suggest that the genre was in the creative hands of community discussants, mostly the members of the Shaker Church, and that it had not often been tried out in relatively formal audience situations except within Shaker groups. It may be an instructive illustration of an exceedingly early stage in the development of a literary genre. Such a stage is characterized by profound social and cultural changes, uprooted, bewildered, and innovative minds which essay amalgams of old and newly acquired ideology, the defensive substitution of such solutions in order to repair insecurity, puzzlement, and uncertain self identity, and the other processes which students of the origins of new cults have long recognized. The exciting thing about the dictation is that it has neither been accepted by many persons nor spread about. It has not crystallized into a standard form even within one group. It is fortunate to have found an embryonic genre. It seems to offer historical and other documentation for a profoundly crushed and perplexed people who seek social acceptance and self-identities as Christians. They are not cognizant of the fact that they are prevailingly Indian in their cosmology and historical perspective.

Editors' Notes

1. See "Wren and His Father's Mother" (Jacobs 1958, 80-105).
2. See "Wren and His Father's Mother" (Jacobs 1958, 80-105). For an analysis of a Puget Sound version of this same story, see Snyder (1964, 362).
3. See Snyder (1964, 237, 244-46) for Sally Snyder's development of the "oldest-dullest" theme.
4. For a more positive evaluation of this genre, see the narrative of Old Pierre from the Katzie Coast Salish people of southeast British Columbia (Jenness 1955) and comments by Suttles, who interviewed Old Pierre's son (Suttles 1955, 6).

12

Mink, Panther, and the Grizzly Sisters

(Mary's River Kalapuya)

This Mary's River Kalapuya myth text was originally dictated by William Hartless to Leo J. Frachtenberg at Chemawa, western Oregon, in 1914. Some twenty-two years later Melville Jacobs re-elicited and checked all of Frachtenberg's transcriptions and translations with his "excellent Santiam dialect informant-interpreter, Mr. John B. Hudson" to eliminate "obvious inconsistencies and errors of various sorts in the Frachtenberg manuscript" (Jacobs 1945, 204). Jacobs subsequently published all of Frachtenberg's Mary's River texts and translations (1945, 204-350), the originals of which are deposited in the Smithsonian Institution's National Anthropological Archives. Jacobs's interpretation is from a previously unpublished manuscript (Jacobs 1959d).

Although neighbors to the Chinookan-speaking peoples of the lower Columbia, the Kalapuya spoke a distinct language of another family of the large Penutian phylum to which the Chinookan family also belongs. Both Mary's River and Santiam Kalapuya (selections 19 and 20 below) are dialects of the Central Kalapuyan language. As Jacobs notes, the Kalapuyans did not enjoy the abundant anadromous fish resources of peoples on the Columbia River or out on the coast so they depended much more heavily on land animals and gathered plant foods. Their social organization seems to have been closer to the more egalitarian Sahaptins of the Plateau than to the Chinookans. For historical and ethnographic information on the Kalapuya Indians see Jacobs (1945) and Zenk (1990b).

Before the nineteenth century some thousands of Kalapuya-speaking Indians, in scores of tiny bands, occupied the Willamette River valley of western Oregon from a point a few miles south of Oregon City to the districts immediately south of Eugene. Because large salmon runs, which benefited most Northwest States Indians, did not go beyond the Willamette River falls at Oregon City, fish granted no considerable food resource to the Kalapuyas. With a few exceptions in southwestern Oregon, Kalapuyas were the economically most limited peoples of all Northwest States groups west of the Cascades Mountains. Among Indians who knew about them, Kalapuyas were notorious for their thankful acceptance of various grubs as foods. Since Kalapuyas' fish resources were meager, their protein intake, which comprised a larger proportion of deer and elk meat and smaller doles of fish than among other Northwest States peoples, was supplemented by fare which revolted their neighbors. The Kalapuya-speaking population was sparse although it occupied an extensive territory. Bands were usually identified with tributaries of the Willamette. The most northerly bands, Tualatins and Yamhills, who lived in districts southwest of Oregon City, spoke slightly divergent dialects of a language which was only partially intelligible to other Kalapuyas. A number of intergrading and very slightly differing dialects south of the Tualatins and Yamhills constituted a second Kalapuya language. The Mary's River bands, around Corvallis, are represented in the speech of Mr. Hartless, who recited this myth. A third Kalapuya language, Yonkalla, was spoken by a small number of bands living near and just south of Eugene.

Mr. Hartless's dictation is a nice example of Kalapuya pre-white myth recitals in every trait of content and style. A close translation of the phonetically recorded text of Dr. Frachtenberg follows.

Panther had a house. His brother Mink lived there. They lived together. Panther customarily hunted and Mink hunted too. He himself (Mink) was cutting wood, and he made a fish trap dam, and he picked acorns and hazelnuts and tarweeds. That was Mink's work. With his brother, Panther, they filled five houses with smoke-dried meat and salmon. And so five houses were filled with all sorts of things (for their winter fare), all kinds of foods. Now then one day his brother (Panther) was going hunting, when a woman arrived. She got stuck in the door, it was quite a while before she came inside. Now then Mink said, "Sit over there." To be sure the woman sat across there. Now Panther's bowstring broke. So then Panther said, "Oh I shall return home." And so he went back, he got to the house, he peeped inside, and there was a woman. He said to her, "Come out." The woman went out. "Come along. Follow me." So they went, they got to water. "Take off your garments!" To be sure, she removed her clothes, she took off her grizzly fur. "Swim! Dive in five times! Come out!" Then she came out, and he changed her garments. Then they went back, they got to the house, they entered it, and now he made her his wife. Then it became dark, they went to sleep.

Now early the next day Panther arose, he built a fire, he told his wife, "Get up." Sure enough she got up, she prepared food. Then Panther went away to hunt. Now the woman worked at the house. The woman dug camas, she picked berries and tarweeds, while Panther was hunting. Now one day Panther was going along hunting. The woman was going along digging camas. Now Mink was there, and Grizzly said, "I shall go visit my sister." The old man (Mink)[1] said, "Oh no! Do not be going." "No. I will go indeed." "Do not be going." The old man said, "But you will not insist on doing it?" "I will take care of my own heart." The old man said, "Oh no! Do stay!" Grizzly went anyway, and then the old fellow wept. Now she (a second Grizzly sister) came along. There were five Grizzly (sisters). Their grandfather was blind. They were that many now. Now that Grizzly woman (the second sister) arrived across (the river), she entered, she got caught (in the door). Then she went in. Now Mink said, "Sit there." Then Mink cooked, and he fed her, and she ate. She chewed up everything, even the bones. Only the knee cap was left. Quite a while she munched at it with her teeth, in her mouth. At length her tooth broke, her big tooth broke. Then she said, "Hm. Whoever killed this deer is going to see something!" Then she went out. She waited for her brother-in-law (Panther) along the trail. Now then Mink climbed up above and he cried out, he said, "Hey hey hey your sister-in-law is waiting for you on your trail!" "Oh go inside! I really do hear you!" said Panther. Mink descended, he went into the house. Now Panther was coming back home, he got himself in readiness, he came back, he was on the lookout, sure enough here Grizzly (his fat sister-in-law) arose before him. And they fought, he killed Grizzly. Then he dragged her aside, he cast her to the back of the house. And he went inside. The woman (his transformed Grizzly wife) got back, there was nothing in her heart (she did not know what had just occurred to her Grizzly sister).

Again early the next day Panther once more went away to hunt indeed. The woman (his wife) went to her work again. Again then another Grizzly (the third sister) said, "I too will go visit my sister." The (blind) old man again said, "Do not be going!" "No! I will go indeed. I will visit my sister." The old man wept again indeed. So now Grizzly went then. She reached the house again indeed, and in the very same way again she got caught in the doorway. Finally she did get inside. Indeed Mink again prepared food, again he gave it to Grizzly. Grizzly ate, she devoured everything, even the bones. Only a knee cap was left. She rolled it round in her mouth quite a while, at length her tooth broke. Grizzly said, "Hm. Whoever killed this deer had better watch out for himself." The Grizzly went out. Now Mink climbed up on top of the house, again indeed Mink said, "Hey hey hey your sister-in-law is lying in wait for you along your trail." Mink called out three times. Panther said (in reply), "Go inside! I heard you indeed." So Mink went in. Then Panther came back home. He really did keep watch. Panther was on his way coming, sure enough Grizzly rose up, and they fought each other. Now Panther killed Grizzly. Again he dragged her, he threw her to the rear of the house. Panther went inside. The woman (his wife) arrived, there was nothing in her heart (no awareness of what had occurred). They did like that five times (Panther killed four Grizzly sisters-in-law).

Now on the last (the fifth) time Panther's wife had a bad dream (a dream wherein a supernatural gave her information). When it was almost daylight Panther's wife arose, she prepared food, and when they were through eating, Panther went away again to work (he hunted). He went off, he went away to hunt. The woman did not now go to work. She circled the house, and she got to the rear, sure enough she saw what she had seen (in her spirit-power dream) when it was dark. Now she became angry, she wept. She put on her grizzly garments, and her (grizzly) teeth, and now she awaited her husband. She got to where her sisters had been killed, she dug a hole in the ground where they lay. Now there she lay down, she waited for her husband. Sure enough Panther's bowstring broke. He heard nothing, though he listened. He heard nothing. He said, "I wonder what it can be, I have heard nothing yet. Oh I had better go back home instead." So he did go back. He took one deer along with him. There was nothing in his heart (no knowledge of what had happened). He was coming along, here Grizzly rose up, and then they fought. Grizzly killed her husband. Then she cut off his penis, and she took it with her. She went back, she got her sisters (the corpses), she threw all of them into the water, and they all rose up (resuscitated). Now they went back to their own home. Then it became dark.

No one came to Panther's house. Mink said, "Wonder what has happened? that no one has gotten here?" He sat up all night long. It became morning again, no one had come. On the fifth day Mink wept (in token of mourning for Panther).

Then this Grizzly became pregnant, she gave birth to two young, one a Panther, the other a Grizzly, a Grizzly girl, a male Panther. Their mother dug camas all the time. The four Grizzly women (her resuscitated sisters) always would make those children do their dance before they could go to play. Now one day the Grizzly girl said, "How is it that our mother here seems as if she were weeping?" Panther (her little brother) said, "Oh no!" Now once again that girl said, "Our mother is weeping." "Oh you notice everything (unnecessarily)," said Panther (boy). Now after a while once again, "Oh our mother is weeping! Look at her eyes!" Panther did indeed look at his mother's eyes. Then Grizzly girl (said), "Let us go see where our mother is digging camas." Panther said, "That is very right." So sure enough they went, they got to where she dug camas. Then they crawled along, and to be sure they heard their mother crying. Then they went still closer indeed, sure enough now they heard their mother plainly crying. She was saying, "My husband! My husband!" (in a high-pitched tone). She held her husband's penis in her mouth. So then the children went back, they got far away from there. Then Grizzly girl said, "Did you hear what our mother was saying?" Panther said, "Yes. I heard." Now Grizzly (girl) said, "Now let us go yonder here! She always said to us, Do not go in that direction there! Well now, let us go see that place." So sure enough they went, they got over to there. "Shoot!" said the girl. Indeed Panther shot. "Looks as if he really must have hit something. Do you hear it?" Panther said, "Yes. I do hear it." "Shoot once again." Sure enough Panther shot. It sounded *paaaak* (a noise like cracking). "Oh did you hear it?" Panther said, "Yes. I did hear it." "Well then let us go back. Let it be tomorrow before we go see." "That is quite right," said Panther. So they went back, they got to the house. Now Grizzly girl said, "Our mother was always saying, Do not go to that place. Maybe it is that which she is hiding from us." The next day they went to look once again indeed. Then, "Our mother again went to her camas-digging place." So the children went then. "Now let us go look." They got over to there indeed. Then they went across.

A house stood there. "Looks as if a little smoke were issuing from it." Now Grizzly girl peeked inside. She said, "Oh an old man is sleeping there." So they went inside. Mink looked back (from where he was lying), he saw his brother (actually, his murdered brother's Panther son) standing there, and thereupon his breath failed (because of surprise and shock). Now the girl quickly took hold of the old man (Mink). She said to her younger brother, "Go fetch water!" Quickly Panther ran indeed, he went to get water, he brought back water. They sprinkled water on his head before his heart got back (before he revived). Then Mink said, "I am not strong enough to explain to you. It will be when I become strong before I will tell you anything." Grizzly girl said, "That is quite all right." Then she said to her brother, "Build a fire! We will give the old man food." To be sure the girl prepared food, she boiled a pheasant, and she fed the old man. The old man ate sure enough. Then the girl said, "We will go back now." Mink said, "Oh that is all right. It will be when I have become strong again before I explain things to you." The girl said, "That is fine." Panther himself said nothing however. Then they went back, they reached the house. They (later) went into the mountains (to seek or strengthen ties with supernaturals). The next day, they worked (at such relationships with supernaturals), they went all over, they worked (at that). Then the fifth day the Grizzly girl said, "Well, we are strong (our relationships with our spirit-powers are maximal) now." So the girl said, "Well then, let us do our traveling now." Panther (replied), "Oh no. Let us not go away now. Let us go see the old man (Mink) first, before we go on," said Panther. Then the girl said, "Well, let us go see the old man." They got there indeed, Mink was there. "Oh so you have gotten here now." "Yes. We have gotten here now," Grizzly girl said. Then Mink said, "This house that is standing here is your father's house. Your mother killed your father. Your mother first came here to where this house is situated." The girl said, "Oh. So that is how it has been." The old man said, "That is actually the way it has been." Then he recounted everything. The girl said, "That is really fine." Now Panther said, "What you have told us is fine."

Now the girl said, "Go hunting!" So Panther hunted indeed, he hunted for five days. The girl meantime smoke-dried meat. Now then they had quantities of food there. "You remain here. We will get back to you again. Do not be going anywhere," Panther said. Mink said, "That is very well indeed." So they went back, they reached home. Grizzly had nothing in her heart (mother Grizzly was unaware of her children's intentions). Then the girl said, "Well now let us kill them all." Panther said, "Very well." So sure enough on the next day they stood to their dance (the two children sang and danced their recently strengthened supernaturals). Their mother went to dig camas indeed, those others (the four Grizzly sisters of their Grizzly mother) stayed at the house. They were all asleep, they were very much asleep. Well now they (the two children) collected pitch, they got a quantity, two together, they tied two (victims) together. They tied the (blind) old man to a log. Then they filled the house with pitch. And also everywhere outside. Well then they set fire to the house. Now Panther took his sister, and he leaped over five mountains before they stood (lit on their feet). Now the Grizzly herself, their mother, she looked back when the house was burning. And then she ran, she went back, she said, "There is no one else who could have done that. They are the ones who must indeed have done that," said Grizzly as she ran along. Then she got there, but there was nothing she could do now. So she circled the house, she looked for her children's tracks. She first went (circled) close to it, at length she went (circled) farther away. Indeed then at the fifth mountain she found their tracks where they had landed. Now then Grizzly (the mother) said, "Children! You could not ever beat me." And she laughed, "Hee Hee Hee," she said.

Well then she went on, she followed the tracks of her children. Indeed then she said in her cry, "My children! My children!" as she followed them. After a while Panther said to his sister, "You look back now!" So the Grizzly girl looked back. She said, "Oh! Our mother is coming along." "That is fine!" said Panther. They kept going along. Panther said again indeed, "Look back!" She did look back. "Oh! Our mother is coming close now!" "Oh," Panther said. Then they made (a patch of) berries, and there Grizzly (halted and) ate, she had gotten hungry. She had been going along for five days, she had eaten nothing. Then Panther (called to her derisively). "What are you doing there? I thought you were following your children, instead." Grizzly came to in her heart (awakened to realization of her absurd delay for the sake of food), she went on again indeed, she again said in her cry, "My children! My children!" She was holding her husband's penis in her mouth. Now for the fourth time Panther said, "Look back again!" Again the girl looked back indeed. "Oh! Our mother is coming closer." "Oh that is fine," said Panther. Then he made a small pond, on it he placed a turtle, and the turtle mocked the way Grizzly wailed. Now Grizzly got mad, so she leaped into the water, she wanted to kill the turtle. The turtle jumped into the water, he transformed into leaves. Now then Grizzly looked for the turtle, she brought everything (that felt solid) out of the water, she could not find him. Then Panther said (derisively to her), "What are you doing there? Are you actually pursuing your children?" Grizzly came to in her heart, she went on again indeed in pursuit, while she cried ("My children!"). Then Panther again said indeed, "Look back!" he told his sister. She did look back. "Oh! Our mother is coming along." Panther said, "That is very good." Now he made a swing, he tied it onto an oak, an oak limb. Then they played there, they were swinging. Now Grizzly got to there, and she said, "My children! My children! I do want to ride there too!" But the children acted as if they had not heard her. Again Grizzly said, "I want to be swinging too!" It was a long time before Panther said, "What is it you said?" "I want to ride," Grizzly said. Panther said, "You might fall down." Grizzly said, "I would not fall." "Well now ride on it then!" So Grizzly did get on, and they pushed her a little at first, and then they pushed her harder, and they pushed her yonder to the west, and then they pushed her yonder to the south. But she came back. Again they pushed her far away there to the east. Now Grizzly said, "I want to get down!" The children would not listen, they just kept pushing her the more. Now then Grizzly sang, her song said,

> "Break off! Break off! oak!
> Break off! Break off! oak limb!"

Then they pushed her yonder here to the north, and then they cut their swing, and now Grizzly dropped far yonder there in the north for all time.

Then the children came back, they got to Mink. He was still there. And they told Mink, "Now we have killed them all. Some of them we burned up. We cast our mother to the north, for all time that will be her place. Then now we will remain here. You now will transform into mink. You will take care of whatever you are fed. Do not break that bone. Be sure you always take care of that." "Oh," said Mink. Then Mink said, "I will feed you salmon. You must always take care of its jaw bone." "Oh. That is very good," Panther said. "My sister will be a grizzly, she will be digging camas, she will gather hazelnuts, she will gather acorns. That is how her work will be." Then Mink went away, he transformed into a mink. And now Grizzly went, she turned into a grizzly. And Panther went, he changed into a panther. Now they had all transformed.

That is all now! Go swim! Always keep (remember) what I have given (told) you.

In typical Northwest States myth style Mr. Hartless's initial phrases introduce, with hardly more than names, the principal actors of the first scene. The recitalist names Panther, who owns a house and who lives with an older man named Mink. Myths of the region often present instances of two wifeless men, one or both of whom are widowers and who live together for a time. Myths also often cite two unmarried women, usually both of whom are widows and who cooperate in a household which lacks adult men. Of course we have no census which would indicate the numbers of households of such unwanted kin. No Northwest society felt that such households were desirable. Younger people who have not yet been married are never portrayed as living apart from their families. When two men of the myth era live in this fashion, the literary style requires that the younger one be the hunter or food-producing mainstay of the household. The older man does some less active work customarily assigned to men, but he is principally a houseworker, that is, a surrogate for a housewife although he is wholly masculine. In Mr. Hartless's dictation Panther and Mink are so industrious and work together so well that they fill "five houses" with smoke-dried venison, salmon trout, and other preserved foods, to tide them through the coming winter. The phrase "five houses" is a stylized way of indicating the men's impressive accumulation of foods in storage. The word "house" may not mean solely a dwelling; in this context it probably connotes a structure of poles with bales of smoke-dried comestibles stored above so that animals cannot get them.

Presently a woman arrives, in the form of a stylized motif, found in many oral literatures of the Northwest States, which I call "bride comes." The woman's advent is unconventional because emissaries have not preceded her to negotiate a bride price and to arrange for a marriage day with its exchanges of gifts and other formal or ceremonial procedures. The woman is noted as corpulent. The mention of her stoutness permits omission of her lineage or community identity, but auditors knew that she was one of the Grizzlies. Her frustration when she tried to squeeze through the small entrance is comical because of the specially woven complex of universal and culturally determined components which here set off a response of amusement—at the expense of females, for we find few references to ludicrously fat males in Northwest States oral literatures. The fun triggered by the Grizzly woman's difficulty in entering includes laughter stimuli among which are slapstick, culturally determined laughter at any female adult, laughter at a woman's successful bypassing of custom by coming unchaperoned and upon her own initiative, laughter at her plight or poor judgment in the doorway, that is, at her stupidity because Grizzly people are not bright, and laughter at stoutness.

Panther is away hunting. Mink is at home like any older man or any housewife. When Mink invites the woman, as he should, to sit on Panther's bed-platform because she has come in order to become that worthy's wife, Panther's bowstring breaks. When a bowstring or a bow snaps when a myth-era gentleman is out hunting, it means that he ought to rush home because something untoward and important has transpired there. The signal is a literary stylization. Every literature represented in this book contains this component of style. I call it "bow breaks."

Panther correctly regards himself as the virile man of the house. When he returns he therefore orders the woman to follow him outside. Men order their housewives around in all the social systems west of the Cascades. In a highly stylized scene Panther tells the woman to undress and to plunge five times in the stream. Of course the clothes which she removes are grizzly skins because she is one of the Grizzly people. (I doubt that in modern Indian bands grizzly furs served in any manner except, perhaps, as blankets and winter capes.) When the woman comes out of the river Panther has her put on the garments, probably of tanned deer hide, which people wear. Now the water, maybe too Panther's supernatural power, produces an inner as well as outer change. The woman is, it seems, henceforth a person, not a Grizzly kind of person, that is, one who is stupid, hostile, cannibalistic, and generally dangerous. At the least, an external change has occurred in her. The lines say, succinctly, that now "he made her his wife. Then it became dark. They went to sleep." That is, they are husband and wife sleeping together on his bed mat, maybe on a bed-platform, while the older man Mink sleeps on the bed opposite.

The aura about the scene must have been peculiarly pleasant to Indians. Witness Grizzly's arrival unaccompanied by a retinue of in-laws, her removal of overt evidence of Grizzly identity, and her acceptance without expensive purchase, burdensome interfamilial gift exchanges, anxiety-generating in-law visitations, and all the tensions attendant upon customary procedure in a marriage. Everything occurs speedily, peacefully, inexpensively, and with only three persons, not scores of visitors, involved!

Next, a few lines indicate that the former Grizzly person is a steady and unobjectionable housewife. The only trouble with her is her kin. While she and Panther are away from home one of her still very Grizzly sisters, a fat one too, comes to the house of Panther and Mink. Her blind grandfather is suggested as a decent old fellow who weeps because he cannot dissuade his cruel daughter from going to Panther's abode. Mink serves food to the second sister, as he must; it is his household work assignment so long as the younger gentleman of the house is hunting for the family. Grizzly's typical orality, omnivorousness, and sadism are shown by her chewing and swallowing everything, meat, bones and all. She is much worse than her oldest sister who has become Panther's reliable and good wife. Stylization appears in the second Grizzly's chewing a deer or elk kneecap last. When she breaks a tooth on it she is angered and at once is set off upon a murderous rampage. I find it curious that her anger is not vented upon old Mink. However, Kalapuyas may long since have felt both stylistic and ideological superiority in a plot which proceeds immediately to the admirable hunter who had produced the venison and who had married her oldest sister. That fine lady's behavior now makes the second sister furious with jealously. Mink calls out to warn Panther who is on his way home and does not know that a fiendish sister-in-law plans to waylay him. Kalapuya anxieties about co-wives and sisters-in-law are thereby indicated, as they are in other ways in this myth. When Panther hears Mink's warning he seems to reply in irritation, and I do not know why. I suspect that a part of it reflects glamorization of the successful hunter, the younger and more active man, and it points to cultural depreciation of older men, one of whose not especially honorific functions is to advise people about things which older persons can no longer do. The modern Kalapuya citizenry may have been as mixed in their feelings about many of the slightly tottery purveyors of advice as they were about in-laws of their own age-generation level.

Panther has so much supernatural power, and he is so able a man, that he kills the stupider person, his Grizzly sister-in-law and potential co-wife. His agreeable wife returns from her daily root-digging and is unaware of her murderous and envious sister's deserved fate.

To heighten the anxiety or terror a third Grizzly sister sets out on the trail to Panther's domicile, like a proper in-law ostensibly come to visit her older and married sister. Again the blind old grandfather of the Grizzly women cannot stop her and so he weeps. Even a Grizzly man is better than a Grizzly woman. Women are less worthy citizens than men. Again, like her older sisters, the third Grizzly is too fat to enter Panther's doorway easily. The spectacle is entertaining and once more it briefly relieves the tension of the dour drama. Mink serves food to the woman. When she goes outside to lie in wait for her brother-in-law, he has already been warned by Mink and so he succeeds in killing her. He kills four sisters-in-law, in four almost identical scenes the only light feature of which is the fat women's squirming and frustration when they go through the door.

The visits, attacks, and deaths work up into a stylized climax. Auditors have identified with the hero who gets rid of iniquitous in-law visitors and furiously rivalrous co-wives, especially those who come unchaperoned and not correctly built into their polygamous husband's family by means of exchanges of gifts and monetary payments. Presently Panther's first and therefore preferred wife, who has survived her younger sisters, has a spirit-power dream which, it seems, informs her about her sisters' deaths at the hands of her husband. What can even a wife feel or do, what is her duty, when her dearest kin, her sisters, have been killed? The recitalist's words say laconically, "She became angry. She wept." Only the loss of kin counts for her. According to custom, she must kill the murderer of her close relatives. In a modern community she would have some man do it for her, very likely a shaman. As a myth woman, that is, a kind of supernatural, she does it herself. What she does symbolizes modern procedure and represents the way in which a killer supernatural may commit a murder. She puts on her grizzly furs and teeth and she lies in wait for her husband, hiding herself near her sisters' corpses. Panther's bowstring breaks and therefore he returns. Along the way, his wife, that is, her murderous spirit-power, attacks and kills him. The raconteur does not offer details of the assault. The situation suggests that Kalapuyas felt that a wife can vanquish a fine man if she is sufficiently and rightly angry. This wife goes far beyond ordinary vengeance. Her fury is so great, because she is a Grizzly, that she severs her deceased spouse's membrum virile and takes only it with her.

The worldwide motif of healing water is introduced to resuscitate the four sisters. The wife casts their corpses into the river, they come from the stream alive and whole, and we hear little more of them in the drama. The wife evidently has had supernatural powers to spare. Only she can defeat Panther, perhaps only because she is morally right about it. And she can bring corpses back to life.

Mink waits five days in vain for Panther to return. Then he weeps in mourning for his noble younger comrade. In a later act Mink steps upon the stage again.

A neat exposition of Oregon Indians' thinking about biological heredity is given in the drama's details that Panther's wife gives birth to a male Panther and a female Grizzly. The little boy identifies with his deceased father, the little girl with her mother! The four resuscitated Grizzly sisters are correctly attentive to their sister's (and co-wife's) children. The words of the myth reveal this tersely by saying only that the sisters make the children "dance" each day. In this context the word signifies holding a baby on one's lap and singing and playing animatedly with it. Such play tells babies that they are liked and wanted. Accordingly, they will be unlikely to consider deserting their new parents and family in order to return to the land from which babies come.

The next scene witnesses one of the many forms taken by the widespread "youngest smartest" motif of Northwest States oral literatures. Here the smaller child, the girl who is dominated by her Grizzly heredity, is especially perspicacious about people's thinking and feelings. She observes, while at first her brother denies, that their mother is weeping.[2]

Myths suggest that, in the Northwest States, elders avoided weeping in the presence of children, it would seem in order not to oppress youngsters with problems and anxieties with which they were too immature to deal.

Observe, too, the way in which a recital leaps through time. The babies are no sooner born than the raconteur is citing events which indicate that the youngsters have gotten to an age when they walk and talk and are pretty well able to take care of themselves. Literary style allows such telescoping of time and it requires verbalization only of situations that are decisive for the plot, without a word to indicate passage of the years.

After the girl persuades her Panther brother that their mother may be crying they spy on her at the root patch where she is working. Sure enough she is weeping, saying "My husband!" and with her late spouse's organ still in her mouth.

Note the orality and oral biting, to use Freudian suggestions, of the Grizzly sisters. I think that the Kalapuyas kept the revived Grizzly woman and the Grizzly widow consistent with one another, without entirely knowing how or why they were doing it. The wife who goes about with her husband's relic in her mouth reflects, I suspect, a native conviction, at a deep psychological level, that she committed fellatio and then she bit off his member. The horror of fellatio and castration is defended against by representing the widow as holding the organ after his death, treasuring it as if it were something of superlative value. Because of mixed feelings she continues to possess, with regressive orality, the most cherished token she has of him. That is, Kalapuya saw some women as mixed in their feelings about marital and love relationships. The point is that they feared such women. Oral sadism is not ascribed to older men of myth eras. Such men are often lustful and unattractive but women go beyond such limits. I know of no Northwest States myth where a man retains a sexual part of his deceased wife.

The children return. They discuss whether they should go in a direction against which their mother had warned them. They ignore the maternal admonition, proceed in the forbidden direction, and when they reach an undescribed place, Panther boy shoots several arrows. The lines do not reveal what he shoots at although a native audience would have known.

Then the children come to a house, enter it, and an old Mink man, whom the recitalist now introduces, faints from surprise when he looks at the boy. The youngster resembles Panther, Mink's brother, who had been murdered. The children presently leave their uncle and go to the mountains. They there strengthen their spirit-power ties in the typical manner of the region's Indians who go far away from settlements, fast, plunge into lakes or streams, pile up rocks and brush, and endeavor to make relationship with or improve relationship with good supernaturals. Upon the fifth day, with the understanding that they have succeeded in their efforts, the children go back to Mink. He informs them that their mother killed their father. Not a word is said to suggest how they respond to such appalling information. At Mink's house the youngsters prepare and store quantities of food, then return to their mother, her Grizzly sisters, and the females' blind grandfather who is introduced again in order to fill in the picture-projection of a family and, later, to add to the pathos. While their mother is digging camas, the children set fire to the house, after tying up the sleeping Grizzly sisters and the well-intentioned blind gentleman. He seems to function in the plot as a contrast to his horrible granddaughters, and to balance blood revenge and justice with pity and the fateful sort of tragic end which overtakes even the innocent whose kin are evildoers. A blood feud spares no member of the family which is under attack.

Panther boy displays prodigious virility, in a symbolic way. He leaps in flight from the settlement, literally flying over five mountains—a stylized phrase denoting distance—with his sister whom he carries. One may not deduce an incestuous relationship unless one adheres to orthodoxy in early Freudian writings.

The children's mother returns, sees the house burning, and pursues her offspring. She finds their tracks "at the fifth mountain"—a thoroughly stylized utterance which again functions to indicate a great distance—and she calls out, "You could not ever beat me." Various stylizations, one after another, maintain the myth-age qualities of the drama. The fleeing children are depicted as guided by the already completely masculine Panther youth who goes along with unturned head, and who tells his Grizzly sister to look back to see if their ominous maternal pursuer is overtaking them. In correct and modern Indian manner, the youth maintains masculine dominance and dignity. He orders females around, when he can. To slow grizzly's advance upon them, they trick her by playing into her orality. They are able to make a berry patch because of their recently strengthened or new supernatural bonds. Their now wholly insane mother, who had been pursuing them for many days, phrased as five of course, and who is famished, halts to eat the tempting berries for she is, after all, a hungry Grizzly. During her trailside meal her son calls out hostilely to her. She again becomes aware of her need to pursue her offspring and she cries out, "My children!" Even at this late point in the drama her deceased husband's member is in her mouth, a motif of regressive oral incorporation and of horror, an act which would be shameful for a normal citizen. No recitalist would think of bothering to explain what she did with the member when she was gulping the berries. Descriptive items which are peripheral to the central projections that guide plot development are severely omitted; their presence would be stylistically so many gaucheries. One wonders if questions about such matters were not raised in unstylized moments apart from formal recitals, when people casually discussed myths.

When the mad mother approaches closer and the daughter reports this, the son makes a pond and places on the water a turtle—a creature which is worthless supernaturally and in almost all other respects. The turtle is a plot expediter. It mocks Grizzly's wails. The sounds it makes must be regarded as the speech of a kind of person, not vocables produced by a normally mute creature. Grizzly is easily distracted, as mad Grizzly people will be, and she leaps into the pond to kill the turtle which is deriding her. At once the turtle metamorphoses into leaves. Grizzly's frenzy does not cease. She drags objects out of the pond in a vain effort to locate her tormenter, while her son ridicules her for failing to chase him and his sister. When his words catch her ear, she pursues, again crying, "My children!" When the daughter reports that the mother is once more approaching, the son makes a swing which he hangs from an oak limb. The children play on the swing. By the time Grizzly reaches them she does not even recognize them as her own. She has so regressed that she asks to be allowed to ride on the swing, too. For a time the children tormentingly ignore the madwoman and her reiterated requests to play. At length her son chides her that if she swings she might fall. She insists because now she is functioning like a little child. She gets on the swing and the children push her more and more energetically back and forth until they cut the rope. Their mother drops far away to the north, never to return. The act, which terminates with the announcement of her and, therefore, other grizzlies' future residence, has ventilated feelings about dangerous madwomen. It has presented a stereotyped picture of the way such people progressively deteriorate until they can more easily be removed from the community. In fact, they can be thrown away.

The children return to the old Mink man as one would to one's sole surviving close kin and, in the absence of close kin, even somewhat remote kin. In the finale the children play a joint role, a stylized one, as announcers of what people will do in future times when the land is fit for human beings of modern kinds with modern customs. The mother, who henceforth represents the Grizzly people as a lineage or community, will stay far away—the direction, to the north, is I think symbolic. Mink, who now represents all the Mink people, will change into a mink. That is, there will be animal minks in the modern world. The children will remain right there, the girl becoming a grizzly who will dig roots and gather hazelnuts and acorns. Old Mink, who has not yet metamorphosed into a mere mink, announces that he, which means any minks in eras to come, will feed the children salmon (or salmon trout) and that they—that is, Indians—must always "take care of" a salmon's jaw bone. I do not know exactly what Kalapuyas customarily did with a salmon's jawbone. Doubtless it was thrown back into the stream or handled in some required manner in order to assure the goodwill of the salmon and their arrival or availability so that the people might have them for food. The announcements by Mink and the children constitute the myth's stylized epilogue. Any actors who are present in a final scene can announce metamorphoses and future customs.

The formal ending, in the last lines, reflects one of the functions which myths played: the recitalist now spoke as if he turned to the children and youths among the auditors. He said, in effect, "Go swim! and always remember this myth." I do not think that he meant that the younger people who had been present should forthwith plunge into the stream nearby. But assigned oldsters lectured pubescent youngsters early in the morning before adults began to stir themselves. At that time, after the morning pedagogy, which almost certainly included myth materials, the youngsters did enter the stream. The words of the formal ending therefore reflect a custom although they are not an order to swim after a myth recital.

This drama is punctuated by only a few light touches to relieve its emphasis upon tragedy and fate. The play contains familiar Northwest States themes about familial relationships and tragedy befalling a nuclear family. One theme deals with society's concern about the chance lest a good man's wife be deeply hostile and murderous, because she is loyal above all, as she has to be, to her parents and siblings. A vital theme treats of the lesser worth of married women. Another, the jealousy and anger felt by co-wives. West-of-mountains antifeminine feelings appear with salient evidence. It is the wife who is mixed in her sentiments about her mate. The husband is wholly fine and manifests no ambivalence. Value ideals receive implicit treatment. For example, a mother who murders a father must be punished by her children. She is not castigated for her sin of fellatio. Such aberrancy functions only to intensify her awfulness and to contrast it with her earlier devotion to her husband. The theme which points to worry about in-laws is clearly exposed.

The structure of the play as a whole is not significant as a well-shaped design. There is only a series of acts and scenes and, as always in Northwest States literatures, not a single backflash. The five-patterns provided by the coming of five sisters and by other and smaller citations of five, for example five mountains, offer important features of style. Dr. Frachtenberg's narrator fortunately displays one of the stylized epilogues and one of the formal endings which good recitalists employed.

Editors' Notes

1. Clearly this exchange between an old man and a Grizzly woman takes place in the Grizzly household from which the Grizzly wife came originally, not in Mink and Panther's place. It is the grandfather of the four Grizzly girls, not Mink, who tries to dissuade the next sister from following the first Grizzly woman to Panther's house. The Editors believe that the preceding sentence, "Now Mink was there, and Grizzly said, 'I shall go visit my sister.' " should read, "Now Mink was there. [new paragraph] And Grizzly said, 'I shall go visit my sister.' " Jacobs's parenthetical identification in the next sentence, "The old man (Mink) said, 'Oh, no. Do not be going' " is an error.
2. Technically, according to the text translation, the Panther boy is the *younger* brother of Grizzly girl, so her perspicacity cannot represent the "youngest smartest" motif here.

13

The Sagandahs People

(Miluk Coos)

Annie Miner Peterson dictated this Miluk Coos tale to Melville
Jacobs at her home near Charleston, Oregon in the summer of
1933. It is an example of Jacobs's genre 4, tales from the period
after whites had come to the region (see "Genres in Northwest
States Oral Literatures," in this volume). The text and translation
were published in *Coos Narrative and Ethnologic Texts* (Jacobs
1939, 59-61). The interpretation and revised translation, published
here for the first time, are from an unpublished manuscript (Jacobs
1959d). Jacobs's new translation differs from the 1939 publication
in only minor details. The Coos language family, which also belongs
to the Penutian phylum, was spoken in south coastal Oregon. Mrs.
Peterson dictated texts to Jacobs in both of the two Coosan
languages, Hanis and Miluk. (see selection 22 below). For
ethnographic and historical background on the Coos Indians see
Jacobs (1939, 1940), Zenk (1990a), and Beckham (1977). Jacobs
published a brief autobiographical sketch by Annie Peterson (1939,
104-14). Youst (1997) has published a book-length biography of
Mrs. Peterson.

This Coos tale about the Sagandahs was dictated by Mrs. Annie
Peterson as a "true story." It exemplifies a genre, which is
identical in form to the genre of pre-white tales. Its content,
ostensibly a product, at least partially so, of nineteenth-century
discussions, exhibits nicely the way in which a community quickly
remodels and "mythicizes" an account of actual events. Mrs. Peterson
said that she heard many Coos people recount the story. No other
example of a nineteenth-century tale is needed in order to display the

characteristics of that genre. Although I make a distinction between pre-white and nineteenth-century tales, the two genres, again, differ only in their kinds and ages of content and therefore in the degree of remodeling and manipulation of actors, situations, and themes. Once more, may I offer the summarization of differences between Northwest States tales and myths. Tales are, on the average, much shorter; they lack myths' introductory and closing formulae, epilogues, and a few other features of style; and tales contain a few more discursive and descriptive utterances, as if the recitalist were aware that an unusually large number of auditors had never heard the plot.

The Sagandahs tale follows.

That (very large) wealthy headman lived at Chetco (River), and their village (the settlement of the Sagandahs Miluk Coos people) was on this side (to the north) of it. The mother of that (Sagandahs) youth came from Crescent City. The young fellow was always sharpening his knife. "Why do you sharpen your knife?" "Oh I am going to go to the south to see my mother's brother." "Do not say so! There are big and powerful people (along the Chetco River) who do not let you pass by. Their wealthy headman is a person of mean disposition. Whoever goes there he kills." But the little fellow (said), "Oh I will rip him with my knife!" "But do not say so! Do just remain here. Do not go there. He will kill you." "Oh he won't kill me."

Indeed then he went, he ran as he proceeded. "Hey! Where are you going?" (It was the big Chetco headman inquiring of him.) "Oh I am going south." "Humph! You won't get there." Then the big man seized him, he grabbed his head, and now he was going to kill him. But then he (the youth) stabbed him first, indeed he split open his abdomen, indeed he killed the wealthy headman. Now then he turned back and reached home. "I killed that wealthy headman." "Now you did something pretty good, to be sure! Now they will be coming and waging war against us."

Indeed people (representatives of the Chetco community) arrived, they brought news. "We will do you no harm if you pay" (because of the headman's death). "Very well. We will pay you." (The Chetco people were satisfied with compensation money) because they had not liked their (deceased) headman, because he had been mean. "Now if indeed you reach the mountain with your money,[1] then everything will be all right. But if you will not (pay so large an amount), then we will fight you." Indeed they tried (measured the strings of) their money, but their money was not long enough (to extend to the mountain) there. "If you will not pay it we will wage war next year." "Oh we will obtain that money by that time." Now they went back home. Now indeed they (the Sagandahs men) made large canoes, far back in the woods they made them so that no one would know. They finished a large number of canoes. Now when the appointed time of year came they went, but the length of their (dentalium strings of) money did not reach to there. "We will give you five (more) days, (and) if you do not come with such a length (of dentalium money), then we will war." "Very well. We will bring it to you." But they did not do that. They merely took their canoes down into the water (from the woods where they had been manufactured), and they simply fled, they went out to the ocean. And wherever they halted, they were driven away from that place. Sometimes they remained an entire year, and then they would be driven off because they (the Sagandahs) were mean. Now they went away to an entirely different ocean.

Then the moving people (the whites) arrived here, and they took with them one of the (Miluk Coos) Indians, the moving people took an Indian to there, to the country where the braided hair (the Japanese) people (live). Now one old man (in Japan), an exceedingly aged man, this Sagandahs man (who lived in Japan) spoke in Miluk to him (to the Indian sailor on the whites' vessel). This is what he said. "I am the only one left of the older generation. I was the child of the Sagandahs." That is what that Sagandahs said to him. That is why they (our people) know that the Sagandahs stopped (and made their home) there in the country of the braided-hair people. The aged Sagandahs man told the (Miluk) Indian everything. He told all that his parents had told him, (about the epic travels of the fugitive Sagandahs people when) they had gone all over there. "We crossed a great river. But after that the ocean changed, and then it got bigger, the whole thing became ocean, when the land sank lower, the whole thing sank. Now it is just ocean there. That is why it is impossible to cross to there now." That is what the Sagandahs told the (other Miluk) Indian. "I am the only one left who can speak the people's language (the Sagandahs dialect of Miluk Coos). When I die there will be no one who can speak the language here. We (the other descendants of the refugees) speak differently (we speak Japanese) now."

As in myths, the first phrases introduce leading actors each of whom receives only one or two strokes of characterization. There is a Chetco Athabaskan headman who is referred to as of giant size. The indication is actually of his great wealth, his ability as a fighter, and therefore of his unusual supernaturals. In other Northwest groups it might also be a projection of virility.

There were many Chetco settlements beside small streams along a lengthy coastline from the Tolowas near the California-Oregon border north almost to the Rogue River. The tale mentions only that the headman "lived at Chetco." The meaning, to a Coos audience, is that he was the wealthiest of all Chetco headman because he lived at the largest village in the district.

The Miluk Coos youth's mother is obviously a lady of highest station because she comes from far away, from a settlement at or near Crescent City, California, where there was a group whose neighbors immediately to the north were Tolowas and, beyond, Chetcos. The mother is married to a man who lives at the Miluk Coos village named Sagandahs. The fact that the youth's mother is from a district south of the Tolowas and Chetcos suggests that she had been bought in marriage by an exceedingly wealthy Miluk. A woman who had been obtained so far away was invariably of wealthy family and had been purchased at an especially high price by very well-to-do folk.

Her son, indicated only as a youth, plans to visit his mother's brother. The journey about which he is thinking appears to be the customary travel of a youth before he settles down in marriage. He knows that in order to pass through Chetco territory he must run a gauntlet of hostile men of wealth, each of whom has armed followers. That is why the youth sharpens his long knife; probably it is the characteristic obsidian blade of northwestern California and southwestern Oregon.

The distortions which quickly effect the remodeling of a tale apparently include the item which makes the most affluent Chetco headman astonishingly tall. Originally I translated the word as "giant," but the man may have been only a burly six-footer. Few or no Oregon and Washington Indians could conceive of giantism of the degree found in European fairy tales. Bigness, when the region's Indians expressed it at all, applied principally to potency of supernaturals, numbers of valuable dentalia, plural wives—the latter were four or five at the most—cavernous swallowing monsters, whales, and ocean-going canoes. Such outlets for feelings about great ability, quantity, or size were so fulfilling that giantism in persons, birds, animals, or fish was really beyond anyone's conception. European dimensions in giantism were inconceivable.

The Chetco headman's murderous hostility to passersby is consistent with scattered evidence that various Northwest States leaders exacted payments from aliens who traveled in canoes or along trails beside villages.

The youth's arrogance and arguments are countered by his fellow villagers, in all likelihood, as well as by his family. Their point is that if he succeeds in his plan to murder the Chetco leader a feud with that celebrity's entourage will ensue. Everyone feared such warfare. But the people who plead with the youth say to him only that he will be killed. In typically Northwest Coast grandiose utterances the youth proclaims his prowess. Since he is the son of a wealthy man he must speak with bumptious pride and jingoistic disdain of the antagonist. A Coos audience certainly identified with the vainglorious youth of well-to-do family. The little play functions, among other things, to celebrate the achievement and memory of the dashing young blade who would not be restrained by the prudent but unadventurous thinking of elders. The play specifically commemorates the combat, in the spirit of Northwest Coast concern about and pride in victory in such affairs.

The elders' mixed feelings are shown by their comments when the surprisingly young combatant returns with the news of his success. They assert that his killing of the Chetco leader was good and they remark, doubtless with enormous anxiety, that war will ensue.

The most frequent kind of resolution of a murder in western Oregon follows. The family of the deceased headman dispatch representatives, probably two men. They journey by canoe for many days north along the coast, to ask for compensation money, because this is a region where cash payments settle any difficulties and erase the deepest animosities. The lines of the play account for the initiation of peaceful negotiation. But observe the function of the scene. It catharsizes feelings about a murder, which is one of the most anxiety-generating types of social relationships in the area. Feelings are strong, too, over the subsequent bargaining about a payment. When the representatives of the two lineages or communities fail to agree on a monetary settlement fighting is inevitable. Individuals will die. An entire settlement may be massacred in an early morning sneak attack. A social order which effects such recurrent if not everpresent terrors expresses its feelings in one or another cultural form, as in the drama of the heroic Sagandahs youth and his fleeing confreres.

Observe the stylized succinctness of the narrator's presentation. As in myths each actor and each situation is tersely noted, with a selection of only one or two facets of people and situations which western civilization's plays and novels refer to in numerous descriptive details, items selected because of the different audience which that civilization provides. For example, a Northwest States recitalist offers no depiction of the youth's appearance and only the citation of bigness, which equates with and points to great wealth and unusually strong supernaturals, of the Chetco headman. The youth's victory implies, without a specific word of description, that his supernaturals are already more potent than his opponent's. Mention of victory is the only expressive need which requires fulfillment on the play's stage, because it carries with it the understanding that victory is given those who possess the better non-material kin, and nothing is more wanted than such kin. The Oregon audience is not even told, nor need it be, that the youth has beautiful, because long, hair. It is sufficient to indicate, indirectly, that he has awesome spirit-power allies, and to show overtly that he has a desirable braggadocio. That fact that he endangers all his people is maybe no demerit.

The poetic reference to reaching the mountain with money is a stylized way of saying that the great man's death must be paid for with a vast sum. Along the Oregon coast the large incised dentalia were strung, ten to a string. A single string of such money beads was approximately equivalent to a hundred pre-Civil War American dollars—in purchasing power many times that of a hundred dollars today. Wealthy men rarely owned more than two or three such strings, each of which had a name and was known far and wide along the coast. One or two strings, at most, constituted payment for a headman's daughter in marriage. Therefore when the Chetco emissaries spoke of reaching the mountain with the compensation money they were boasting, with a metaphor about strings of money beads, about their unfortunate headman's fame and value, his lineage's worth, and the merits of his village and people. Again, such tall talk is typical Northwest Coast bluster. Both sides in the tale were allowed, in fact required, to ventilate their needs to exhibit and express high status, and the members of the evening's audience identified with each successive speaker of grandiloquent utterances.

Since warfare might mean village slaughter, the Chetcos really retreated, but without shame, when they allowed their opponents a year to accumulate the demanded sum. The harried Sagandahs people bluffed it out. They said, without complete conviction, that they would have the money within the year. Probably they hoped that one or several among them would "find" an "encounter power," that is, a southwestern Oregon class of supernatural whom one met by sheer accident and who presently left, at the very spot, a nice supply of money dentalia.

The reprieve permitted the Sagandahs to construct ocean-going canoes in the forest where the intent to flee would not be witnessed. The last-ditch effort to stay in the village was unavailing. The ill-fated Sagandahs were unable to produce the required sum and, in the stylized five-day period before they were to be attacked, they took to the ocean. They remained at one or another place along the Oregon coast north of the Coos-speaking country. But they were driven away because they were "mean." I am unable to interpret why they were "mean." Maybe inability to amass the money connected with meanness of disposition: admirable people would surely have been able to relate to the excellent supernaturals who somehow would have provided the valuable dentalia. Or, the brave youth's adventure and his kin's inability to prevent him from making the journey added up to "meanness" in the lineage and populace.

The scene which limns the flight "to an entirely different ocean" expresses anxiety about warfare, the occasional need for an exodus in order to avoid being massacred, and the worrisome problems when establishing residence in an alien and therefore suspicious or unfriendly district. The scene is an ultra-compact depiction of a saga-like flight to a foreign country.

The last scene tells about an early nineteenth-century sailing ship which had one Miluk Coos Indian in its crew. Of course, a few coastal and Columbia River Chinook Indians shipped out in trading vessels in those days. I do not doubt that the tale is a partial consequence of what this sailor reported when he returned to his people after a voyage across the Pacific or far up the Pacific coast of North America. Mrs. Peterson thought that it was to Japan. The sailor asserted that he found one aged surviving speaker of Sagandahs Miluk Coos in Japan, and that other descendants of the boatloads of Sagandahs refugees spoke only Japanese. I find it of interest that the words of the play say nothing about differences in anatomy of the Sagandahs and the people in whose land they obtained sanctuary, and that the lines refer only to the braided hair of the country's native inhabitants. The point is that Oregon Indians were extraordinarily sensitized to hair and barely perceived other anatomical details. Again, a person was beautiful or notable in appearance not because of complexion, curves, eyes, mouth, ears or anything but long, long hair.

If the tale refers to an actual flight by sea, and I think it does, it is inconceivable (not withstanding Mr. Thor Heyerdahl and other buoyant protagonists of trans-Pacific pre-white romances) that the refugees reached an Oceanian or Asiatic haven, least of all, Japan. A much more plausible deduction, one which is consistent with everything we know about coastal Oregon Indians, is that very late in the eighteenth century or in the first years of the nineteenth a few canoes with members of a Coos lineage or settlement went far to the north and kept close to the North American coast and coastal islands. The people of the Straits of Juan de Fuca, Puget Sound, and Vancouver Island were unknown to Coos or other residents of the Oregon coast south of the Alseas and Tillamooks. Mrs. Peterson said that she had heard her people refer to the natives of northwestern Washington as Eskimos! That is why I urge that the tale of the fugitive Sagandahs stands for a group of Miluk Coos who settled in some district hundreds of miles to the north, perhaps on Vancouver Island or on coastal mainland British Columbia where coastal shipping of the early to mid nineteenth century would have allowed a Coos sailor to find people with whom he could converse in his native tongue. He might well misinterpret the neighbors of such people as Japanese, who were far away, too.

The content of this modern tale, which encloses a folklorized drama rooted in the immediately stylized outlines accorded memories of recent events, is distinctively Northwest Coast in its central themes. Like other myths and tales of the Oregon coast, it jubilates about wealthy men, their mortal combat, vast monetary payments, properly grandiloquent public discourse in the forms of threats and claims, success in building secretly some big war-and-ocean-going craft, romantic travel over a perilous ocean, and ability to survive in distant lands where, naturally, the new arrivals are unwanted. Even the "meanness" ascribed to them is not wholly bad. The ascription may function as a defense against feelings that they were unjustly treated. There is an implication that the fugitives are sensible, tough, and resourceful when against unbeatable odds. War, killing, money, stilted phraseology when negotiating, a dangerous journey, and survival are some of the themes, all of them arising in anxieties universally felt in the region.

The sole woman in the play is a mere plot expediter. Her natal community and wealthy parentage are beyond the Chetco country and that is why her precocious and imperious son must journey through it no matter what the risk.

The style of the play is exactly like other myths and tales in its sharply limited selections of items which refer to status, personalities, and situations. To be sure, the introductory and ending formulae of myths are absent.

The title, "The Sagandahs people," is Mrs. Peterson's phrasing. Northwest States titles of myths and tales are concrete and succinct. The means by which people referred to oral-literature plays were, as in this instance, by selection of an aspect of plot action or by the name or names of the actors of the first scene or scenes. An abstraction or quality is never included in the words of a title.

Editors' Notes

1. Money consisted of strings of dentalia shells. Dentalia, or elephant's tusk shells, are mollusks of the class scaphopoda that have tube-shaped shells. Although scaphopoda are found world wide, the beds in Nootkan territory off the west coast of Vancouver Island were apparently the source for those shells treasured by Northwest Coast Indians. (See Drucker 1951, 111-12.)

14

An Historical Event Text From a Galice Athabaskan in Southwestern Oregon

(Galice Creek Athabaskan)

Hoxie Simmons dictated this text to Melville Jacobs at Logsden, Oregon. It is one of a number they recorded in 1938 and 1939. Galice belongs to the very large and closely related Athabaskan family of languages found in the interior of Alaska and Canada, in two isolated positions on either side of the Columbia River, in southwest Oregon and northwest California, and in the Southwest (Navajo and the Apachean languages). Jacobs had hoped to collaborate with the Athabaskanist Harry Hoijer in preparing a volume of Simmons's Galice Creek texts and translations, with content-and-style analyses by Jacobs, but the project was never realized. This narrative was prepared as a contribution to a festschrift for the linguist Fang-Kuei Li and is reprinted from the *International Journal of American Linguistics* 34.3:183-91 (1968). Although Jacobs refers to it as "one genre of connected speech," it does not fall into any of the literary genres he describes in selection 4, above. Jacobs's phonetic transcription of the text as well as some introductory remarks have been omitted from this reprinting.

In 1938 and 1939 at Logsden, near Siletz, Oregon, I obtained texts from the last well-informed person who could speak Galice Creek Athabaskan. He was an able man, named Hoxie Simmons, aged about sixty. His ancestors spoke a language that was used in bands that dwelled along the Galice, Applegate, and Illinois Creeks, tributaries of the Rogue River in its central course.

I hope to prepare a volume of Mr. Simmons's admirably dictated and translated texts. I offer in this paper the first of the texts that I have attempted to copy out of the field note books. With it I present a tentative content and style commentary. After I have completed such observations on the other Simmons texts, I may be able to perceive additional features of expressive content and style in the text that is printed here. Regard it as an example of one genre of connected speech about an historical event. To it is appended a preliminary examination of its nonlinguistic traits of content and style. The paper is primarily a sample of a suggested method of multifaceted content-and-style exploration. I believe that this method may be able to expose more of what is structured and expressed in connected speech, whether casual or memorized, than has heretofore been often ventured.

Most analysts of nonwestern language texts have worked with relatively purely linguistic premises and orientations. But a field recorder himself is the person who can, and should, offer much more than the phonemic, morphophonemic, grammatical, syntactic, and semantic observations that, since the 1890s, have been the stock in trade of anthropological linguists and that they have customarily appended to their published text-and-translation materials. ...

Commentary that follows treats of expressive content and extra-linguistic traits of style which utilize content for formal purposes. Of course, there are always at least some few features of style that are manipulated with linguistic devices, for example the Galice enclitic h^{w}a^n- *so people say.* Mr. Simmons tagged it unpredictably to one or another word, more often a phrase final, in every third or fourth utterance in both myth and non-myth dictations. I have not labored with detailed attention so as to identify other linguistic features of style. But style in Oregon Athabaskan speech genres appears to me to resemble style in other Northwest States genres in, first, a relatively modest array of purely linguistic features that are of stylistic service and, second, a patent multiplicity of the sets of expressive content features that effect stylistic ends. The latter have escaped the attention of most linguists.

Numbers in parentheses connect with the same numbers in the translation and commentary. ...

The English translation of the text ("Klamath River Men Murdered a Shasta") now follows:

(1) Long ago, one of the Klamath River people was named Percy Wash. He bought—so they say—a woman (to be his wife), he

bought—so they say—a Shasta woman from that place there while both of them were still young. (But) these Klamath River and Shasta (peoples) were constantly ambushing and murdering one another, they killed each other—so they say—there on both sides. (2) That is the way they did to one another—so they say. That is the way it got to be later on—so they say. Wherever they saw one another well (a good chance to ambush successfully) they killed one another—so they say. That is why later on Percy Wash's oldest (Shasta) brother-in-law came from Yreka to visit him. There were ten such (Shasta) brothers—so they say. (3) It was early in the morning at about that time that some of Percy Wash's own (Klamath River) kin came over to visit. "We have come to go hunting," they said to him—it is said. "Let's hunt elk. Let's see. But first let's do target practice shooting," the Klamath River fellows said to him—it is said. They all had whites' rifles (by this time, which was about 1852 or 1853)—so they say. He (the Shasta brother-in-law) helped Percy Wash's (Shasta) wife cook (breakfast)—it is said. (4) His (Shasta) brother-in-law was in the house there. Now he said to his brother-in-law—it is said, "Don't go over to there" (where my Klamath kin are practicing shooting at a target). A bit later Percy Wash turned and noticed, his brother-in-law was (in spite of the warning) quite far over there standing among them where they were target shooting. Now the Klamath River people realized—it is said—that Percy Wash's brother-in-law was staying here (visiting) with him. (5) That is the reason why the Klamath River fellows had come to there—so they say, they wanted to go kill him. It was in this manner that they deceived him. "Let's shoot at the target" they said to him. Now then they shot in succession (one man after another) at a tree. One Klamath River fellow sighted his rifle, now then it appeared as if he were about to shoot (at the target). Now he swung the gun around toward the Shasta—so they say. (6) He shot at him—they say, (but) he dodged—so they say. Now another one of those (Klamath) people shot at him—they say, but he dodged it too—so they say. All those (Klamath) people shot at him—they say, but he dodged all of them too—so they say. But it was that one last (Klamath) who shot him—they say. It was at the moment when he slipped when he dodged. That is how they at length shot (and killed) him—so they say. (7) Now Percy Wash perceived what his own people had done. He told his people—they say, "Begone quickly! Go back home! I might shoot you to pieces. You have caused me trouble now. Get going quickly! All of you go back home!" He spoke like that to his people—they say. He had gotten extremely infuriated. Now then he and his wife took (the body of) his brother-in-law back (to the deceased's home)—so they say, to his own people's land, to the Shasta people, to his father, to his brothers, to his own people. (8) Now then he covered him with money (he decorated the body with currency shells). That is the way he brought (the body of) his brother-in-law back with money (to compensate for the frightful wrong done)—so they say. That is the way that long ago the people were glad about it (a murder that was so compensated and resolved with a proper payment in shell money). That is why he did like that with it—so they say. Now he got near to there, he got to be only a short distance away, close to the house of his father-in-law (and) his brothers-in-law. Now then he became very frightened—so they say. But he braced up his heart (courage) again now—so they say. (9) At some distance from (the house) there he spoke out (in a loud voice)—so they say, in the way that people customarily did (in a situation such as carrying back a deceased resident and relative). He exhibited all of this (money beads on the corpse) to them here according to custom. The old man (father of the murdered man), his (Percy Wash's) brothers-in-law, (and) the hearts of his relatives (his in-laws who lived there) were as if melted. He knew how to speak (upon such an occasion). He spoke (exceedingly well because it took) a long time. Now the old man his father-in-law said—so they say, "You have spoken well. (But) that one (my youngest son there) who is walking about (and stalking you with his rifle cocked), address your words to him! It is possible that he will listen to you (and accept your explanation)." (10) He was referring to the smallest (and youngest) of his sons—so they say. (Others of) these people were walking about back and forth (too), all of them were carrying guns. He felt almost as if one of them would shoot him—they say. He could hardly feel himself (because he was numb with terror), he said (in later years)—so they say. (11) Now the old man said—they say, "(It was) long long ago that I used to drink human blood early in the morning, and (only) then I would eat well," he said—so they say. His (Percy Wash's) wife forced herself to remain close beside him the entire time, it was as if she was fastened tightly to him. That is the way it happened once upon a time to that person named Percy Wash. Now they buried him (his murdered brother-in- law). Then he and his wife returned (without further threat of retaliatory violence) to their country—it is said. They never did anything (further) to him—they say. Now that is all.

(1) Like the stylistic requirement that characterizes introductions to myths in the Northwest States, the first sentence cites the leading actor in the event. As in myths, the sentence tells no more than the name and Klamath River provenience of this actor. These two references in the text are suitable because of the terseness and limited selection of things that may receive mention that appear in that standard for elegant expression, the myth literature. There is another propriety for such references in the Siletz Reservation area. There, people from various western Oregon language communities had been congregated since the 1850s. The first sentence does not make note of which among five or six language groups the actor came from on the long Klamath River of northern California. It was apparently sufficient, in conversation too, to identify him as a Klamath River person.

Mr. Simmons later told me that Percy Wash also was a "big man," that is, a brave man in feuding or fighting. After the Siletz area Indians came to know English, that is, very likely by the 1860s, they therefore referred to Wash with the English word "chief." Of course, a chief to Northwest States Indians was not necessarily a lone headman. He was among the several, in a community or band, who were especially respected or well-to-do. This kind of narrative might not have been told about a man who was less well regarded for his wealth and status. The second sentence cites a fact that is relevant to and introduces the tragic mood of the action. It is that Wash also had a wife. Later I ascertained that she was a Yreka Shasta. In the next place, it is stylistically right to say that he not only was married to her, but that he had done so in an admired way. Tragic fate is all the more impressive when the right kind of upperclass marriage had transpired. That is, Wash had purchased his wife, as a man of wealth and standing had to do.

We may never be able to ascertain whether females were slightly or considerably lower in status in upriver bands, or on a parity of status with men, by contrast with wealthier downriver and coastal hamlets of the Rogue River region. The latter saltwater hamlets apparently witnessed a lower level of status for women, again how much lower is unclear. Inclusion of *he bought her* functions to grant the narration and its actors something of status and respectability, also deeper tragedy because the subsequent event was in so exemplary a couple and family. A narrator of a myth or anything else almost never told whether the husband and his kin had bought his wife with a tiny, modest, or large quantity of money dentalia and other money beads. Perhaps such specification was unimportant in a narrative that dealt with a group that was fifty to eighty miles upriver from the more modish coastal or downriver hamlets. Sufficient respectability accrued, and sensitivities and identifications were intensified, with a simple stroke: *he purchased her.*

Dismissal of almost all possible descriptive items, and selection of only one or two, was evidently a central stylistic characteristic of both myth and historical-event genres. Every myth genre of the Oregon-Washington Indians was depictively parsimonious and laconic. In this respect the text, although not a myth, is typical of a region's myths and one or more other oral genres. Mr. Simmons seemed loquacious, if not prolix, among Northwest States Indians that I knew over a period of years. But when he dictated this historical narrative, it came out as stark as myths in its few delineative items. I deduce that his casual speech exhibited the hold of the myth style, with its omissions of almost all of the possible depictive details. Mr. Simmons seemed no more inclined than any other informant to break through the narrow boundaries of that style.

The period referred to in this text is 1852 or 1853, just before the heartbreaking debacle called the Rogue River War. We are not informed that, when Wash married, he received aid in money beads from his Klamath River relatives or that he, rather than one or several go-betweens, negotiated the purchase agreement and marriage. Everything about such arrangements is omitted. An informant asserted that he purchased his wife when the procedure did not constitute a simple purchase. We do not know that Wash himself broached the proposition to the Yreka girl. The point is that stylistic requirements felt by Mr. Simmons precluded mention of all matters other than the fact of an unspecified monetary payment. Information about anything else in the pre-marital period was a verbose intrusion of items that everyone knew about anyway.

The genre guides a speaker directly to the theme of the tragedy, which is about the murder of the good brother of Wash's wife. Therefore Mr. Simmons proceeded, in the next sentence, to explain that Klamath River and Shasta Indians chronically feuded. Feuding that took principally the form of employment of so-called magical lethal substances, that "bad" shamans sent with supernaturals, doubtless continued long after the establishing of Reservations during the 1850s. The Whites did not regard seriously such "bad magic." They did not track down persons who resorted to nonmaterial devices for mayhem and murder, because they did not believe such means ever hurt or killed anyone. From Indians' point of view, Whites were naive. Murder was murder. The methods were not necessarily with arrows, bullets, or blades. On the Reservation after 1855, it was safer and surer to rely upon techniques which Whites would not recognize as competent.

(2) *That is the way it got to be later on* may seem to be an error. But I think it is a preface to a statement, by Mr. Simmons, that he at once bypassed in order to continue with his theme. The sentence that he omitted was, I think, about the fact that in Reservation times pre-1855 feuding presently ceased. The next sentence adds the notion that people committed a murder when they managed to effect a fine ambush. They did little or no murdering out in full view, or not much unless they were in numbers.

That is why Wash's brother-in-law came to visit is probably not a gauche utterance. In this context the *that is why* amounts to *that is how it happened that*. In casual speech or a spontaneous events genre, people may have peppered their sentences with such words. I therefore regard *that is why* as a stylistic juncture. We can worry unduly about style junctures because a great many, or most, of our Pacific Northwest texts have been more or less verbatim memorized myths and tales. Everyday American English offers analogous fillers such as "Y'see what I mean ...," "Y'understand," "I mean ...," and other colloquial expressions. They function like Northwest Indians' *that is why* and *that is how* morphemes, which are sometimes demonstrative pronouns. What is present here is best regarded as an item from a category of junctures of style.

(3) *Early in the morning* probably functions in two ways. One is as a juncture of style from a set of time rather than a set of causal or explanatory items. It is a stylistically pressured, preferred, or required introduction to a new action. How firmly it may be pressured is unclear. Junctures of a stylistic kind, whether explanatory (e.g. *that is why or how*), temporal (e.g. *that is when*), or of other kinds, contrast with linguistics' now familiar phonemic junctures, which are members of wholly different sets of units. A second function of *early in the morning* is to transmit a morsel of meaning. The given translation must not be

taken as literal. The word connotes something like *not along in the afternoon* or *not later in the day*.

The proposal by kin of Wash to hunt elk greatly enhances tension and moves the plot forward to a new scene. Wash's virtually unarmed brother-in-law is now confronted by armed, traditionally suspicious, and always murderously hostile Klamath River kin of Wash. Tension arises in the sensing of Wash's helplessness about the posture of his fractious kinsmen. Tension also develops in each hearer's undoubted identifications both with Wash and Wash's doomed brother-in-law. Tension is increased, too, by the society's custom or requirement, if it was that, to practice at target shooting before going out for elk. Still more intensification is consequent upon possession of rifles, which are more fearsome than bows.

A dramatic contrast in feelings, an emphasis upon the inequity in the tragedy about to occur, follows in mention of the brother-in-law assisting at cooking. Such pacific, innocent, and helpful behavior expresses the man's acceptance of peace with his Klamath River brother-in-law, Wash. The tragedy is that two traditional enemies who are now friends are to suffer for their amity, one with his life, the other in mourning, grief, guilt, shame, and costs. Each auditor's identification with the well-meaning victim becomes more lamentable because of his helpfulness in cooking. The auditor who identifies with Wash suffers the anguish that worthy must have felt in his inability to curb the fury of his own kin.

(4) When his wife is assisted in her chores, Wash reciprocates with a protective utterance that also furthers the consuming sentiment of tragedy: he admonishes his brother-in-law to keep apart from the target shooting. It means that he is alarmed by the unreliability, hotheadedness, and corrosive hate of his own kin. He realizes that, no matter what he says, they are driven to cause him suffering most unfairly. The tragic finale is inevitable. What Wash says and does to protect his wife's brother only deepens the odious feeling of irresistible and irreparable tragedy.

Instead of describing the brother-in-law, who is either reckless or feckless, Mr. Simmons says, I think skillfully and effectively, that Wash turns and sees the luckless fellow standing close to the murderous marksmen. In the Northwest, a verb morpheme *turn* often connotes no more than *glance* or *look a little to the side rather than directly ahead*. It usually does not mean a ninety degree or greater turn of body and head.

Several expressive items are imbedded here. One is the lamentable destiny of a person who ignores warnings, even of lethal danger. Throughout the oral literatures of the bands and hamlets of the Northwest States, myth actors who, in a regional kind of bullheadedness that verged on suicidal compulsion, were proceeding to their doom were admonished and at once blandly disregarded what they heard. I think that the region accepted a premise that was at once of a psychological kind about persons' autonomous choices, and of a philosophically fatalistic kind. Narrators expressed it frequently in the oral genres. It exhibits a conviction that no person can be persuaded, certainly he can never be forced, to halt or protect himself if, in a kind of extremity of individual autonomy that is abetted, even straitjacketed, by his personal supernaturals, he chooses to march into a situation from which withdrawal is impossible. Indians therefore would not think of forcibly halting a person who had advanced in the direction of a denouement that was certain death. Such respect for other persons' choices, such conviction that they could not and would not listen to advice to be cautious, such fatalism from the point of view of Western ideology, are alien to most Euro-Americans. Accordingly, observe that Wash did not call out to his brother-in-law to return. He had done all that an Indian could do: he had warned the hapless man before he chose to wander over and mingle with the marksmen. Good man that he was, Wash therefore said no more. It would have been stupid, or in bad taste, to say more. Such policy expressed acceptance of a tragic destiny, in a frame of proper Northwest States Indian etiquette, values, and orientation about people's self-identities. They were unchangeably what they were. They did what they did. Their direction was unalterable. Nothing could change such people, such events, such reality. The behavior, so sparely described in the narrative, encloses portions of a philosophy, an ethics, and a theory of a psychological kind. That is, it expresses a "world view," or in the terms of Ruth Benedict during the 1930s, a "culture pattern."

The content of the next sentence offers a transition. It is like a new scene in a short play. The spotlight shifts to the villains, who are said to perceive that Wash's brother-in-law is there. But the next sentence (5), which may be somewhat contradictory as is casual conversation anywhere, says that the fellows came deliberately to deceive and kill him. They say to him in seeming decency of intent, *"Let's shoot at the target."* But they are hypocritical. They use the situation to attack him. Now one of the men turns and shoots at the victim. The narrator does not reveal that the prey ever anticipated his peril. No verb represents his feelings when he is shot at. Tension is heightened (6) only with the terse citation of dodgings of shots. He dies only when he slips while trying to dodge. His ability and excellence are indicated by his series of successful evasions of the bullets. Slipping or tripping is an accident of tragic destiny. He had nearly escaped.

That is how (they shot him) is a stylistically favored and regionally typical, although probably not required, utterance that follows a description of how some deed was done or how an event occurred. This kind of *that is the manner* utterance may be present, to be sure, without a single item of description of the manner. *That is the manner* required filling or projection by the auditors who, of course, knew what transpired, perhaps not in every detail. *That is the manner* therefore must not be translated as *that is precisely the manner,* any more than *five* means a numerical *five* in the Northwest States.

(7) The notation that Wash saw the entire affair is obvious. It is depictively unnecessary. Nevertheless, it is proper literary style to say that *he perceived.* ... Then, obviously in utmost anger, he tells the killers to depart. He follows at once with a *"Go home!"* The sequence of *depart* and *return home* is a regionally characteristic selection, in correct style, of two facets of movement homeward. First, you leave, or you go. After that, you go homeward. Either in casual utterances or in myths, a speaker selected two such successive verbs, and had to.

Next, observe that not one descriptive word has as yet reported Wash's anger. Instead, the style allows indication, in an indirect way, of the fact of anger but it does it by placing the feeling in direct discourse which asserts what the person threatens to do. That is, Mr. Simmons reports what Wash said to his murdering kin, *"I might shoot you to pieces."* Literally he would do nothing of the sort, although a musket shot of the 1850s probably tore a rather large hole through a person. *Shoot to pieces* is a stylized device in direct discourse, and it functions to express an extreme of fury.

Then note Wash's regionally typical complaint: *"You have caused me trouble."* Anger is not stressed. Anger is not the trouble. The cultural heritage emphasized humiliations, fines, and status trouble. Trouble is to have to pay a large sum for an injury inflicted, and trouble is to collect from disapproving kin in order to amass the compensation sum that is required. No fieldworker has ascertained just how hard-nosed were kin who had to be loyal to one of their own, who did not like it a bit, and who grumbled, growled, and criticized the unhappy collector.

Research has not revealed how flattened by humiliation a man became because of his kin's feelings toward him, or how awful he felt because of others' insults.

A murder was probably the biggest kind of trouble because it called for the largest of all amounts in compensation money. Only a wealthy person could pay weregild forthwith. Others had to go to their kin for loans and sentiments of disapproval that cut to the quick. In western Oregon, all offenses could be wiped away with a requisite sum, and what was a customary rate for each type of offense was registered, to a bead, in the memories of elders. The offender had to make a huge payment in beads to his wife's kin for their loss, even though it was his kin, not he, who perpetrated the crime. It was as if he had committed it.

Later, one sentence does say, *he had gotten extremely infuriated*. I believe that had this been a myth, literary style might have omitted such a comment. But this is a spontaneous reporting, and to a cultural outsider to whom things ought to be explained. This is no highly stylized, verbatim memorized Northwest States myth wherein notations of sentiments usually gave way to laconic reportings of overt acts.

The next sentence, which is about Wash and his wife taking her murdered brother back to her people's community, omits mention of helpers who carried the body. A reporter-raconteur felt no warrant in commenting on something that almost everyone would understand by projection of custom and familiar imagery. Of course, helpers from kin and community volunteered in the task of carrying the body if a trail had to be followed. Or they would take it to a dugout if that was sufficient for the journey. On this occasion, we do not know how Wash traveled, or how the corpse was prepared and wrapped. The sole expression of cultural content is (8) a citation that the journey was properly undertaken with compensation money sewed on or attached to the corpse wrappings in some unrevealed manner. The pressure in expression is to state that a quantity of money beads large enough to constitute compensation for the murder accompanied the body on its trip to its home. Mr. Simmons in effect is also explaining, again to a cultural alien, the central theme of proper payment and resolution when an offense has been committed. It did not occur to Mr. Simmons to clutter his report with descriptive items that a Euro-American would like to have.

Next, Wash becomes fearful of the response at his wife's hamlet, because the people there might not regard the weregild as sufficient.

They might turn against him in mortal vengeance (9). Whatever he may feel, his call to the residents of the hamlet, made as he approaches and at a short distance, is correct etiquette, Mr. Simmons himself states. Then Wash displays the money beads, it is not clear whether still at a distance or when he has entered a house: a detail like this was self-evident to an Indian.

The expression about melting the hearts of people is arresting. I do not know if it is a metaphor that was borrowed from speakers of English.

The observations that Wash *knew how to speak*, and that he *spoke for a long time* state, of course, that in this situation he spoke adequately, if not eloquently. It appears that ability to speak for a long time was admired and effective. Wash gains stature because he speaks well and at length. Dramatic tension is thereby enhanced.

The deceased's father assures Wash of personal acceptance but at once warns about a youth who is *walking about*. Mr. Simmons explained (10) that this is a younger brother of the murdered man, and the implication is that the father cannot control his possibly hothead son. Mr. Simmons went on, in effect, to say that other armed men are stalking the hero, too. The expression *he could hardly feel himself* nicely phrases how even a fine and brave man, who supposed that he had paid all the compensation that was called for, might nevertheless be almost paralyzed with terror. There was nothing shameful in the Northwest about being so scared as to be almost catatonic. The bravest man might respond like that.

(11) The deceased's unwarlike father now enunciates his former capacity to drink human blood, I suppose through acquisition of, or identification of self with, a powerful personal supernatural. I have no clue about the literal meaning of this kind of bragging by the old man. A breakfast aperitif of human blood, or one at a later time of day, is not reported from any group in the Northwest States. In all likelihood the claim is metaphorical. It symbolizes admirable ferocity and savage courage when he was a younger man. Perhaps he is telling his younger sons and other armed followers that he once was a bloodthirsty fellow and that he outgrew it. They ought to respect him because although he was once that way he had matured enough to avoid silly keeping up of trouble. Maybe he is also saying that he might still have rather strong supernatural power. If so, he is trying to control them, almost by threatening them. One may ask, too, if he is not also shaming his followers into laying down their guns. All in all, the statement about drinking blood is not clear, although it points to an effort by the older

man to control testy young fellows. It also functions as a climactic announcement, a final effort, that may intercept generation of a feud. A peak of intensity here is further expressed in the statement that the wife of Wash stays loyally, of course dutifully and properly like a fine wife, beside her nearly paralyzed husband.

The remaining utterances are laconic, in the manner of the style of myths in the Northwest States: *That is the way it happened, they buried him, he and his wife returned,* and *they never did anything to him.* Observe these typical selections of four wholly stark surface facets of the total situation, and the omission of citations of emotions in the finale. Such terseness and bypassing of expressions about sentiments are exactly like style in the region's mythologies. The carriers of this cultural heritage were almost eloquent in the sense of unexampled parsimony in depiction of actions, and they pointed to feelings almost entirely with their spare citations of actions.

Oral Traditional and Ethnographic Texts

15

Coyote, Eagle, and the Wolves

(Upper Cowlitz Sahaptin)

The myth text, "Coyote, Eagle, and the Wolves," was dictated to Melville Jacobs by Jim Yoke in July of 1927. It was translated by Sam N. Eyley, Jr. "in Yoke's presence in the latter's tipi at Lewis, Washington" (Jacobs 1934, 177). The phonetic text and its translation were subsequently published in Jacobs (1937, 167-76; 1934, 191-202); the interpretation and revised translation, published here for the first time, are from an unpublished manuscript (Jacobs 1959d). Jacobs's new translation differs from the 1934 translation in only minor details. Brief biographical notes on Yoke and Eyley and the circumstances of Jacobs's Sahaptin fieldwork can be found in Jacobs (1929, v, 241-244) and Jacobs (1934, ix-xi, 102, 177). See Hunn (1990) for historical and ethnographic information about the Sahaptin Indians.

In the summer of 1927 an interpreter introduced me to a bed-ridden old man, Jim Yoke, who was living in a plains-area kind of canvas-covered tipi at Lewis, Washington, far up the Cowlitz River. His people were almost one hundred miles north of the Klikitats. He was one of the few informed survivors of the Upper Cowlitz River dialect group which alone, among Washington State Sahaptins, resided wholly west of the mountains. He dictated this and other myths, or parts of myths.[1]

The lower and middle courses of the Cowlitz River had Salish-speaking settlements that may have numbered, all in all, a thousand or more persons. The upper fifty-odd miles of the river, closer to the mountains, probably had only a few hundred people; some spoke both Cowlitz Salish and Cowlitz Sahaptin, others only Sahaptin. In terms

Sam Eyley, Jr., Morton, Washington, 1927

of their self-awareness they were close, by way of a well-marked trail through the mountains, to the Ellensburg area's Sahaptins. Mr. Yoke's people spoke a dialect that is almost identical with that of their east-of-Cascades Ellensburg neighbors. In social structure and culture the resemblances were such that we may regard this myth as an east-of-mountains play which is colored, maybe not in its tellers' eyes, by awareness and values which arise in Salish culture.

Only Thelma Adamson, in 1926 and 1927, obtained meaningful ethnographic notes on both the Salish and Sahaptin settlements along the Cowlitz. I have been informed that her manuscripts may be lost.[2] The sole background observation which I can offer to illumine Upper Cowlitz oral literature is that its transmitters and developers had intermarried with both the more well-to-do and socially stratified Salish families just west of them and the unstratified Sahaptins east of the divide. Therefore the Upper Cowlitz Sahaptins' mythology, if it was distinctive from Sahaptin literature to the east and I think it was slightly so, partook of both social systems and cultural heritages.

The text follows.

Coyote and his son Eagle were persons. His son Eagle had four wives. When away hunting, Coyote went to a high rock cliff, Coyote defecated, and he came back home. And his son came home again also. Eagle had a valuable shirt. Coyote said to his son, "Oh. Yonder are young ones of an Eagle, with feathers for these arrows." His son replied, "Well, so you did find feathers. Let us go tomorrow."

When the sun rose they went away to that place, they reached it. There Coyote said to his son, "Look!" He had made the feathers, that was how Coyote had wished them. He said, "Look!" He told his son, "Take off your shirt and all of that. You might spoil it." That shirt had dentalia. He took it off, placed it there, and left it before going on. Then Eagle climbed up the cliff there to fetch those feathers. He climbed up, at length he reached the place. Two tiny feces of Coyote lay there, that was what Coyote had wished. There was no way to descend. He took his son's shirt, he put it on. "Yah ah ah aaaaah yah ah ah aaaaah," he ran on singing, "Father found some feathers!" His son said shouting down to him, "Dirty-scabby face!"

Coyote came near to the home where the four wives of his son were. Eagle had one son, a boy. When he came near to them, "Papa papa!" it cried as it went along, "papa papa!" Pretending he (Coyote) had been caught up above Coyote came to the two women.[3] They were comrades, Mouse and Cricket. He had (also) as wives Turtle Dove and her comrade Dove, these two women were his (Eagle's) favorites. He returned to there, to Mouse and to Cricket, while he let alone the wives who were dear to his son, Turtle Dove and Dove.

The Doves said to each other, "He is Coyote. He caused his son to be marooned up above there." Turtle Dove and Dove wept on account of their husband. "There's too much talk now! (Coyote said, pretending that he was Eagle and that Coyote was lost on the bluff). But they did not like their father-in-law! Let him be there. The old man is marooned up above there." When they moved away (from the temporary camp), Coyote took those two Mouse and Cricket wives of his son.

When they had moved away, he said to them, "Go camp over there now." Turtle Dove baked white camas in ashes, she put in the food, she covered it over. She left one (camas root) in plain view there, because in some way or other it was possible he might escape, descend, reach there, and find food at the fireplace. Coyote hunted as they went along. "You are to camp at that place yonder!" The women reached that precise place, Turtle Dove and Dove themselves camped at a distance away, while at the other site were Mouse and Cricket, the wives of Coyote, they were the wives he had taken from his son. Along the way Coyote had shot and killed a fawn, Coyote brought it home, he offered a foreleg to Dove and her comrade. That boy, Eagle's son, cried and cried, they camped with the child at a distance away, they were making it cry. "They love and want their father-in-law a very great deal!" (Coyote explained to Mouse and Cricket).

Meantime he (Eagle) could not get down from that place. When the sun rose, they (Coyote, the four wives, and the infant) moved away. "You are to camp yonder at that place!" Again in the same manner Turtle Dove prepared and cached white camas for his (Eagle's) food before going on. Again they made their camp at a distance apart. Going along Coyote had shot and killed another fawn, he brought it there, again he gave them a foreleg. The boy cried and cried. "Ah, they loved their father-in-law." They camped with the child a distance away (away from Coyote, Mouse and Cricket).

When the sun rose, they moved on. Coyote said, "You are to camp yonder at that place after a while." As he went along he hunted, he shot and killed another fawn, he brought it back to there, and again he gave a foreleg to Turtle Dove and her comrade. They camped overnight.

When the sun rose, they moved away. Again in the same manner Turtle Dove prepared food, she covered over white camas roots close to the fire before going on. Coyote had said to them, "You are to move to yonder place after a while." That was where they camped. On his way Coyote had shot another fawn, and again he proffered a foreleg (to the Dove wives).

When the sun rose he said, "Let us move now." He said to them, "We will camp at that site yonder." Before going Turtle Dove covered over white camas roots for his (Eagle's) food close to the fireplace, and left one (root) there in plain view for him. That was the third night they had made camp.

When it dawned, they moved on. He said, "You are to camp at that place yonder after a while." They moved on. Coyote hunted, he shot and killed still another fawn. Turtle Dove and her comrade always camped at a distance away. Again he packed home a fawn and gave them a foreleg.

When it dawned they moved away. This was the fifth time now.[4] He told them, "You are to camp at that site yonder." When they made camp there, Coyote brought another fawn home, and he shared another foreleg with them. The boy had been crying. Coyote said, "For what purpose do you camp with it?" But they loved their father-in-law. "Never mind the old man stuck up there!"

Spider had a trap set and there he found Eagle, now just about completely starved. "What has happened to you," he said to him, "to be caught up here?" "Ah yes. Coyote did it to me." He said to him, "Grandfather! You let me down!" Spider took and tied Eagle, and he let him down below. When he stood on the ground Eagle untied himself and went away.

He arrived (at a deserted camp), nothing there any more. He found the food, ate it, went away, and reached another campsite. Again he searched for food, again found it, and ate it. Then he became stronger. Again he went on, again he found it. "This is the place where they made a camp." Again he found food, ate it, again he went on. He became strong now. "They must have been camping right about here." He found food. "They must have moved away from this place just a short while ago." He followed them. Then Eagle ran on and caught up to them.

She was going along carrying the child on its cradleboard. Mm mm mm mm it cried as they went along. He went on to catch up with them. Turtle Dove was going along in the rear with the child on its cradle board. The little boy on the cradleboard turned his head, "Ta ta ta ta takum," the little boy (said when he) saw his father coming. Turtle Dove said, "He (your father) is dead." Five times, that many, he watched him coming (and each time the child cried out), "Tatatatata!" "Hush! He has died!" The pack rope hung from his wife Turtle Dove's pack, he took it there, he tugged at it, he pulled her head back, the woman turned toward him, and she saw him coming. Her comrade Dove was ahead. "Ah. So you have caught up to us!"

They rested at that place, and there the women told about themselves, and how Coyote had taken them here and there. He said to his (two) wives, "After a while, when he gives you the foreleg, you will throw it back at him directly then." The women packed him along with them.

When they came to where they made their camp, Eagle was not in view. Coyote returned from hunting, and he brought a fawn. They went to share the foreleg with them. Eagle had told them (the Doves), "You should make camp farther at a distance (from the others)." When Coyote arrived, he said to those two women (to the Doves), "Oh indeed you are camping with the baby at too great a distance away (from us). But they loved their father-in-law!" The son, Eagle, listened. The person appeared who gave the foreleg to them. The woman took the foreleg, she threw it back at her. "Ah! but they did love their father-in-law so dearly!"

Eagle was about to pick up a stick and go to him then. Father Coyote saw Eagle. He (Eagle) could have whipped him for it there. He (Coyote) said to him, "Take care! You might break the valuables (the shell money on Eagle's shirt); I will take off yours, my son! don't do it!" He took his shirt off, and Coyote told his son, "The women (all four) are yours, of course, my son! Here are your women, my son!" His son said to him, "Let them be yours! I don't want them! You can have them for your own wives now." They became amicable again; Coyote's son gave him the women.

Then the women and all moved away. As they went along Eagle hunted, he shot and killed a large deer. They lived there for some time. When Coyote went hunting he shot and killed mere fawns. Eagle shot and killed large things. Eagle went hunting, and he shot and killed two, he left one of them there, the other he carried home. He said to his father Coyote, "You go fetch it yourself now! I left a packstrap there with which to pack it." Coyote went away, he waded through streams, he crossed five streams, small streams. Rain was coming, and then it did rain. Eagle had wished for rain to come to him. Coyote came this way with his pack. His son had put out for him entrails that exactly resembled a packstrap, deer entrails. He packed it, he came this way with his pack, while it rained and rained.

He came down to a stream that was rising and already becoming large, he waded across to the other side with some difficulty. He came down to another river, waded to the other side, but it was already a large river. His packstrap broke, he caught it, dragged it ashore, with difficulty packed it away. He packed it along, came down to a river, waded across, the packstrap broke in the very middle of the river, with difficulty did he drag it from the water to the shore. There he packed it on again, and he packed it along in this direction. He came down to still another river, waded across to this side, when it broke in the river, he caught it, he tugged it ashore, packed it, and came on. He came down to a stream that was already quite large, and he waded across to this side, it broke, he pulled it ashore, he packed it by hand, he packed it on in this direction. With his pack he had forded as many as four rivers on his way here.

He now came down to the last of the rivers, he waded across to this side with the pack, but he now waded over in water too deep, the pack broke apart, he caught it, he dragged it to shore, but it became too much for him, he lost his hold on it in the stream, and that pack floated away. When Coyote got ashore, he said, "What am I to do? I will float downstream." He searched for wood, found it, it was a concave piece of wood like this, he laid himself on it, he put himself on it as if on a cradle board, he put himself into the water, and he floated away.

There was a fish dam of earth blocking the stream. There were five Wild Duck girls, that fish dam was theirs, it was at that place that Chinook salmon were held in. Every kind of as many fish as there were belonged to those girls in their water place, and it was at that place in the water that Coyote was caught.

He was working his tongue (like a baby), when the youngest Wild Duck came down to the water and saw that a child was stuck there. She went ashore, she brought water from the river, and she said, "An infant is stuck in the water," to her older sisters. The oldest one said, "It ought to be nice to have it for a child, its relatives must have drowned, and apparently it came floating downstream from there." All five of them came down to the river then. "Oh it is a nice child!" They brought it from the river to their house, they fed it (said in a ludicrous blustering monotone), it worked its tongue. "hwis hwis hwis." "Dear oh dear! It's a cunning tot, and it's hungry." They went to sleep, they took it with them to sleep.

When the sun rose, they set it on a cradleboard, they tied it on a stick, they placed food before it near its mouth, and they fixed its little hands where it could see them. Then they left it; they went to dig white camas. When they had gone out of sight, Coyote untied himself, went down to the fish dam, caught a Chinook salmon, took it ashore, butchered it, roasted it, when it was all done he ate it. Then when he had finished eating, he made a wooden ladle; he made a root digger. Then he realized, "They are going to return pretty soon." He put himself on the cradleboard, in the same way again he set himself on it, but that food was still there. The women arrived. "Dear oh dear! how cutely he had been staying all alone here!" They went to sleep.

When the sun rose they treated him in precisely the same manner again, they prepared food for him before they went, they left him. He untied himself, went down to the water, seized one, took it ashore, butchered it, roasted it, finished cooking it, and ate it. He made a ladle, and a root digger, there were two ladles, two root diggers now. And the same way again he put himself on the cradleboard, he set himself there, and he fixed himself in just the same manner again. Those five came back home. "Oh dear! How cutely he stays all alone!" They went to sleep.

When the sun rose they went away to dig roots. They left Coyote fastened on the cradleboard there. He untied himself, went down to the river, caught a Chinook salmon, butchered it, roasted it, ate it, came back, and made a ladle and a root digger. That was the fourth ladle he had completed, and also the fourth root digger. They came home, they went to sleep.

Before going away they set him there, and they left him in the very same fashion. He loosened himself, went to the river, caught a Chinook salmon, roasted it, finished cooking it, ate it all, came back, made a ladle and finished it, made another root digger and finished it. That then was the last of the five ladles, and also the fifth of the root diggers. They slept through the night.

They left him; they went to dig white camas. Coyote untied himself, went to the river and caught a Chinook salmon, took it to shore, butchered it. That was the last one of them now. When cooked, he ate it.

He went and took a root digger, put a ladle on top of his head, and dug in the soil; he dug to make an opening through that fish dam. He dug all day long; he dug to open up that fish dam. When he was deep down there in it, he reflected that it was pretty nearly opened through. Then the oldest woman while digging (at the root patch) broke her root digger, the oldest Wild Duck woman said to her younger sisters, "Some people or other must have reached that child. Let us go home." They reached home, but no Coyote, no baby. They ran here, they ran there, but no baby. They searched for it.

They ran down to the water, they saw him digging, they ran to him, they struck him, they struck him five times, when they struck him that ladle was bent thoroughly out of shape, and at the same time the root digger was broken. He took another ladle, placed the ladle on his head; they took another root digger. He dug, again they struck five times at that cup, that cup was smashed, and again the root digger was broken. He took another one and placed it on top of himself, they took a root digger. He put more vim into the digging. They struck him as many as five times, that ladle was smashed, and at the same time the root digger was broken. He took another one and put it on top of himself, and they likewise took a root digger. He dug with still more energy. Five times they struck him, smash! and likewise the root digger broke.

Only one more ladle, only one more root digger. He placed it on top of himself; they took the last root digger. Then he dug, they struck him four times, they struck him, bent, smashed! he wedged through it and opened it, that water flowed through and out. "Hurrah! hurrah! the younger brother has arrived!" Apparently in the meantime the younger Wild Duck had known, so she headed off the Chinook salmon, but nevertheless they escaped some distance past her.

Coyote stood there and shouted, "Of all the fish only a few will be yours. The people (the modern Indians) who are coming are near now. You are to be Wild Ducks, and when Chinook salmon go upstream, you will follow them. You will be mere birds. You will follow crying, 'wid wid wid wid'."

Coyote went on in this direction; he came up the great river. He had come up along the river to that place. "I am becoming hungry. I will cry out." There was gravel by the side of the river, there he stood and he shouted, "Get yourself ashore! thing I have made!" Chinook salmon came ashore haapapppppp, he stooped here and there, but he could not catch them, all the Chinook salmon went back into the water. Five times he went (and did that), that was how it occurred (each time).

He went and defecated his two younger sisters. "You explain, my younger sisters!" One younger sister's name was Huckleberry; the other's name was Pine Nut. They replied, "Go figure it out yourself now! You will say, 'That is precisely what I had been forgetting,'" "tututututu tamiyu tamiyu tamiyu!"[5] "Oh be careful older brother! We'll explain what you are to do when you go. You are to stand on the sand, you will take a club, when it (a fish) has come out of the water, and when it is flapping here and there on the sand, you will strike with this club, and it will die, you will strike it on its head till it dies." "That is just what I forgot."

He went away, he went down on the river sand, he took a club, and he shouted, "Get yourself ashore! thing I have made!" A Chinook salmon came out of the water, he struck it on the head, he struck it absolutely to death. He took hold of it, carried it away from the water, prepared firewood, made a fire, butchered it, roasted it, and when it was thoroughly done he became sleepy. "I'll take a little nap." He leaned against some wood and slept. Meantime Wolves were going by, there were five Wolves, they had made sleep (with their supernatural power) for Coyote. They came to him, and while he was sleeping they ate up all that of his. And they daubed his hands and mouth with salmon, they heaped up the remains of it for him, they left him. Coyote woke up hungry. "Although I am at my eating place, I am still hungry."

He went away, again he went upstream, there again he shouted, he cried out holding a club, "Get yourself ashore! thing I have made!" It came out of the water, he clubbed it on the head to death, he went away, prepared a fire, butchered it, roasted it, became sleepy, and fell tight asleep. Those same Wolves came to him, there were five of them, they ate up that of his, they did the same thing again to his mouth, they left him. Coyote woke up. "I am hungry, and nevertheless I have remains of food on my hands and mouth." They had daubed him with it.

He went on, but he was even sooner hungry now. He went on, and there again he shouted, "Get yourself ashore! thing I have made!" A Chinook salmon came out of the water, he clubbed it, caught hold of it, brought it ashore, prepared firewood, made a fire, butchered it, roasted it, and then when the cooking was nearly done, "Oh dear I'm becoming sleepy." He leaned against some wood, and he must have slept soundly indeed. The Wolves came to him, they ate up all that of his, all of it. He was sleeping. They daubed his hands and mouth with salmon. He woke up. "I'm hungry, but anyhow I do have remains of food on me." They had left him.

Coyote went away, again he sat down on the dirt, and he shouted, "Get yourself ashore! thing I have made!" A Chinook salmon came out of the water, he clubbed it, brought it ashore, prepared a fire, butchered it, roasted it, and when it was nearly cooked, he became sleepy, and then he fell sound asleep. That was sleep the Wolves had made for him. They came to him, they ate up all of his, they themselves were just Wolves who were traveling along some distance back from the river bank. They just daubed some on his hands and mouth. He was hungry. "Anyhow I am at my eating place."

He went away again, and he became hungry directly. No food at all. He sat down on the sand and he shouted, "Get yourself ashore! thing I have made!" A Chinook salmon came out of the water thlapppppp, he clubbed it on the head, brought it ashore, prepared firewood, made a fire, butchered it, roasted it, it was nearly cooked, it was cooked now, he fell asleep. The Wolves came to him, they ate all of his while he was sleeping, they smeared it on his mouth and hands. Coyote woke up. "I am hungry, but still I have remains of food on me."

Then he was very, very hungry. He went, sat on the sand right by the water, and shouted, "Get yourself out of the water! thing I have made!" It came out of the water happpppppp, he clubbed it to death, brought it ashore, prepared a fire, roasted it, it became done, Coyote became very sleepy, he slept. The Wolves came to him, ate all of his, smeared it on his hands and mouth, left him. He woke up. "Really I must have eaten anyhow, and nevertheless I am hungry again."

Coyote went away a short distance, that was how he went (he was famished now). "I'll defecate and inquire before I go farther." He defecated, one younger sister of his was Huckleberry, another younger sister of his was Pine Nut. "Now explain it to me, my younger sisters!" "Think it out for yourself before you go on. You will be saying, 'That is really just what I had been forgetting!'" "Ttttt tamiyu tamiyu tamiyu!" "Oh don't! older brother! We'll explain to you! It is Wolves who are traveling by. They are the ones who bake eggs up from the riverbank; they are the ones who have been making sleep for you. And when you are asleep they come to you, they eat up yours, and they smear it on your mouth and hands. Now you yourself cause them to sleep. They bake those eggs up from the river bank." "Very well indeed! That is exactly what I had been forgetting."

Coyote went on, he made sleep for the Wolves, they slept, Coyote reached the Wolves, the eggs were being baked, all five of them lay about, asleep, Coyote took them out of the bake oven Coyote ate them. He left one remaining one for each of them, that is how he did it to them, he deposited such a leftover for each of the five of them, he himself gave each of them just a smear of it on their mouths and hands, and he left them. The Wolves woke up hungry, they said to one another, "But we really must have been eating. And still I am hungry. Nevertheless we all have remains of the food right on our mouths and hands." They baked those eggs of grouse and pheasant.

Coyote went on, he went up the river, he had eaten now. He came to the sand near the river, he shouted, "Get yourself out of the water! thing I have made!" It came out of the water, he clubbed the Chinook salmon, he brought it ashore, he burned firewood, he roasted it, it became cooked, and then he felt sleepy. "I shall not fall asleep any more." He strolled here and there around the roast, when it was done he took it away from the fire, and he ate it up. He did not sleep any more.

When he finished eating, Coyote found out where the Wolves were baking eggs. He made sleep for them, they went to sleep, Coyote reached them, they were sleeping, he took it out of the bake oven, Coyote ate it up. He daubed it on their hands and mouths, he collected the leftovers for them, he left them. The five Wolves woke up famished. "We are hungry, although there are remains of food on our hands and mouths."

Coyote went on, and the Wolves themselves went along. Coyote stood close to the river holding a club, and he shouted, "Get yourself ashore! thing I have made!" A Chinook salmon came out of the water haaappppp, he clubbed it, brought it ashore, threw it down, prepared firewood, made a fire, roasted it, it was finished cooking. When it was done, he felt as if he wanted to sleep, but he went here, he went there, and he did not go to sleep. Since it was cooked, he ate it, he finished eating, he went on, he went upstream.

He found out that the Wolves were baking eggs. He made sleep for them, the Wolves went to sleep, Coyote came to them, took it from the bake oven, ate the eggs, collected five leftovers for the five of them, smeared it on the mouths of all of them and on the hands of all of them, and he left them. The Wolves woke up hungry. "And yet there are remains of food smeared right over all our hands, and we are famished."

Coyote had left them, and he had gone away. "I'll call out." He shouted, "Get yourself out of the water! thing I have made!" A Chinook salmon came out of the water, he roasted it, it was done, he felt like sleeping, "I must not sleep at all now." He took the cooked Chinook salmon from the fire, ate it, finished eating, and went away.

He found out that the Wolves were baking eggs. He made sleep for them, the Wolves became sleepy. He reached them, the Wolves were asleep, Coyote took it out of the bake oven, ate it, ate all of it. He collected the leftovers in five piles for the five of them, smeared it on all their mouths and hands, and left them. The Wolves woke up, he (one of them) said to his younger brothers, "Anyhow we do have remains of food on all our mouths, and still we are hungry. How can it be that we are like that here? Very probably Coyote has been doing it to us."

Meantime Coyote had gone on for a certain amount of time, and then he became hungry. He stood on the sand right by the water, and he shouted, "Get yourself out of the water! thing I have made!" A Chinook salmon came out of the water haappppp, he struck it on the head with a club, he brought it ashore, roasted it, it became done, he felt as if he wanted to sleep. It was the sleep the Wolves were making for him. But he did not sleep now by any means. "I certainly shall not sleep now." Coyote ate, he ate it all, he went away.

Ah, he found out that they were baking eggs, he made sleep for them, the Wolves went to sleep, he reached them, he took their eggs out of the oven, he ate all of theirs, he smeared in on all their mouths and hands, he left them. They woke up. "And still there are remains of food." The oldest one said to them, "But we do have remains of food on us, and still I am hungry. Suppose we bake, and no longer go to sleep." They planned it, Coyote found it out. "The damned things! They no longer want to go to sleep. They did it as many as five time to me, and I myself would be satisfied if I too could eat theirs five times also."[6]

He went for the last (the fifth) time. The Wolves were very hungry now. Coyote went on, he was hungry. "I will call out to the thing I made." He stood close to the water, he shouted, "Get yourself out of the water! thing I have made!" A Chinook salmon came out of the water haapppppp, he clubbed it, brought it ashore, built a fire, roasted it, it became done, he felt sleepy. "I certainly will not sleep now." He went here, he went there, he took it out of the fire, ate it, and left there as much of the remains as he had eaten. It seems that Coyote was not asleep when they arrived, and apparently they were eating Coyote's leftovers. He had just about finished his repast, when he heard thlhhhhh, he stood up, he looked, and he saw one Wolf peeking here at him. Coyote grabbed a club, Coyote ran at them, he scared the Wolves away, they scattered. "Wherever you may be, that is exactly how you will come, and you will eat leftovers."

Coyote went away, but they just followed behind Coyote some distance back from the riverbank, while Coyote himself traveled along by the side of the river. "I am hungry now. I will call out to the thing I have made." He went down to the stream, he stood at the very edge, and he shouted, "Get yourself out of the water! thing I have made!" A Chinook salmon came out of the water, he clubbed it, brought it ashore, made a fire, roasted it, now it was roasting, now it was done, it was almost finished cooking. He heard thlhhhhhh. "Aha!" Wolves came into view from the thickets, they wanted to bite and kill him. Coyote quickly arose, snatched a club, and chased them. The Wolves fled. Coyote ate, he left some of it there, and then he went on. "They might bite and kill me, indeed!" He came on from there and then at that place Coyote quit (halted).

Editors' Notes

1. See Jacobs (1934).
2. Carbon copies of some of Thelma Adamson's Cowlitz Salish ethnographic notes are deposited in the Melville Jacobs Collection, Division of Manuscripts and University Archives, University of Washington Libraries. Whereabouts of Adamson's original field notebooks is unknown.
3. Coyote here takes on Eagle's identity.
4. The narrator has already detailed five episodes. This is actually the sixth.
5. Jacobs does not translate this, presumably because neither Yoke nor Eyley knew what it meant or because it represented untranslatable vocables. It may be in another Indian language.
6. Coyote has already cheated the Wolves of their eggs five times; this is the sixth. The Wolves had previously deprived Coyote of his cooked salmon six times before he consulted his "advisers" for the solution to the mystery. Either the narrator has repeatedly lost count (see note 4 above) or begins his count with the first repetition, not the first instance of an episode.

16

The Basket Ogress Took the Child

(Clackamas Chinook)

Victoria Howard dictated the myth, "The Basket Ogress Took the Child," to Melville Jacobs in the Clackamas Chinook language in 1929 at Howard's home in West Linn, Oregon. She had learned it from her mother-in-law. Mrs. Howard also provided the English translation; the phonetic text and translation were published in *Clackamas Chinook Texts, Part 2* (Jacobs 1959a, 388-409). Only the translation is reprinted here. A content-and-style analysis appears in Jacobs (1960a, 284-307). The Basket Ogress, a terrifying figure, is found throughout Northwest states' oral literatures.

They lived there. Their village was large. Their headman's house was in the center. He and his wife were separated. Their son was small. It became winter, and then he danced (gave a spirit power dance). She had five slaves.

Now on the last (of the five nights of spirit power singing and dancing) she said, she told her slaves, "I shall go for a little while. I shall go look on (at the dance)." Her slaves admonished her not to, they said to her, "Are you not ashamed that you should go look at your husband?" She replied to them, "I shall merely stand beside the door." So then she went, she got to there, she stood by the door. Now they (the crowd) pushed her right to the place where her husband sat. And she stayed there.

She forgot that she had left her son. The infant woke up, he cried. They (her slaves) carried him around fruitlessly. He cried all the more. Now one of them (a slave girl) said to (another one of) them, "Go! go fetch her!" She went, she went to the place there where they were dancing. She said, "Your son is crying." They (persons in the crowd) took hold of her, they threw her far over to the end (of the house).[1] Yonder then another (slave) said, "Now you go too! Hurry! The child is crying." She (a second slave girl) went, she got to there, and she called out, "Your son is crying." They seized her, and they also did that to her. They threw her far over to the end. Now two (slave girls had tried to get her attention). A third one ran, they did that same sort of thing to her also. They did the same way too to the fourth.

Now only one of them was taking care of the baby. And she thought, "Where have they gone? Now then I shall go too." She put down the cradle board, and she ran on. She got to there where they were dancing. She entered, she called out, she said to her, "Your son is almost dead now!" They seized her, she began to scream, she (the infant's mother) heard, she thought, "Oh! my son!" Now she went, she went back home, she got there. No one at all. Only the cradle board stood there (empty). She took hold of it, she said, "Sonny! my son! Sonny! my son!" She opened it (the hide covers on the cradle). Nothing whatever (inside them). Only a stick of rotten wood was inside it there. She screamed, she cried. Her slaves (who had been released and had just then) returned, said to her, "Why are you crying (because it no longer avails you to weep)? You went away. You said to us, I shall be gone for only a little while. You did not come back all night. The child cried. We did everything for him but uselessly. He did not quit crying."

Actually it was in the (early) morning that it had gotten to be a heavy dark fog. Then the Basket Ogress passed through the village, she heard some infant crying, she went inside, she took it, she put it inside her basket. She got a stick of rotten wood, she put it in (the cradle). Then she ran away, she went away with the infant.[2] She took him with her right to the place where her house was. She brought him with her. Now she gave him things to suck on, (mashed) snakes, (mashed) bull frogs, (mashed) common frogs. And that was how she did to him. Now he became big. Then wherever she went, she packed him (on her back) in her basket. He sat on it there (riding on her) wherever she went.[3]

Next door (in an adjacent house) there was one man. He (the child) never went to there. She said to him, "Do not go there. He eats all sorts of bad things." So he did not go to that place.

He was becoming a large youth now. And he thought, "Supposing I go see that person (the neighbor whom I have never seen).” He went inside, he (Crane) was roasting (trouts on spits). He (Crane) looked at him, and at once he said to him, “You must indeed be a person (not a kind of creature like the Basket Ogress). Come inside!” He said to him, “Be seated.” He conversed with him as loudly as he could (in order not to be overheard by her). He said to him, “Very likely your mother has been telling you that you should not come here. Now I shall tell you all about it. What has she been giving you to eat?” He told him. “Hm,” he replied to him, “yes.” “When we two go somewhere or other. . . .”

When they would go somewhere she would pack him with her. Whatever they (she) would find, she would throw it to the rear into her pack basket where he sat. Whatever she picked up (such as snakes and frogs) would then be crawling over him. Then when they would go back home, when they got back those were the things she would serve to him, he would eat snakes, bull frogs, common frogs. She would say to him, “Here are your eels (which were actually snakes), your potatoes (which were actually frogs).” Those are what I recall (of the non-human kinds of foods which she ate and which she fed to him).

“Now when she picks up small potatoes, then she says to me, Here are potatoes. And also when she gets (other) things, then she says to me, Here are your eels. When we get back then those are the things that she gives me. I eat them.”

They went where there were woods, and then he would take hold of a limb (of a tree above). Now she would try to go on, (and as she strained to proceed) her neck would become small (and stretched extremely thin). That is the way he did to her all the time. One white fir stood there, it had large long limbs right close to the ground. When they passed underneath he would take hold of a limb, and that is how it got, her neck got very very small (stretched thin). She would say (as she pulled to go forward), *i'ya i'ya i'ya*. He would (then) let her go. Then they (the two of them) would proceed again. “We have been living like that for so long a time.”

He (Crane) told him, “What she has been giving you is not (edible) food. This here is what we (human beings) eat.” He took out a trout. He said to him, “Now eat this.” He ate it. He finished all of it. He said to him, “Very likely you are supposing that I am angry at you. But if I were speaking quietly to you, she would be hearing it all. On the other hand I am speaking loudly to you, and so she does not hear it. Whenever you become hungry, then come to here. Now I will let you know that you should not believe that she is actually your mother. She merely took you away when you were small."

They sat there for a little while, and then he went to the place where his (foster) mother was. He lay down at once. She said to him, "Sonny! Here are things now for you to eat." He replied to her, "No. I am not hungry." Now she thought, "He (Crane) has told him something then." She called over to him (to Crane), she said to him, "Whatever may you have been telling him?" He replied to her, "But why should I have informed him? I only said to him, (When) your mother gave birth to you, her little anus became turned completely inside out." "Yes yes! that is the way (it was with me)!" And she spoke to him like this, "Your sister's son."[4]

Now they continued to live there, and that is the way then that he was becoming a big youth. When he became hungry, then he would go to the adjacent place there, and he (Crane) would give him (decent because human kinds of) food. He would eat, when he finished eating then he (Crane) would ask him, "Where do you go? Do you not see something or other, or do you do something to her?" He replied to him, "Yes. We go yonder, a very large white fir stands there. When we pass (under) it I take hold of its branch, and her neck becomes very very small (stretched thin). Then I let go, we proceed, and when we get back, then those are the things (snakes and frogs) which she gives me. I eat them." He said to him, "In a little while I shall make arrows for you. Whenever you decide then that you will go back (to your original home), say so to me, and I shall tell you the place where you should go.[5]

Now that indeed is what he (the youth) did. He thought, "Now I shall go back home." So then he went and told him, "I want to go home now." "When you go (with her) tomorrow, when you get to that white fir, take hold of its limb. When you see how she has become (with her neck stretched thin). . . . Where you hold on to the branch, do like that. When her neck has become very small, and you suppose, Now I could cut it, then cut her neck. Then run up it (up the tree) quickly. All those trees are her relatives. They will topple down on one another (when she dies). Then run up on that white fir. When you get up above there, if it is a little too short, then you should join your arrows and your bow together (to make a chain which will reach the sky)."

And so that is what he actually did. The two of them reached the white fir, he held onto a branch, and her neck became as small (thin) as a hair. He had that flint which he (Crane) had given him. Now he cut her neck, and he climbed up the white fir. Then those trees and everything toppled. They said, "Oh! my father's mother!"[6] "Oh! my mother's sister!" "Oh! my father's sister!" "Oh! my mother's mother!" "Oh! my older sister!" "Oh! my younger sister!" "Oh! . . . ." All of them cited it (the relationship to her). He on the other hand had gone on up, he got to the top, and then he joined together his arrows and his bow. He reached the top, he had really gotten to another land.

As he went along he saw people approaching. Short flat and white were their bodies. They were saying, "As we go we crawl all over their vulvas." He met them. He said to them, "Where are you going?" They replied to him, "We shall be crawling all over their vulvas." He thought, "Ah (it should) not (be) like that." He said to them, "I believe you ought not to be like that. Once in a while a person might think, What is crawling over me? It is actually only you. Your name is Greyback Louse. A person might think, What is crawling on me? He will scratch himself. It will be only you. He will take hold of you, he will turn you (like this), he will crack you." He took hold of several of them, he cracked them. Now only a few of them went on (and escaped him). "You are not to be like that (in future eras when the Indians enter this land)!"[7] Then he proceeded.

Pretty soon again as he was going along, then again he saw people coming, all women, blackish ones. He met them. He said to them, "Where are you going?" They replied to him, "No (not to any important place). We shall just be getting on heads (of people)." "Ah," he said to them, "You shall not be like that. Sometimes a person will become lousy. They will look at it, they will take it (off) with a fingernail, they will crack her, sometimes in their teeth." And that is exactly the way he took hold of some of them, he cracked them. Just a few of the others went away (alive).[8] Then he proceeded again.

Now again some more girls came along, white ones. He met them. He said to them, "Where are you going?" They replied to him, "We are merely going to go hang on some big trees (that is, on persons' head hair)." "Ah," he said to them. "(It is) not (to be) like that. They will merely say that your name is nit (louse larva)."

He took hold of (some of) them, he said to them, "They will just do like this to you. They will pull you out from head hairs." He cracked them, he did it to some of them,[9] they (the survivors) went on.

Now he went along again, farther on then again people were approaching, all men, youths, reddish ones. They were just jumping as they went. He met them. He asked them, "Where are you going?" They replied to him, "Yeh! on their ribs." "Indeed," he said to them. "You are not to do that. Your name is flea. You will merely occasionally crawl on them, you will bite them. They will make a movement, they will get you, they will crack you. But you will not bite them (and kill them)." Now he again proceeded.

Then as he went along he again saw an old person (a woman) approaching, she was packing something. He met her, he said to her, "What are you taking along with you?" She said to him, "No, dearie! I am of the Darkness Ones." He said to her, "In spite of that, give me what you are taking along. I am hungry."

Then she again said to him, "Oh no. I am a Darkness One, my dear!" So then he went around to the rear of her, he saw where the plug was, he pulled it out. It became total darkness. She said to him, "Plug it back in so that it will become daylight! Plug it in so that it will become light! Plug it in!" He sought unsuccessfully for her plug. He did not see it. So he merely pulled out grass, he plugged it in, it became daylight. Then he said to her. "But it will not be like that (in future eras). The people (the Indians coming) are close by now. They will not see you. It will merely become dark then, and then it will become daylight. But you yourself will not be going around." He proceeded then, he left her, and he went away.[10]

Now as he went on again, shortly afterward as he went along, then he saw a person coming, and an arrow was stuck in him (through his side). He was groaning "ah, ah." He observed him approaching, and then he (the wounded man) fell, he died.

He went along, a little farther then another person (a Sky Cannibal hunter) came along. He met him, he (the Cannibal) said to him, "Did you not see my quarry?" He replied to him, "No. Only a person was going yonder with an arrow pierced through him. And he fell and died." He (the Cannibal) replied (angrily) to him, "But that was not your quarry!" He passed by him. Then he (the Cannibal) said to him, "Where are you going?" He replied to him, "I am merely traveling around." "Indeed. When you reach two trails (at a fork in the trail), do not go along the right-hand trail. Do not go to the right. Go along the left-hand trail, it is our trail." "Very well," he replied to him.

He proceeded, and he again saw something approaching. It must have been a (wounded) deer (with an arrow pierced through it). It went by him, it fell at that place there, a large deer.

He went somewhat farther, and he encountered a man going along. He (the man) asked him, "Did you not see my quarry?" He replied to him, "Yes. It fell way over there." "Indeed," he said to him, and he went on. But he also (first) said to him (to the youth), "Where are you going?" He said, "I am merely traveling around." He (the hunter) said to him. "Watch carefully when you get to (a fork leading to) two trails. Our trail (the right-hand one) has paint poured over it. Various valuables (money beads) and fine feathers are mixed in it (in the paint on the trail). On the other hand you will see various bones on the other trail. Our (human) flesh, our hair, blood and various things are mixed together (on that left-hand trail)." "Indeed," he replied to him. Then he went on.

As he went along he came to (the fork) where those trails were. He stood there, he thought, "Which trail should I go along?" He stood there for quite a while, then he went along that left-hand trail (which led to the house of Sky Cannibals).

That other man had said to him, "Go along our trail. When you see such things as paint, valuables, feathers mingled and poured onto it, that is the one along which you should proceed. But he did not go along the (preferable) trail. That man (the human who was hunting) went on, he got back (later) to the house, he asked his children (whether the youth had arrived), they told him, "Why no. He has not come!"

Now he (the youth) went along, he came to a house, he arrived. He went inside. No one at all. Goodness he saw our (human) skins, and various sorts of (human) heads were there. He sat down.

He thought, "Wonder where I might find urine (so that) I might clean (shampoo) my hair with it."[11] He looked around for it. (When he failed to find it) he got water, and he cleaned his hair, although at first he looked for urine. He had found none.

Now he also looked for a comb. None at all. He looked around for it. Then he saw something (a hide bag) that was hanging up above (from a rafter). He stood up, he took it off (in order to find a comb inside it), it was covered with (human) skins. He took them off (the hanging bag), she (a girl inside it) turned to him, she looked at him, she said to him, "What are you looking for?" He said to her, "A comb." "To be sure," she replied to him. "Take this which I have inserted in (my hair)." He did not see a comb (in her hair). Only a (human) infant's (dried) hand was inserted in it (in her hair). He took it out, he combed himself with it. He finished (combing), he gave her back her comb.[12] He enclosed her (again in her hides in the basket hanging from the roof), he hung up her carrying basket. Then he strolled about. That was indeed an unmarried (Cannibal) girl to whom he had come.[13]

Presently as he was going around, then he heard persons (four Cannibal girls) coming, they were laughing, they were giggling, the four girls went along.[14] They said, "Goodness! Some person has gotten to our younger sister." Soon afterward then their (Cannibal) father arrived, he brought (packed) with him a dead person (his human "deer"). He said to them forthwith, "Why not make (cook) something? The person (our guest) is probably hungry." Then he butchered that person (his game which he had brought home). Now they fixed everything (for the dinner).

Then he said to them further, "Why do you not take out your younger sister? Set her beside her husband (that is, our youthful guest)." So then they took her out (from her hanging container), they spread out skins (of human beings, to serve as dinner mats), some of them the skins of (human) children. Then they served as food our (murdered human beings') toes, our toes were their camas. Our teeth were their nuts. Our eyes, the center black parts, these were their huckleberries. They served all sorts of things.

He thought, "What could I eat?" So then he got a (stalk of) wild celery, he inserted it into himself clear through to the ground, and then he ate. It went clear through and out of him onto the ground. He did not feel well (because of his feelings about eating human flesh). On the other hand she herself ate. They finished, they finished eating.

Then their father said to them further, "Now go fix a bed for the two of them so that they may sleep together." And so they fixed a bed for them (using human skins for blankets). Then the two of them went to bed. He thought, she was probably like a woman (anatomically), so that he might do something to her (have sexual intercourse). However there was actually nothing (that is, she lacked genitals).[15] He left her alone.

When it dawned the following morning he thought, "I shall not remain here." Then the (four) girls went again, they went to dig (human eyes, toes, and the like). On the other hand their father himself went to hunt. Now they left only the two of them.

He arose, he turned and went back to the place where the two trails forked. He reached that place, and then he went along on that other trail. He proceeded, he got to a house. He arrived, he went inside. No one at all (was at home). Now he again thought, "I shall look around for the urine (bowl)." He found it standing there, and so he washed his hair, he bathed (in it), he made his body clean all over (with water).

Then he sought further for a comb, he looked around for it. Then once again he saw a pack basket that was hanging there, and again he took it down. It was covered (with hides), he took it (the cover) off, and another unmarried girl was covered over inside it. She turned and looked, she looked up, she said to him, "What are you seeking?" He replied to her, "A comb." "Take this one inserted in my hair." It was a fine copper comb. He combed and combed himself (in his pleasure at having the use of so extraordinarily valuable a comb). All done, and then he took it back to her. He covered her over well, he hung her up (inside her pack basket).

Now he strolled about. He noticed that everything was just like the sun. On the trail (and all over the house, too) valuables (money beads), (red) paint, feathers were all mixed together, they were scattered about. Meat was smoke-drying there. He strolled around.

Then it became evening, and they came back home singing and laughing. Four (human) girls got to there. They said at once, "Indeed this one must be the one our father told us about (when he described) the person he had seen." He heard them (talking), and right away they made a fire, they made (cooked) things (for dinner).

Presently then their father returned, he brought a deer with him. He entered, he saw him (the young guest). He said to his daughters, "Hurry! fix things (for dinner)! The person is hungry. And take down your younger sister. Set her beside him."

Now they fixed a spread (of furs) for them, they stretched it out for them, everything was very fine. Then they placed their younger sister there beside him. They said to him, "Sit right here." So then he went, he sat there, they served food to the two of them, the two of them ate. He ate (with pleasure because the food was excellent and the family admirable). The two finished eating.

They made a spread (bed) there for the two of them, the two of them went to bed together (and engaged in normal sexual relationship).

It became light on the following morning. He said to his daughters, "Gather up all the (deer) bones. Pretty soon the Cannibal people will come here. Smoke them out with them (with the scorched bones). They will be coming here out of jealousy." He said, "Let it be tomorrow before you go to dig (camas)." And so they did. Meantime he himself went away, he went hunting. A little while afterward then they said, "Now the (four) Cannibal people (the girls) are approaching!" And sure enough they got to there. They (the four Cannibal girls) said to them (to the four human girls), "He got to our younger sister first. You took her husband from her!" They stood there, and they said (and sang insultingly),

> *"Holes you have you have!*
> *Split you are you are!"*

That is the way they spoke (as they sang and danced in this song of mockery). Then they (the human girls) said, "Be quick! Now we shall make smoke for them!" They burned those bones and everything, it became thick dark smoke. They (the Cannibal girls who were sickened by the fumes from deer bones) fled, they went back toward (their own) home. Then they (the human girls) made their trail clean (by smoke from burning boughs), and their house (too). They did that all day long, they worked at it.

In the evening their father got back, again he brought a deer with him. Now that is the way they were, they lived there (and the youth married and remained with the youngest sister).

Quite some time afterward and then she became pregnant, and now she became ill (in labor), she gave birth, she took out (gave birth to) twins. They were stuck together.[16] Now their grandfather made a cradleboard for them. Then they continued to live there. Now they (the Siamese twins) got a little larger, they sat up, they made them sit up, they sat together. Now they (the twins) began to take steps, and they began to walk about. They became a little bigger, and then their grandfather made arrows for them. Now they played (shooting at a) target. When they threw (shot) their arrows, both of them ran, both now did like that.

Now her father said to her, "Take care! When you (and your husband) are outside, when you are looking for his head lice, he should not lie face down there." And so she did to him. When he would say to her, "Let me lie face down," she would reply to him, "No. There is nothing (there are no lice) there (on the back of your head)." She had the better of him in that. They would go inside.

In the evening her older sisters would get back home. Now that is the way they were doing. And the two children were becoming big. The following day the children went outside to play.

Then he would again say to her, "Look for my head lice." "All right," she replied to him, "go lie down." He lay down (head in her lap). She forgot, he lay turned face down. As he lay there he dug at the ground, he dug out grass and their roots.

He looked down below, he saw a village.[17] Presently then (he observed far below) a child was going along, as it went along (he noticed that) it was blind,[18] he was saying, "Long long ago it was before I was a person yet (before I was born), when the Basket Ogress took my older brother." He (the blind boy) wept. That was what he was saying. Then presently Blue Jay ran ahead of him, he (Blue Jay) said to him, "Here I have come! younger brother!"[19] "Begone! Blue Jay!" he said to him.

His heart (the older brother watching above felt badly) was not right about it. He said to her, "That is sufficient now (your looking for my head lice)." He got up, he went inside, he lay down at once on his bed.[20] His father-in-law got back, he noticed him lying there. He (the father-in-law) said nothing. The (four) girls got back. He (their father) said to them, "Prepare things (dinner) now." Then to be sure they made haste. Their father said, "Now give food to them and to your younger sister. Awaken him!" Their younger sister replied to them, "He is not sleeping." Her father said to her, "Perhaps you did (quarreled about) something or other." She replied to him, "No." Then the old man thought immediately, "He has seen his (home) village."

Now the next day he said to him, "What is doing it to (troubling) your heart? Do not hide it from me. You should tell me what you are thinking."

Then he asked his daughter, "Did he not turn face down there?" "Yes," she said to him. "Yes," he said to her, "he must have seen his village. Now go tell the two old persons (the Spiders who are neighbors of ours) that they should make a large basket, and ropes." They went and said that to the two of them. Not at all long after then they had already brought the (completed) basket and ropes. Then he said to his daughters, "Now make very tiny packs of various tanned buckskins and deer-hide." And they did that. He said, "Tomorrow then we shall take them (below)."

Then when it dawned the following morning, they put it (the baggage composed of tiny packs) into the basket, they filled it, they let it down below (through the hole in the ground), they brought it down to the bottom there. They emptied it, they pulled it (the emptied basket) up, they brought it back above. Then they themselves (the young man and his family) sat on it. He (the old man) said to his daughter, "Be careful. Take good care of the two children. I had (mistakenly) supposed that it would be a while yet before he (your husband) would go back (when his children had become bigger) to his own village."

Now they went, they put them down below (in the Spiders' basket). They got below. Their food (the many small packs) stood there, the things they had brought were full, those tiny things became big and full. They got out of the basket beside a spring. She jerked on it (on the rope), and they pulled it (the empty basket) up.

Presently as they were seated there, then a (blind) child approached and was crying. He was saying, "Long long ago the Basket Ogress stole my older brother, when I was not yet a person (and was not yet born)." He (the older brother) felt bad at heart (again, when he heard these words). He went to him, he said to him, "My poor poor younger brother! my younger brother! my poor poor younger brother! my younger brother!" He (the blind boy) said, "Oh Blue Jay! do not do like that to me! I am pitiable." He said to him, "Oh no. This is me. Just take hold of me, feel me." Then he actually felt him. "These two are your brother's two sons here." He felt them, he said to him, "Is it truly you my older brother?" He said to him, "Yes." "Our parents, our slaves, half the village, our father, they are all blind (from weeping)." He informed him about everything.

She said to her husband, "Bring him here to the water." He took him with him, he led him by the hand, he brought him to her. She got water, and she also poured it on his eyes. The fifth time she threw the water at him, he saw. She said to him, "Now bathe yourself. Wash your head."

He turned and looked, he saw that everything (all those large packs) was full there. He went to fetch a long pole. He said to his younger brother, "How many slaves are there?" He replied to him, "Ten." He said to him, "Fetch five first."

He went, he got there, he said to his parents, "My older brother arrived." They replied to him, "Oh it is only Blue Jay who is playing with you." He replied, "No. It is truly my older brother, his wife, and their two sons. She restored my eyes. I came to fetch slaves."

He took them with him, he led all those blind ones (while they held on to the pole), he took them to the water (spring). And she did that (same way) to them, she poured water on them, they all got their eyes (sight restored).

Now he again said to his younger brother, "Fetch the others also. These may go, they should clean up the house." And that is what they did. They went and cleaned up the house. He brought them (the second group of five blind slaves), and again she did that to them, she restored their eyes. He told them, "Now pack everything (from the spring to my parents' house)." Then the slaves worked. She said to her husband, "(It will be) Tomorrow before I shall work on (restoring the sight of) those two old persons (your parents)." He replied to her, "All right." It became night.

Then the following day she took them (the blind parents) to the water, and she did like that to them too. She restored their eyes. Now she worked on all those people of her father-in-law, she fixed their eyes. Then they fixed up their houses, they cleaned them, they made them clean, they fixed their village.

Now they lived there. They fixed up the ground there where the two children might play. All day long they watched them as they ran about together. When they would run together to one side over there, they would throw (shoot) both their arrows together. When it became evening then they would go inside. Now they were becoming large. The two children came outside, they took them the following day to play, they waited and watched for them, they took care of them as they played.

Now Blue Jay was going about. He thought, "If they cut them, then they would become separated into two. When they turn, they (their connecting membrane) becomes very very thin like hide."[21] Now he thought about it more and more. "Probably if they did only that to them, then they would become two." And that is what he was thinking, as he went about.

Then when on each successive day they took them again to play, the people came there, they kept watch on the two of them. Presently then Blue Jay himself followed them about. Then he thought, "Now I shall strike them with my feather crest." And now he did just that to them. When they (the watchers) had forgotten (to keep constant watch on the twins), they ran to one side, they passed by where Blue Jay stood. He hit at them with his crest, one went this way, one that way. They fell, they died. Their entrails came out. The people stood up, they took hold of the two of them, they took them to the house. Their mother said nothing. The people wept.

Blue Jay himself tried to weep, he wanted to but was unable to cry, no. So then he went to purchase a cry, he bought it from an old woman. When he purchased it she said to him, "What can be making your heart like that? Just say it tomorrow (as follows), When will I be again like that, that they will say to me, You too Blue Jay may eat the leftovers in the bucket. Say that!" So Blue Jay went, he wept, and he spoke in that manner what she had told him (to say in order to make him cry). But presently as he was dashing along he fell down, and he forgot it. Now he forgot her cry. In vain he did woo ah. He said, "No (that is not the cry I purchased)." He had forgotten her cry.

All done. The people quit (now). Then she said to him, "I shall go back home now. I shall take our two (dead) sons with me. If they had lived longer, then they would have become separate (without surgery). But now Blue Jay spoiled (and killed) them."

She made preparations, she went. She pulled at the (Spiders') rope, and they let the basket down forthwith. It dropped down. She took her two sons, (she held one) in one of her arms, she held the other in the other (arm). She held both of them under her arms. She said to him (to her husband), "The people (Indians) are close by now and they will see me (for I am Sun) when something (very bad) happens to a headman (or to a very wealthy man), and they will then see me and both my sons one on either side (of me at sunrise). Sometimes if only one (star is beside me at dawn), it will be just not so much of an upperclass man (some less well-to-do man will have suffered misfortune then). (Then) only one of my sons (only one star) will they see. I shall bring him out (into view then)." Now she went, they took her up above.

And then they (the villagers below) lived like that, they (again) became blind (because of their weeping over the twins' deaths).

Now story story.

Notes

1. This first slave girl entered and called out to her mistress, "Your son is crying." Before the mother noticed the presence of her slave, the crowd at the dance jostled the girl away to the other end of the house.
2. This dangerous being, whom I have termed the Basket Ogress, is a solitary figure who should be distinguished from the numerous Grizzly Women of Clackamas mythology. The Basket Ogress is a cognate of the Washington Sahaptins' ťaťaɫíya ogress and in changing features may be traced in mythologies hundreds of miles from the Columbia River. Clackamas thought of her as a woman with a pack basket who sought babies or children whom she might steal. When there was a heavy fog children were warned to stay inside lest she steal them. See also the short ethnographic text 88.
3. Mrs. Howard's grandmother used the morpheme -štiwɫ for "basket." Her mother-in-law, whose people came from villages along the Columbia River east of the Willamette, employed the morpheme -šḱali.
4. She was so pleased at Crane's sally about her manner of giving birth that she called the boy Crane's nephew. By such means she expressed acceptance of Crane as if he were her brother.
5. During the period of these secret visits to Crane, that worthy was making a bow, arrows, and an arrow-tool container or quiver for the youth, who did not know that these were to be given him for use on his trip back to his original home. Although the youth was now as tall as a man, the ogress did not allow him to walk with her. She insisted that he ride in her pack basket as if he were still an infant. When the youth decided to get rid of his foster mother, Crane also gave him a flint with which to sever her neck.
6. This is what wa'mqu, "Big Fir" said. Because each tree in the forest was her relative, each lamented her death in this manner. Each claimed her as a relative and as it fell it specified its relationship to her. Mrs. Howard remarked that older Clackamas storytellers would have gone through a fuller inventory of relationships than she was able to recall.
7. That is, "You must not crawl over people freely and in large numbers. There will be comparatively few of you." This is what he implied. Note that Greyback Louse people were thought of as feminine and whitish. The myth does not mention waqší'ti, "Black Louse."
8. He cracked and killed most of the Lice Women. That is why people since that time found few head lice and these were harmless. If he had not killed some

of the Lice, the Indians who were shortly to enter the land would have been killed by head lice. He decreed that head lice would be infrequent, harmless, and easily disposed of.

9. He killed most of these Nit Girls, but he allowed a few to survive and they were to annoy the Indians later on.

10. Had he not done this to Old Woman Darkness the Indians who were presently to come would have had a long period of daylight followed by a long period of darkness. His treatment of Darkness resulted in the modern tempo of succession of daytime and nighttime.

11. A Clackamas family collected urine of both sexes in *atǫi'kwal,* the "urine bowl" which was almost certainly of wood. Urine "made the hair feel good." Urine that stood a day or two was preferred for head hair. After a urine rinse the hair was cleaned with water. Urine was also rubbed over the body and it made the skin feel good and soft. Of course, the Indians washed with water after such a rub. The myth suggests that a dusty traveler availed himself of the host family's urine bowl. After he washed off the urine with fresh water, he obtained a comb from *iǫwa'ƛba,* a hide "bag" or "pocket," in which the host family kept several implements. Combs were perhaps of several kinds, of bone or of hard arrowwood slivers, the latter tied with sinew onto a central piece.

12. Mrs. Howard explained that he only pretended to comb with the murdered infant's shriveled hand, because no one could comb efficiently with such an implement. Neither the myth nor Mrs. Howard's explanation expresses explicitly the idea that the young traveler felt horror because he had to handle such a comb. It may be that Clackamas supposed, on a rational level, that the youthful traveler of the Myth Age reacted with frustration or irritation because the comb was inefficient rather than with horror because the comb was a dead infant's fingers.

13. The girl in the bag was the youngest of the five daughters of the first hunter whom he had encountered. The four older sisters put their younger sister in the bag when they went elsewhere. The so-called deer felled by the hunter was a human being. The hunter and his hideous family were *čúyušt,* which is a general term for Cannibal Persons of the Myth Age. The Sky Cannibal family depicted in this episode were only one type of Myth Age cannibal folk.

14. They giggled *hahe'··y²ana,* a stylized laugh that was peculiar to Sky Cannibal Girls. It occurred at the end of their spasms of laughter and adolescent girlish giggling.

15. The Sky Cannibal Hunter People, both male and female, lacked excretory and sexual organs. Their sole orifice was a mouth. No wonder that the young traveler found no urine bowl! The creatures he was visiting neither urinated nor defecated.

16. These Siamese twins were joined by flesh from hip to shoulder.

17. He pretended that he was asleep. But for a while, as she worked over his head in order to find lice, he peered below through the aperture and he observed various things in the land beneath.

18. The blind boy had been born of the reunited parents after the theft of the older brother who was now looking below.

19. Blue Jay pretended that he was the older brother who was in the sky country.
20. Mrs. Howard subsequently added the following, which explained why he was so upset. ... "He (Crane) had (long before) informed him, Your father's people are all blind (now). She (your true mother) gave birth to your one younger brother, but not until after this mother ... of yours had brought you to here." Now, when he saw and overheard the blind boy below, he inferred that it must be his younger brother, because Crane had told him that his entire family had become blind. He was also disturbed because of the manner in which Blue Jay attempted to dupe the blind boy. Clackamas believed that in the Myth Era the people cried and cried until they became blind.
21. Blue Jay observed that the membrane connecting the twins became thinner the older they got.

17

Coyote and Skunk. He Tied His Musk Sac

(Clackamas Chinook)

This story is a good example of Clackamas humor utilizing a variety of the stimuli Jacobs identified (in "Humor in Clackamas Chinook Oral Literature," in this volume), such as trickiness (Coyote), anality (Skunk), gullibility (animal victims), and greed (Coyote). Victoria Howard dictated the myth, "Coyote and Skunk. He Tied His Musk Sac,"[1] to Melville Jacobs in 1930 at Howard's home in West Linn, Oregon. Mrs. Howard also provided the English translation; the phonetic text and translation were originally published in *Clackamas Chinook Texts, Part 1* (Jacobs 1958, 13-18). Only the translation is reprinted here. A slightly different translation and a content-and-style analysis were published in Jacobs (1959b, 17-26). Footnotes are from Jacobs (1958, 268). Parallels can be found in the following: from Wishram Chinook (Sapir 1909, 149-53); from Klikitat Sahaptin (Jacobs 1934, 98-100); from Upper Cowlitz (Jacobs 1934, 177-79).

C oyote and Skunk lived there. They would look for something, they would eat it. I do not know how long they did like that. Then he (Coyote) said to him, "Younger brother. Supposing I tie you (your anus), and then I summon everyone, they will come to see you." "Oh no!" (in a pained tone). I do not know how many times he spoke to him (urging him), before he permitted him to. Then he (Coyote) tied him (his anus). He (Skunk) lay down. Then he (Coyote) went outside, he hallooed and hallooed,

> *"Who will come?*
> *Our younger brother might die (because of) his stomach."*[2]

Pretty soon a Doe came. "Oh dear! my older brother! oh dear! my older brother!" She came, she got to there. There Skunk lay. He was saying, "It is coming out! Hurry! It is coming out!" "Yes. Yes. You see him now. His spirit-power is getting ready to go out of him now (and when it does he will be dead).[3] Some shaman or other did like that to him" (said Coyote to Doe). "Indeed." He said to her, "Let us move him from there." "All right," she said to him. He said to her, "Hold his legs toward you, he is light on that side." She took hold of him, while Coyote (held) his head. They moved him. He untied him (Skunk's anus). He broke wind. Doe fell there. Coyote (and Skunk) had killed her. Now then Skunk's breath had all gone out of him there.[4]

Coyote butchered her, he roasted her (on spits), he ate her, he ate her all up. Some little pieces of bones remained lying there.

Skunk came to. There was absolutely nothing left in their house. He (Coyote) told him, "Here are a few small things (left for you). (Not just) one person got here, lots of them got to us." He (Skunk) took and ate the bones. Now again they were living there. They looked for various things, (and) that is what they ate.

After quite a while now again he (Coyote) said to him, "Younger brother. We are hungry. I will tie you again." "Oh dear no!" (in a pained voice). Then he said to him again, "There is nothing now for us to eat." "Oh no!" (pained voice again). So many times (Coyote urged him), and then he (Skunk) permitted him. He tied him (his anus). He lay down. He (Coyote) went outside, he hallooed,

"Who will come?
Our younger brother might die (on account of) his stomach."

I do not know how long, and then Buck came along. "Oh dear! my younger brother! Oh dear! my younger brother!" He got to them there. He said to him, "Observe what our younger brother is saying. I do not know where he has been going around, (and now) that is what some shaman has done to him." Now Skunk himself (said), "It is coming out! Hurry! It is coming out!" "Indeed" (Buck said). "Now that is his spirit-power speaking. Will you please help me." "Yes," he (Buck) said to him. "You take hold of him toward his legs, I by his head." They took hold of him, they moved him, he (Coyote) untied it, he broke wind at him. Buck fell back there (unconscious), Coyote killed him. He butchered him, he roasted him, he ate him, he finished eating all of him.

Only some few small pieces remained. Soon now Skunk came to. He looked around. (There was) nothing at all, only bones were there. He (Skunk) said to him, "Where is something for me?" He (Coyote) said to him, "Oh dear oh dear. People got to us. They took away absolutely all the meat" (and I had to share it with these guests). Skunk got up, he took the bones, he gnawed on them.

Now again they lived on (there). Coyote would go away, he would bring back some mice. That is what they would eat. As for Skunk, he would dig out yellow jackets, he would bring them back. They would eat them.

After a while then he again said to him, "Younger brother. Now there is nothing for us to eat." "Oh no!" (in a pained voice). After a while he (Coyote) spoke to him again. "Oh no! (pained voice). Something (bad) might come to us" (said in fear). He (Coyote) said to him, "No. Now I will (for safety sake) shut our house." After some time he (Skunk) said to him, "All right." So now he tied him again. He went outside, and he hallooed,

> "Who will come?
> Our younger brother might die (because of) his stomach!"

Even as he was hallooing, then along came a big Horned Buck. He came along, he got there. Then Skunk was saying, "It is coming out! Hurry! It is coming out!" "Yes yes yes yes! (said Coyote). Do you hear him? Now the spirit-power is leaving him (and he will die). I do not know where he was going about, (and then) some shaman did that to him." "It is going out!" (Skunk howled again). "Assist me (said Coyote). Let us take him close to the door." "All right," he (Horned Buck) said to him. They took hold of him, and then while they were taking him, he (Coyote) untied him. There Buck fell back (unconscious), he (Coyote) killed him too. He butchered him, he roasted him, he ate him, he ate him all up.

Shortly Skunk revived. He (Skunk) said to him, "What have you saved for me?" He said to him, "I was outside, people got to us, (and because they were guests) they took everything away." He (Skunk) said to him, "So! You are not going to tie me again." "No no younger brother! I have saved lots of things for you." "Hm! It is nothing." (But) he took the bones, those are what he chewed on.

The next day Skunk went somewhere or other to look for things (to eat). In the evening they came back. He (Coyote) said to him, "Younger brother. Now there are no more mice where I go." He

(Skunk) paid no heed. They lived on for a while, and then again he said to him, "Dear oh dear. Younger brother. We have nothing to eat now." He paid absolutely no heed. Skunk thought, "There is nothing (to eat) now. (But) I will not let him tie me." I do not know when it was, but it was a long time before he let him tie him (again). Coyote went outside, he hallooed,

> "Who will come?
> Our younger brother might die (because of) his stomach."

After some time now an Elk came along, he was weeping. He was saying, "Oh dear! my younger brother!" He got there. Skunk now was nearly dead (from waiting and from being tied for so long). He (Coyote) said to him (to Elk), "Come closer! come sit down! Now it (the spirit-power) is getting ready, the spirit-power is going to leave him." "Indeed" (said Elk). Now Skunk was dying (to all appearances). He was saying, "It is going out! Hurry! It is going out!" "To be sure. To be sure. Listen to him. Wherever he was going about, there some shaman did like that to him. Do assist me. We will lay him by the doorway." They took hold of him, they dragged him. He (Coyote) said to him, "Hold him by the legs." Coyote took hold of him, he untied him, he broke wind, Elk fell back there (unconscious). Coyote made haste, he killed him, he butchered him, he roasted him, he ate him.

Shortly then Skunk revived. He said to him, "Younger brother. I saved a lot of things for you." Skunk got up, he picked up bones and sinew and things, he ate them.

The fifth time, now I do not know what came. Maybe Grizzly, maybe something or other. It killed Coyote, but I think not Skunk. I recall only that much of it now.[5]

It told Skunk, "Your flatus will not kill people (after the Indians enter this land). You will just scare them somewhere or other by rotten logs. Then you will break wind, (and) they will only smell your vile odor. You will not kill people."

Notes

1. Mrs. Howard heard this myth told by her mother-in-law, Mrs. Watcheeno, whose Clackamas names were *wásusgani* and *wašʔa'wt*. The myth was recorded and translated toward the end of the second season of field research, in my notebook 16. For each story told by Mrs. Howard I indicate, as here, whether the specific source was her mother-in-law, her mother's

mother who was named *waga'yuɬn,* or some other Clackamas person or persons. Mrs. Howard believed that her mother's mother spoke the Clackamas dialect that was used at and near Oregon City, and that the relatives of her mother-in-law came from dialects spoken in villages just to the east of the Willamette River and along the Columbia River. Mrs. Watcheeno was in fact part Klikitat Sahaptin. I gather that her Chinook ancestry was largely from persons in the intergrading dialects between the Willamette River Clackamas and the Cascades Chinooks.

2. This call or song of Coyote was recorded on my Ediphone cylinder numbered 14547d. It was dubbed onto a tape numbered 11 in my collection. The recitalist repeated words and refrain many times.

3. See "Ethnographic texts on Shamanism and Spirit Powers," in this volume, where the narrator reports the belief that losing or being robbed of one's spirit power would cause death. Coyote persuades his intended victims to help him move Skunk because a dying person was moved either out of the house or at least close to the door so the corpse could be easily removed lest its presence lure the dangerous spirit back inside the house. [Eds.]

4. Mrs. Howard explained that Skunk "died a little" from the effort of discharging. Soon after he lost consciousness he came to.

5. Mrs. Howard regrettably failed to remember the fifth episode and conclusion. However, she added the final paragraph a few days later.

18

A Girls' Game

(Clackamas Chinook/Chinook Jargon)

This short ethnographic text was dictated to Melville Jacobs in Chinook Jargon and translated into English by Victoria Howard, Jacobs's Clackamas Chinook consultant. It was originally published in *Texts in Chinook Jargon* (1936, 12-13). It offers a glimpse into the domestic life of Chinook children. Descriptions of informal children's games are rare in Northwest ethnography, and descriptions of little girls at play especially so.

My mother told me how they used to play a game long ago. They would go get flowers, they would break off just the flowers, and they would tie them to a long rope. Then of as many of them as were there, one would stand a little apart. One of them hung the flowers on her, they placed them all over her, until her body was just covered with flowers. Then they danced.

One of those young girls would go to where that one was standing, and the one who was standing there would say, "Well, come! I see you are playing. What is the matter with your nose? It does not seem to be right. What is the matter with your eyes? One side is small. What is the matter with your head? It's crooked. What is the matter with your mouth? It is sort of twisted. Now you laugh! Look at me! Don't make your eyes crooked." Until at last if the young woman would laugh, at the one who did the talking, when she had not yet reached her, then she might laugh. "Now I have beaten you. Come now!"

Then they would make another one of them stand, and they would treat her the very same way. That one would go towards her, and she did it to her the same way. She would enumerate everything, for some time, and then the young girl would laugh too. She would say to her, "Now I have beaten you." But if the young woman did not laugh until she reached where she stood, then she (they) won from her.

19

Ethnographic Texts on Spirit-powers and Shamanism

(Santiam Kalapuya)

Jacobs, as his mentor Franz Boas had done, elicited non-traditional impromptu ethnographic texts in the Native language. Both he and Boas felt that Native language dictations contained fewer distortions of features of content and style than such texts told directly in English. These short ethnographic texts on aspects of Kalapuya religion were relayed to Melville Jacobs in the Santiam Kalapuya language, then translated into English by his principal Santiam consultant, John B. Hudson. Jacobs explained that "[n]o planned procedure guided the obtaining of these [ethnographic] texts. Whenever I supposed that … [Mr. Hudson] might give in his native speech some especially valuable rendering of an ethnologic point he had already phrased in English, I asked him to retell it in Santiam. This he always did unhesitatingly and rapidly. His translations were also apt and speedy" (Jacobs 1945, 5). Only the English translations of the texts are reprinted from *Kalapuya Texts* (Jacobs 1945, 51-52, 55-72).

49. Shamans can tell about missing people

Long ago the people used to say, "A shaman knows everything through his dreams. He sends out his dream-power when he wants to know what people are doing at some different place. If anyone went away to another place, (and) if he did not get back, then the people would say to a shaman, "Try (to see) what has become of that person. He has not gotten back. Maybe he will die." Then the shaman would say, "Done! (Very well!) Pretty soon I will try (to see with my dream-power) tonight."

Then if that person was not to die, then the next day the shaman would say, "Oh he is living. He is quite all right. He did not die." That is what he would say to the people. Now further then the people would learn when a person had died in a stream, when he had gone down in it, (and) the people could not find him, then they would send for a shaman who had dead people for his dream-power.[1] They would speak to that shaman—when that shaman had dead people for his dream-power, they would say, "He can converse easily enough in the dead people's language"—(saying to the shaman) "Speak to him! (to the drowned person). Where is he lying in the water?" Then the shaman would go at night to the water, and he would talk the language of dead people. Then he would say, "Ah yes. He is lying down below here." And so the people would go look where he said he (the drowned person) lay down below in the water, and sure enough they would find him there. Once in a while when they missed a person, then they would take what clothes that person had, and they would give them to the shaman (saying), "Can you try to see if that person is going to die?" They said (that) to the shaman. Then when the shaman would put that person's clothes under his head, when he was asleep at night, then the next day when he awakened, he said, "Oh I saw him last night. He is still living. He has not died." That is what the shaman would say it is said. Sure enough that person would return. That is what they used to do long ago it is said.

51. After a bad dream blow ashes on your child

Long ago the people, a person who had a child, once in a while he would sing to his child, just alone he would sing to his child. They would say that such a man (did that) when he had had a bad dream, when his dream was no good, then he would sing (one or more of his dream-power songs) to his child. And a woman would do the very same way too, she would (also) sing (her dream-power songs) once in a while (after a night of bad dreaming) to her child. When they sang (thus) to their children, they would take ashes, and they would slap the ashes together in their hands, and the ashes would go up in a puff, and they would blow the ash dust (on their child). It is said that that is the way they did. That is how they did if they had had a bad dream. Then they would scatter the ash dust about, and when they blew on the ashes, they would say in their hearts, "May it not become like that, like it was in my dream last night!" That is how they did it is said.

52. Seeking spirit-power

Always a boy who wanted to become a shaman, he was always swimming in the early morning. And when it became dark (at night), (and) the moon was full, then he would go to the mountain. He would fix up that spirit-power place on the mountain. He would go five nights. Always in the early morning he would be swimming. And then he would find his spirit-power, while he slept he would see his dream-power, his spirit-power. That is how he was (did) all the time. Then to be sure sometimes he would become a shaman, and he might be a big shaman. (But before that time) they would tell him, when he went away in the nighttime (to seek shamanistic spirit-powers), "Do not be fearful when you go about. You must get to where you have gone to." They told him, "If you are frightened, if you return before you have yet arrived at where you have gone to, it is not good for you to come back. You are cutting off your life" (if you do that).

53. Illness due to non-acceptance of new dream-power

The people used to say long ago that once in a while some one man who had not made good (had not carried out the instructions of) his dream-power, then that person would become ill. And he would continue to be ill all the time. Now then his relatives would say to that person who was sick, "It is better if we go fetch a shaman at once, (to see) what is making you like that. We will go get a shaman. What is your heart (your opinion)?" So then the sick person would say, "Your hearts (suit yourselves)!" Now then his relatives would fetch a shaman. Now when the shaman came to doctor him at nighttime, then the person who was ill, all his relatives came. And so the shaman doctored. Now then he said, "Oh but there is indeed nothing I can do. He himself knows what is doing that to him. It is his own spirit-power which is doing that. His dream told him, You are to do that! But then he did not do what his dream had told him. (To the patient:) Sing your (dream-power) song! Stand up at your dance! (dance!) Pay these people when they help you (by singing and dancing your dream-power song dance with you)!" That is what that shaman would tell the sick person. The shaman would say of that person, "If he will stand up to his dance maybe he will become well." Then when the shaman went back home, now those people discussed it with one another. And then they said, "It may be better if we get (more) people together now" (to help in the dream-power song dance to be given). They said to the sick person, "It will be good now for you to sing." So then the sick person said, "Done! I will sing!" And then sure enough they would assemble (more) people, and they went to fetch that shaman again (to have him present to assist at the dream-power dance). Now then when the sick person was to sing, once in a while the sick person would say, "I have no dream-power song of my own!" Then the shaman would say, "Oh you do have a dream-power song. Now I myself will sing your song!" So then the shaman would sing. And the sick person who had said that he had no song, he himself would sing. It was as if he (the shaman) were indeed not in his heart (as if he were out of his mind), when he sang the song, when the shaman sang it. Now then the shaman remained by the sick person. When the person stood dancing, the shaman stood right there (by him) too, he watched the sick person closely. And the rest of the people were all singing and standing dancing (his song, too). That is how they used to do. They stood at their dancing (they danced) for five nights. And now on the fifth night, when it was in the middle of the night during the night, the people took a rest, they ate, when they finished eating then they (again) stood up to their dancing. And now when it became morning, then that was the time that they ceased their dancing. Now they (the sick person and his relatives) paid all those people who had stood at the dancing, who had assisted the sick person (by singing and dancing his dream-power song dance with him). And sure enough that sick person would become well again. That is how they used to do. If that is what the shaman had said, and they did that, then he would get well again. And the people said, "It was his dream-power to be sure. That is what did it. It was his singing and his standing at his dance, and then he got well again." They also paid that shaman.

54. Taking the dream-power of another person

They used to say that once in a while if a shaman knew in his heart (sensed, believed) that he would not be good in heart (would not live much longer), he would give his dream-power to some one who was his very best (his closest) relative. And so then when he (the shaman) gave it to him, and when that shaman died, the person to whom he had given it, he himself would take (obtain, receive) that dream-power, (and) he (too) might become a shaman. That is the way they used to do so they say.

Long ago they used to say that some shamans would take another person's dream-power, from this person who had always sung his (dream-power) song (at winter power-renewal dances), and then when he died, then later some other shaman would sing that (dream-power) song of his, the song of the person who had died. Thereupon they said, "This shaman is singing that (deceased) person's song. Maybe he himself had taken that man's dream-power" (and so killed him). That is what they said.

55. Shamans and spirit-powers

Long ago when a shaman wanted to kill a person, he would hit (shoot) him with whatever spirit-power he possessed (that was fatal). If his spirit-power was rattlesnake he would strike (shoot) a person with it. And if his spirit-power was grizzly rather, he would send grizzly to kill that person. Those grizzly and rattlesnake (spirit-powers) were very bad spirit-powers of theirs. Some other people had dead persons for their spirit-power, (and) they would shoot with dead people, who were their spirit-power. The shamans, some of the shamans, were bad. They were always killing people with their (death-dealing) spirit-power. Then some other shamans would say, "It is the spirit-power of that (bad) shaman (whom they then named). That is what has caused it for this (sick and doomed) man." Then they (people) would go fetch that (accused bad) shaman, they would say to him, "They say it is your own dream (your bad dream-power or spirit-power) which has been doing this in this manner." And then that (accused) shaman sure enough would (judge it safer and wiser for himself to) go to doctor that person, (he would extract his own bad spirit-power from the sick person) and the person then would become well again. But on the other hand sometimes that (accused and guilty) shaman would say (denying complicity), "It is his own spirit-power that has done this (which is making him ill)." And so then when that shaman would not (go to) cure that (sick) person (remove the fatal spirit- power from his body), and when the person died, then they might kill that shaman. That is what long ago those people always used to do it is said. They would always kill shamans, when they said in their hearts (when the people believed) they were bad shamans (had fatal spirit-powers which were killing people). That is what they always did.

The shamans themselves would say, there was nothing indeed that they could do in their heart (they could not entirely control their own powerful spirit-powers), if their spirit-powers told them, "Kill a person! We want to eat blood. And well now if you do not kill a person, we will kill you. But then if you do kill a person now (so that we can feed on some blood), you will live long, if you do what we tell you. If you do that, you will live always (a very long time)." That is how the shamans spoke (explained about themselves) long ago.

The other people who were not shamans, those who just had (non-shamanistic) spirit-powers, they would sing (the songs of their dream-powers too). But a shaman's spirit-power however was extremely strong (stronger than non-shamanistic dream-power). Some of these shamans whose spirit-power was dead people, they would sing (their dream-power songs) at night. Then they would go outside, they would address themselves to dead people. That is what they said. Whatever they wanted to learn, they would ask the dead people. If a man (a shaman) had a dead person for his spirit-power, he would address his words to the dead person. That is what they said. But as for an ordinary person (who had no powerful or shamanistic dream-power), he did not know very much (i.e., had no powerful dream-power guardian). He would merely sing his (ordinary, weak) spirit-power song, he would stand up to his dance (too). If he saw gambling in his (spirit-power) dream, then he might know (well) how to gamble. That is what they used to say.

Some of the shamans would address their spirit-powers, when they wanted to learn (something), at the place where they sent their dream-power off to a distance so they say. Then their dream-power would go (to there), and it would come back again, and it would tell the shaman what was the matter with the people at the place to where he had sent his dream-power. That is what they say. When his spirit-power came back, then it told the shaman what they were doing yonder where the spirit-power came from.

56. Winter dances to strengthen dream-powers

Long ago the shamans fixed up their (own) dream-powers during the wintertime. When some one shaman wanted to fix up his spirit-power, he got together a lot of people, and he (and they) stood at his dance (he danced), he stood at his dance for five nights. Everybody came. Those who had assembled stood up at their own dance (too). Of all those people when they stood at their dance, the older (bigger, wealthier) people themselves sang their own (dream-power) songs, (and) in the very same manner the women sang their own songs. The shaman (who was giving the dance) himself sang his own songs first, and those others who were also shamans, when they came to their own dance, they (also) sang ahead (of non-shamans). These mere common people (who lacked shamanistic dream-powers) sang after (the shamans). Always when they sang one song, they would throw (sing) that song five times (before proceeding to another song). Always on the fifth night in the middle of the night, they would all eat when they rested. And then they would stand up to their dancing again, and (only) when morning came they would cease their dancing. Once in a while the shaman sent off a relative of his, he told him to kill one ox. Then those people would skin it, and they would distribute pieces of it, they would (thus) pay them for (assisting by) standing at their dancing. To some of the men and women they would give out clothes, with this they paid them for their standing at their dancing. They would say of that shaman, "Now indeed he has been making good (bettering, strengthening) his spirit-power." That is what the shamans always did in the wintertime, when they stood up to their dance.

57. Canes and feathers for shamans' spirit-powers

Long long ago shamans got spirit-powers. For their spirit-powers some of them painted canes, (and) they called them their spirit-powers. On the other hand some of them had what they called their feathers which were their spirit powers. It is said that this is the way they always used to speak. "The one who is wearing his feather, that thing (bird) is his spirit-power." And on the other hand some of those who were holding their canes when they stood at their (spirit power) dance, they would say (of such persons). "That is his spirit-power, which he is holding (represented) on his cane, when he stands at his (spirit-power) dance." That is the way those people of long ago commented.

58. Shamans extract poison-powers

They said that when a shaman was doctoring a person, and when he saw what made the person (ill) that way, (and) it was just an ordinary (non poison-power caused) sickness, he would say, "No one did this like that (by shooting a poison-power at him). He is just ill (of some non poison-power caused sickness)." Then if he had a sickness, (caused by a poison-power) which the shaman extracted with his mouth, and he sucked on the place where he had the ailment, and he extracted it, then the shaman would say, "Now he will get well again." And sure enough that person would become well again. But sometimes doctors would say, when he doctored a person, that he could see another shaman's poison-power residing in him (inside the patient) as poison-power. Then the shaman would say, "That poison-power is in him there. I myself do not know it (I myself do not have that same type of poison-spirit-power). I could never extract it. I must cease doctoring him. Go fetch another shaman. Perhaps he may readily know (have for his own spirit-power) that poison-power." Then the people would go fetch another shaman. Now when that shaman arrived, and he doctored, and then when he saw the poison-power residing in there, then he would say, "Oh I know (I myself have and have power over) this poison-power! It is that (yonder) shaman's poison-power. What shall I do with it now? Shall I take it out?" That is what that shaman would say. Then the sick person's relatives would say, "Take out that poison-power if you know it (if you have it for your own dream-power and can handle it)!" Then sure enough that shaman would extract the poison-power. And then he would say, "I shall kill this poison-power!" (also thus weakening the life of its malevolent sender). But sometimes he would (just) throw the poison-power some (safe) distance away, the shaman would throw it away when he extracted the poison-power. That so they say is what they used to do.

59. The shaman's interlocutor-speaker

Long ago whenever a shaman doctored, another person always talked to the shaman. He would say to him, "Now make yourself strong of heart (get your spirit-power to its fullest strength)! (Cure) make that (sick) person good! You are a shaman! So now cure that person!" And then when the shaman talked, that other person repeated the words of the shaman. That is the way they always did they said.

60. Shamans can take away guardian-powers from people

A shaman would take away the spirit-power of another person. That shaman would sing the spirit-power song of that person, he would make it his own spirit-power song. Then the rest of the people, when they heard (him sing) the spirit-power song, they would say, "That was his song first, and now this shaman is singing the song."

A shaman would do that to some people. Then they would call him a mean shaman. "He is no good. He takes away guardian-power from people." Not all shamans did like that. They said that some of them were good. That is what the people used to say long ago.

Long ago when a shaman would sing some of the spirit-power songs, they would say, "What he is singing is from long ago. He merely knows from long ago that power song that he is singing now. That one is not his own guardian power." That is the way the people would speak. These shamans would take away the guardian-power from the mere common people (who were not shamans). They could not take away the guardian-power from a shaman. That is what they said.

The people said, "His guardian-spirit-power is gone. Now he is going to die soon." That is how it was with those people when they forgot their power song and could not sing their song. They would say, "Maybe now he is pretty nearly dead. He does not know his own spirit-power song." (Some shaman had stolen it.)

61. Shamans poisoned drinking water

Long ago some of the shamans, they said, got water, and then they blew upon the water, it turned into blood. Then when they gave that water, and the people drank that water, they would die.

62. Visiting shamans paint their faces

Long ago the shamans and the people (who accompanied them), when they went off (to visit) to another place (village), the shamans would paint their faces, all of those shamans (would do that).[2] It is said that they said (to their own people who went along with them), "Now we are taking care of you," those shamans (would say that) to their own people. That is how they did it is said. The other (visited) people's shaman would know, now then he would not try to do anything (ill) to these (visiting) people, when he saw that those other shamans had their faces painted (indicating that their dream-powers were strong and alertly on the defense). Now they would know that their faces were not just painted for nothing. That is what they used to say.

63. The Americans prohibit killing shamans

These (Indian) people used to say that when the Americans got to this country, then the shamans became somewhat stronger of heart (their dream-powers increased in strength). These Americans did not want the (Indian) people to kill a shaman. The Indians would tell an American, "That shaman killed my relative." The Americans would say, "What did he do when he killed your relative?" Then our people would say, "That Indian shaman poisoned my relative. It is that shaman who killed my relative." "Oh," the American would say. "He could never kill a person! That shaman is just the same as any ordinary person. There is nothing he could kill, such as you are telling me about." That is what the Americans said. So then we quit killing shamans. The Americans said, "If you should kill a person for nothing, we will hang you." That is how they used to speak to the Indians long ago. They did not want to know (anything about) the Indians' dream-powers. They (the Americans) said, "It could never be like that. A shaman is only an ordinary (not possessed of special powers) person."

64. Shamans could not kill Americans

Long ago (among) the Indians the shaman would say, that he was unable to kill an American, with his guardian-dream-power, when he threw (shot) his fatal poison-power at the American, it would just go right through his body (without causing him to become ill). They could never kill Americans with their dream-powers. Many shamans tried to kill Americans. Once in a while, they would say, the fatal-poison-power would hurt them a little bit, when it was shot into their knee. But then in a very little time they would become well again. That fatal-poison-power did not stay in them at all. They would say that an American's body was not at all like an Indian's body. They would say that an American's body, and their blood, were sort of thinner. It was not thick like an Indian's body (hence the poison-power would pass right through). Americans' bodies were like that (they were of thinner blood and texture). That is what the Indian shamans used to say.

65. Joseph Zangretter's spirit-powers

One man, a shaman (Zangretter—he was part Mary's River Kalapuya), said, long long ago when there were many people (Indians) here, he always knew who was going to die—a man, a child, (or) a woman, he knew it first. He said, "I have two spirit-powers. One is a black man, the other one is like us in body (in appearance an Indian)." They always came in his dream, always when he had a bad dream, he would see those two people in his dream. In his dream they would tell him, "I know who is the person's name." Then they would name that person's name. "Now that one has (virtually) died." They would tell him, "Now he will die." Sure enough such persons would get sick (and) they would

John B. Hudson, Jacobs's Santiam Kalapuya consultant.
(photo courtesy National Archives and Records Administration,
Pacific Alaska Region, Seattle)

die. And now "That (other) person will get sick. (But) he will not die. He will get well again." Sure enough such a one would always be like that (become ill and then recover). When a shaman saw a person's spirit-power, they said that the person would die. So now (too) he (Zangretter) would say in his heart (would say to himself), " It is a long time now that you have been (virtually) dead." Now then when that person's (Zangretter's) dream-powers told him, "That person will be ill, (but) he will not die," and when he heard of it he would get a shaman to doctor on that person. When his (Zangretter's) spirit-powers told him, "That person will not die," then that shaman (Zangretter) would say in his heart (say to himself), "Oh that shaman will cure that person now when he doctors him." But when they fetched a shaman to doctor on a sick person, if his (Zangretter's) spirit-powers had said to him, "He is (really) dead a long time now," then he (Zangretter) would say in his heart (say to himself), "Oh he is doctoring him in vain. He cannot make that person well." Now then he (Zangretter) told us, that was how it was he always knew who would die. On the other hand those others who were not going to die, when they became ill, he always knew it. "But now those two dream-powers of mine never talk to me any more. They are always hiding on the other side of a tree. If I talk to them my two spirit-powers never talk to me any more in my dreams. They never address me. Now my heart tells me (I think that) I am now near death. That is what my heart says (that is what I believe)."

66. Peter Selky. Jack Pícimin

There was one Yamhill man who had strong spirit-power. Now his spirit-power was so very strong, they said, that when he became angry his spirit-power shook. They say that his spirit-power was thunder, when the thunder roared, and when it rained down quantities of water. And another too of his spirit-powers, his spirit-power was deer they say. And very well did he know how to hunt. He always killed many deer. When the people wanted deer (meat) they went to his house, there they bought deer. That is how the people did. The name of that man was se'lkya (Peter Selky, husband of Louisa). At the time that I (first) saw him he was (already) a large man. Now when he was getting old he would always go on horse (horseback). He would ride a horse when he went hunting. When he stood at his (spirit-power) dance he did not hold in hand his spirit-power (such as a cane or feather). He merely stood at his dance when he sang what was his own spirit-power song.

Another man whom I saw was named Jack pícimin. They said he too had a very strong spirit-power. He was a shaman. His (home) place (village) was Yonkalla. Jack pícimin was a shaman, his spirit-power was strong. If he wanted it to rain he moved his spirit-power (i.e. he "shook" it, he thought about it while he danced and sang its songs). And then it would rain. I saw that man. That is how that man was. He was a Yonkalla man. His wife was a Molale woman.

67. A shaman dreamed the earth became black like ploughed land

Long ago the people used to say that one great shaman in his dream had seen all the land black in his dream. That is what he told the people. "This earth was all black (in my dream)." He saw it in a dream at night. Just what that was likely to be he did not know. And then (later on) the rest of the people saw the whites plough up the ground. Now then they said, "That must have been what it was that the shaman saw long ago in his sleep."

68. Large black woodpecker dream-power

They used to say long ago that the large black woodpecker knew (learned of) everything, he observed everything. If some one was coming from the rear, then he would notice it at once. They said that he knew a (another) person's heart (could see another person's dream-powers). Should some one want to kill him (to kill a person who had this woodpecker for a dream-power guardian), he (this woodpecker) would know it they say (and would tell of the danger). That is what the people said.

69. Dead person spirit-power

They said that one of the shamans knew how to converse with dead people. It is said that once he did try his heart (tried using his dead person dream-power) there at Yamhill where those (Yamhill) Indians lived. One man (a Yamhill named Frank Bond) had gone yonder to the ocean coast. And he did not come back at the time that he had said he would return. Now then that man's mother (named Mrs. Miller) wept. She said in her heart (she thought to herself) that her son had perhaps been killed there yonder where he had gone away to the seacoast. Now then the old man (a Yamhill shaman named Gílya; white name, Amos) who knew how to speak with dead people (had a dream-power giving him that ability) said to the old woman (Mrs. Miller), "Now I will try to find out in my heart (with my dead person dream-power) what is the matter with your son. Give me his old coat, the one he always wears. I will make it my pillow. I will sleep here now. Pretty soon then I will see (through my spirit-power) what has become of him, if he is still living or if he is dead." And then when it became morning the old man said, "I did see him. He is staying there at Garibaldi. It is all right. There is really nothing the matter at all. Maybe he will be back pretty soon." The man (shaman) said this to his (Frank Bond's) mother when it became morning. That is how one woman (Adeline Bond, a cousin of Mr. Hudson's—the Santiams called her ɛ'Dəlyɛn)—told me about it. That is all I know of it. Sure enough the (missing) man did come back to his home here where he had started from when he had gone off to the seacoast.

70. Shamanistic power over rain and thunder

Long ago the people used to say, if a big shaman had thunder for his dream-power, if that shaman were killed, the thunder would sound very hard (loud), (and) it would rain directly. Then when the people heard the thunder's voice like that, they would say, "Maybe they have killed someone who is a shaman."

Once in a while indeed when the thunder sounded (rumbled) on a fine day, when it sounded, and when it rained, and then it cleared up again, they would say, "Maybe some one who is a man who has a big heart (has a powerful dream-power), who has a (powerful) dream-power, maybe he has been stabbed." When that one with a big heart (a strong guardian-power) was injured, (and) it would rain, and the thunder would sound (roar), and then it cleared up again, then the people would say every time, "Maybe some one who has a big heart has been injured. Or maybe he has been stabbed." That is what the people would say.

That is what the people said every time. They carefully noticed the thunder when it sounded. Right away that is what the people would say. Once in a while if it rained hard, they would say each time, "A, shaman is doing that." (Thus) every time that it kept raining. Then they would tell a shaman, "Can you not try to stop this raining?" Then the shaman would try to halt this rain. Sure enough once in a while it would clear up again. But once in a while it just kept on raining. They would always say, "The shaman who is causing this up above here," they would say, "he has great dream-power, it is big (and) it is strong. This (other) shaman cannot clear it up above here." That is how the people spoke. When the shaman did like that (tried to stop rain), they would not pay him.

All these people were merely good (felt happy) in their hearts towards the shaman who tried to clear it up above again. On the other hand when the shaman doctored a person, they always paid him. He could not just doctor him for nothing.

71. The ghost dance (warm house dance) at Grand Ronde

Long ago these people (here at Grand Ronde) always used to stand at their dance (to dance here, the warm house dance). There was a large house of theirs, there they stood at their dance (they danced). They built a fire in the center of the house. Now then all who would stand at their dance danced. They had all painted themselves. They striped (themselves) with the paint. There was white paint, and there was black paint, and there was red paint. Then they would dance. They ran (around the fire) ..., all those who were dancing would run around the fire. And then they would stop their dancing, and they would kick (stamp) their foot on the ground. Then the rest of the people would be standing at the side, they were all singing. Some of the men held small split sticks, and they hit their hands with them.

Notes

1. Jacobs uses two English words, "dream power" or "spirit power" for the same Kalapuya word. Some spirit helpers were acquired through dreams and some, for example shamans' powers, from questing in the wilderness, but Kalapuyans seem to have used the same word for both. [Eds.}
2. No doubt the shamans' face paint is the overt aspect of their technique for keeping their spirit-powers at full strength; this in order to ward off the other shamans' spirit-powers which might cause injury to the visitors.

20

Some Shakers Find the Body of My Brother's Child

(Santiam Kalapuya)

John B. Hudson, one of Jacobs's Santiam Kalapuya consultants, dictated this historical event text in the Santiam language. The text recounts the tragic drowning of Mr. Hudson's young nephew, Lloyd F. Hudson (1919-1928), and the Indian Shakers' successful efforts to find and retrieve his body from the Yamhill River. Believing themselves inspired by the Holy Spirit, or spirit of the Christian God, Shakers cured and divined much as shamans, but unlike shamans did not accept pay for their work. Success depended less on an individual Shaker's inspiration than on a unified effort by all the Shakers present. Jacobs implies that the Shakers were guided by their aboriginal-style dream powers. Although some converts to Shakerism were able to "convert" their dream powers, others had to abandon their old spirit helpers as a condition of embracing the new faith. For information on the Indian Shaker Church, see Barnett (1957), Amoss (1990), and Ruby and Brown (1996). The English translation of this text, reprinted below, is from *Kalapuya Texts* (Jacobs 1945, 52-55).

Now I will briefly recount how it once happened to one of my relatives (my brother Abe) here at this place (Grand Ronde) where we live. My brother's child (a boy aged about six or eight) fell into the water from a foot log bridge (over the Yamhill River). He slipped on it, and then he fell into the water.

Now then we were unable to find him. We sought him there in the water. We did not know where to find him. We searched for him perhaps two days.

Two whites arrived from the place we call *tcami'GiDε,* and (which) the whites now (call) Salem. They call the place that now. They looked for that child that had fallen into the water. They could not find him. So then when it became dark they went back (to Salem).

Now that brother of mine said to me, "What do you think if I go get those whom they call Shakers?" Well then I said to him, "(Follow) your own heart (suit yourself). If you go get them, it might perhaps be good if they do find the child." So then sure enough he went to fetch them. He threw (sent off) a paper (letter). Indeed those people (Shakers living at Siletz) came (in several autos) on the next morning. Now I will tell you who (what) were those (Shaker) people's names who came. One man's name was Jakie Johnson. I do not quite know just where that man's place (his native group's locale) was. Perhaps he is part seashore-people (anywhere from Nehalem Tillamook south to Coos Bay), (and) he is part Siletz (i.e. from the Takelma, Lower Coquille Miluk Coos, or any southwestern Oregon Athabaskan). I myself do not quite well know.

There was another one whose name is Hank Johnson.[1] Maybe he is part Alsea and (part) Umpqua. That is his place (the original village homes of his parents) maybe. And there was another whose name (was) Tommy Jackson,[2] he was an Alsea person. And another person's name was Orton. He is a Siletz (from one of the Siletz Reservation bands) they say. And another person too whose name is Oscar Wood. He perhaps—I do not quite well know—(is) a Klikitat (southern Washington Sahaptin) person. And another person too, I do not know what her name is."[3] That (latter) elderly woman said this, "I saw the child in my dream this morning. He was brought (dead) into the house." That is as much as I know of (this part of) my narrative, this that I am relating.

Now then they (these Shakers from Siletz Reservation) sang. They had with them many small bells (large hand gongs[4] such as are used in elementary schools), and whites' pitch (i.e. candles). These they lit. They held the burning pitch (candles). That is how they did (they sang and danced, holding candles or ringing gongs) on that day when they got there (they danced and sang outside the Grand Ronde schoolhouse). And then when it became dark they stood at their dance (danced), those (Shakers) who had come from Siletz, those people who had arrived (they continued dancing into the night). They were all Shakers they say. People say that those who are that kind of person (who are Shakers and have Shaker spirit-powers)[5] know all (sorts of) things (have many strong dream-powers), when they sing (and) they stand at their dance. And indeed (later) during that night they (the Shakers) had much discussion (among themselves), and then they said, "We do know that he fell into the water. He slipped on the foot log bridge, he fell into the water. Perhaps we may not find him now. We do not know (what our dream-powers indicate) that it is all good how we work (we seem to be of unfortunately different dream-power knowledge as to where his body may be lying). Some of us people are different here in our hearts, we are not all one at heart (our dream-powers differ in their information)." That is how they spoke when those people discussed it that evening.

So then the next morning they wanted to return (to their Siletz homes, feeling that they had failed). Now then my brother said to them, "Better if you try it once again (sing and dance and try to learn from your dream-powers)." And indeed one woman of those Shakers (possibly Mrs. Albert) in the morning said then, "Yes. Now we may find him pretty soon. Maybe I did see him in my dream this (early) morning. He was brought inside. The little child was laid here. He had on trousers. And he also had his coat on him. That is how I saw him in my dream this morning. Now let us go try to find him." Then sure enough they all went away. Some went to the other side of the stream. They crossed on the foot log bridge. But some others did not cross over. Now then they went on down below, they sang (seeking the aid of their dream-powers) as they went along. Now three persons got into a canoe, they too went along by canoe. Then they went on a little below there where I live (downriver from my house), and sure enough below that place they found the child lying in the water. He was lying they say face down in the water when they found him.

And those three persons who were in the boat, one of them saw him first. Those two (others who) were seated in the boat, they did not see him, they had not noticed. Only that one (who had the best dream-power) saw him. Now then he got out of the boat, and he went in the water, and then he got near to it where it was lying. Then those two (other) persons saw it indeed. Now the one who had gone into the water took hold of the child, and he drew him out of the water. Then they took the child back to his house where he had lived.

Notes

1. Hank Johnson was one of Dr. Frachtenberg's interpreters for the Lower Umpqua-Siuslaw language.
2. Tommy Jackson was Dr. Frachtenberg's principal informant for the Alsea language. He died in 1929.
3. I think that this may be the present wife of John Albert, the last speaker of Alsea. Like her husband, Mrs. Albert is today a devout Shaker; natively she is from an Athabaskan dialect spoken on the seacoast between Euchre Creek and Miluk Coos.
4. Jacobs has chosen a peculiar and inaccurate descriptor. Bells have clappers that strike the sides of the chamber when the bell is swung; gongs do not. The Shakers use bells. [Eds.]
5. Note that all reference to "dream power" or "spirit power" appears in Jacobs's interpolations, not in the actual text. The one reference to "dream" appears below when Mrs. Albert reported that she saw the child's body "in my dream." This is an example of Jacobs's tendency to extrapolate beyond the text. [Eds.]

21

The Origin of Death

(Upper Coquille Athabaskan/Chinook Jargon)

The myth text, "The Origin of Death," was dictated to Melville Jacobs in Chinook Jargon and translated into English by Coquelle Thompson, Sr. at the Siletz Reservation, Oregon, in December 1935. The phonetic text and translation were published in *Texts in Chinook Jargon* (Jacobs 1936, 26-27); only the translation is reprinted here. Chinook Jargon was a trade language developed on the lower Columbia incorporating a simplified grammar from Chinook and adding vocabulary items from other Indian languages and later from English and French. During the fur trade period it was used along the coast north to southeast Alaska and south to California. Elizabeth D. Jacobs, who elicited the same story from Thompson in English only, recorded in her fieldnotes his explanation for the name "Coyote Jim": "Started calling Coyote Jim every since White people came in cause White people didn't understand Coyote was person. So they tacked on 'Jim'. They really just call him Coyote" (E. Jacobs 1935). In Western Oregon there are cognate texts from the Alsea (Frachtenberg 1920, 116-17), the Coos (Frachtenberg 1913, 42-45; 1922, 419-22; Jacobs 1940, 135-36), the Kalapuya (Jacobs 1936, 18-19; 1945, 137-38; 226-27), and the Takelma (Sapir 1909, 98-101). For the wider distribution of this tale-type see Boas (1917).

They dwelt some distance apart in their (respective) houses. Well, that person had a son, (and) that one yonder (also) had a son. Well, the son of that man became ill, well, the youngster was sick perhaps two days, and then the young man died. Well, that man was extremely sick at heart. He cried. Well, he put him in the ground, he had the ground covered over. Well then, he went back home, he was sick at heart.

Well, now (when it was) four days he went to Coyote Jim, he went to see him. He found him at home. Now then that man said, "It will be well if when a person dies, it will be well if that dead person comes back on the fifth day after, (it will be well) if he returns in five days." That is how he spoke to Coyote Jim.

Now then Coyote Jim did not (at once) respond to these words. Well then, after a while Coyote Jim replied, "So thus you say a person is to come back, if then a dead person is to return in five days." "Well, that is what I wish to say." "Well, my friend, I say to you that if persons return within five days, wherever you live, if they return in five days, it will be bad for the people like that because there will be no ground to stand on, there will be an extreme lack of food, you will be unable to sleep for lack of ground." That is the way Coyote Jim spoke to the man. "Now then, now those dead people will not return after five days, they will not come back in five days."

Well, now Coyote Jim's son became ill, and then he died. Well, now Coyote Jim was very sick at heart. Well, now he put him in the ground. That was how he went outside, he fell down on the ground (in a transport of grief). Well, now then four days passed. His partner (neighbor) lived a short distance away. Now then he went yonder to that man's house.

Well, he said, "I want my child to return. Now it is four days, and tomorrow it is five days. That is how I wish my child to return on the fifth day. That is what I want. I am unable to sleep, I am sick at heart. Now it is for that that I have come to see you, I am so sick at heart. Let dead persons return on the fifth day. That is what I wish now."

Then that man said in reply, "Well, now I myself am becoming black (bug).[1] This is how I feel no longer sad, now my heart has become good again (no longer sad)." Well, so then that man said, "You gave that word (law) to me. Well, what you said was right. Now I have become black (bug), and now it has become the law."

Editors' Notes

1. Several Indian groups in western Oregon and northwestern California associated the origin of death with an insect: Clackamas Chinook (see "Badger and Coyote Were Neighbors," this volume), Takelma (Sapir 1909, 99-101), and Yurok (Kroeber 1976, 47-54).

22

Small Bird Hawk Had His Head Cut Off

(Hanis Coos)

This myth adventure recounts how two brothers ascend to the Sky country by means of an arrow chain ladder in order to avenge the murder of their father and retrieve his severed head. Annie Miner Peterson dictated the myth, "Small Bird Hawk Had His Head Cut Off," in the Hanis Coos language to Melville Jacobs in 1933 at Charleston, Oregon. Mrs. Peterson also provided the English translation; the phonetically-recorded text and translation were first published in *Coos Myth Texts* (Jacobs 1940, 235-38). Only the English translation is reprinted below. According to a note by Jacobs, Mrs. Peterson had heard this story from Old Dick, a Hanis Indian, when she was about ten or twelve years old. A cognate Hanis version, "The Revenge of the Sky People," was published by Frachtenberg (1913, 149-57). See Hymes (1981, 274-308) and Ramsey (1983, 76-95) for an extended discussion of this and a related Clackamas Chinook text, "Seal and Her Younger Brother Dwelt There" (Jacobs 1959a: 340-41). Parallel texts can be found among the Alsea (Frachtenberg 1920, 137-49) and the Tillamook (Boas 1898, 136-38 and E. Jacobs 1990, 24-28).

Many people lived there. There were five brothers (small bird hawks). Now one of them married, and then he had two (male) children. He made canoes all the time. One day he did not return. Now they (his two sons) searched for him. He was just in that canoe, headless. Only his dog looked upward when it barked. No one knew why. "I wonder why the dog looks above." Then one of the youngsters dreamed thus, "They took your father's head up above. If you want him do not bury your father.

Annie Miner Peterson, Jacobs's Coos consultant, 1934, Charleston, Oregon

Just let him be lying. Both of you go, you will find your father's head. Now you must shoot up above." So they did. "Your arrows will join together, and then you may climb up to there." That is what the young man dreamed. Indeed that is what they did. So the next day this is what he said to his older brother, "That was the way I dreamed. Let us try it." Indeed they went to there where he made the canoe, there they went. Indeed they shot (up to the sky), and sure enough their arrows joined together. Now indeed they stood straight up (from the ground to the sky, a chain ladder), and so then they climbed up on it, and they ascended to a different country.

Now they went along, they went over a prairie, and then they found a trail. Then they went along it, and now they heard a person singing. So they went to there, and there were girls, they were digging for roots. Now the girls saw the young man. Then this is what the young man said, "What is it? What are you digging for there?" "*Hú‥* there is going to be a big time. Our husband brought back a below world head, and they are dancing on account of it, they are going to have a big time and feast (a return-from-war dance)." That is what the girl explained to the young man. Now this is what the young man said, 'We want you (to be our wives)." "Very good. We ourselves desire you too." "If you want us you

must explain to us what your people do." Of course then the girls
explained it all. "Up above on the rafter slats is where they keep the
head of your father. And when we cross (the river here) the
ferryman does not land, he comes only just so far to here, and then
we jump into it." That is what the girls explained to the youths.
"When we have been taken across," this is how they explained to
the youths, "And when we have gotten home, then they cook,
because there will be a big (return-from-war) dance. People will
come from all over." That is how they explained to the youths.
"And when it is getting towards evening, we give food to all the old
people, and wood similarly. But one house standing at the end (of
the village), old people live in it there, we never give them anything.

And when we go to bed then we play (mere play) with our
husband until he goes to sleep. Then we do not bother with him
any more. Because of the (return-from-war) dance he has nothing
to do (sexually) with us then, for he is their chief, and it is he who
got your father's head." That is what they explained to them. And
now the young men (spoke) thus, "Let us wear your garments.
Then when we return home we will take you back with us."

Indeed so it was. Now the young men put on the girls' garments,
and then they went along. Indeed the ferryman came across, and
sure enough it was just so far, and the (one) young man jumped,
and to be sure he got into it. Then the other one jumped too, oh,
one of his feet dragged on one side of it. "ʾú· my pack is too heavy
today. That is why my foot missed it." Indeed he (the ferryman)
said nothing (deceived by the alibi). Just the way the girls told
them, they did just as the girls had told them. Now they gave food
to the old people. Oh they had forgotten what the girls had told
them. "You should not give them food." Now they had forgotten
that, and they gave them food. Those old people (who were
possibly storks) began to call out. "Hɛ·ʾ···i I saw a down-below
face." That is what the old people cried out. "Oh we forgot! (about
the warning to give them no food). But no one heard, so it is all
right anyway, no one has heard them."

Now the people began dancing. It was after midnight when they
ceased dancing. Then they were going to go to bed. They went up
above (to sleep on a bed in the house rafters). Now their husband's
younger brother and their husband's mother (were sleeping below).
Now (when) they were going up above to bed, the boy (the man's
younger brother) looked up at them as they ascended (and then he

cried out), "Mother! My sister-in-law has testicles!" "Keep quiet! do not be talking every which way! Do not say such a thing about my daughter-in-law. Don't! Don't!" "Well she does have testicles!" "Keep silent!" Indeed then the boy ceased, he said nothing more. Now they went to bed with their husband. Indeed they played with him, and then he fell asleep. Now they obtained their own father's head, and then they severed his (the chief's) head. Now they were going to flee. But now this is what the boy said. "Mother! one of them (my sister-in-law) urinated (on me)." That is what the youngster said (because blood of his decapitated older brother dripped on him). "Keep quiet! you talk too much. Your older brother might hear you." Indeed the boy said no more.

Now the youths escaped, and they ran, and then they obtained a canoe, they went across, they got ashore. Now they pushed the canoe away from the shore, and indeed the canoe drifted away. Now they ran on, and they got to there where the girls were. Then they put on their own garments, and the girls put on their own clothes too. Now they ran on, and they went down below (on the arrow ladder), and they got home. Then they did not put his own head on him (because it was too dried), but the smaller head (of the man just murdered above) they put on him there. Indeed now he had a head. That is why that kind (of small bird hawk) has a small head now. Then their father got well. That is the way they became their wives.

That is how the myth ends.

23

The Girl Who Had a Dog Husband

(Miluk Coos)

Annie Miner Peterson dictated this Coos myth text in the Miluk Coos language to Melville Jacobs in 1933 at Charleston, Oregon. She also provided the English translation. The text and translation were published in *Coos Myth Texts* (Jacobs 1940, 159-62); only the translation is reprinted below. Jacobs noted that this story was "[t]old to Mrs. Peterson by a Hanis, Old Dick; but probably generally told by all Coos" (Jacobs 1940, 159). Another Coos version was published by Frachtenberg (1913, 167-71). The Dog Husband tale-type has a wide distribution in North American Indian oral traditions: see Boas (1916), Thompson (1929, 347), Sheppard (1983), and Amoss (1984). This version differs from the others because the Coos Dog Husband is not really a dog at all. Versions from other areas relate to stories of sibling incest and celebrate the paradox that a forbidden marriage produces supernaturally potent offspring. The Coos version radically reinterprets the widespread plot elements.

The girl was the wealthy head man's child. They all desired her, but she wanted no husband. No matter how much they offered as marriage payment, she would not concede. The girl had a big dog. She never remained at home, it was her dog that was her companion. She dug fern roots all the time. Once when she was digging fern roots she came upon a young man. "Oh what are you doing here?" The girl became embarrassed. "Oh I am not doing anything. I am only digging fern roots." "And why, when you are indeed so very pretty? And then you are all the time merely digging fern roots?" The girl said nothing more.

Now she was going to return home. "Are you going to be here again tomorrow?" "Yes." "I will be seeing you." The girl did not speak. Then she returned. She just thought and thought about the young man. "That was so nice looking a young man." She just kept on thinking about him, she did not sleep. Early in the morning she arose, and she ate in a hurry, and then off she went. To be sure, the young man was already there. "Oh I have been waiting for you so long." The girl was embarrassed, because she also desired to see him quickly herself. "Why do you keep your head bowed?" "Oh I was just thinking." "û· come quick and dig those fern roots of yours. I will help you." Indeed the young man assisted.

They filled up the girl's basket. Now she was going to pack her load. "ś· do not go! Let us sit down and talk. You can go back after a while." The girl did so. And then now they met constantly (daily), that is what they did indeed.

One time he spoke thus, "I will go back to your home (with you)." "You must not come to there! (without having made a marriage payment). My parents would not want you!" "Well what do you think? Suppose we kill your dog, and I will get inside it, and I will be just like the dog." "All right. We will kill it." Then indeed they killed the girl's dog, and they fixed it, and then the young man got inside it. It became winter. The young man was still inside it. Whatever was good of their food, she gave it to her dog. Now her brothers spoke about it. One time they went out, her youngest brother shot the dog. The dog screamed as it went. The girl followed it, indeed when she reached her dog it was almost dead. Then her husband spoke to her thus, "Here is my (large) bow, and here is my fire drill, and here is my pipe. Take them all, and my money (large dentalia) here. Take it all." Then she buried her husband. When she had finished burying him she started to go, and then she cried in this manner,

> "Oh I am so grieved,[1] my husband husband!
> My heart is just so sick."

The girl did not go back home. She just continued to live at the head of a small bay. She started in trapping for food and everything. In no long time she had quantities of everything, of food, of hides, of all sorts of furs (of small animals, to use for baby clothes). She became big with child. Then she was going to have baby clothes when she would give birth. Indeed the girl had quantities of all sorts

Coos artifacts owned by Annie Miner Peterson, 1934.

of things. Then she gave birth to three boy babies. Now she sat (got along) well because she had everything (well prepared). In no long time the babies went along rapidly in their growth, it was not long at all, about a few years, before they began to hunt. The girl herself did not hunt any more, just her children hunted. They became young men.

Now (one day) they came back from hunting. "Mother! why are you quite alone here? We have seen two old people, and they weep all the time, whenever we see them. We kill something or other, we place it there where they travel, and we hide and then sure enough they find it. We give them other things and indeed they find them. Maybe we kill an elk, and we give it to them. They are so very glad when they find it. That is why we are asking you." That is what they said, that is what they told their mother. The girl began to cry. "Those are my own parents whom you saw. We will go back home (to them)." Indeed that was what they did. She informed her children of how they had killed her husband. Then she took out the possessions that her husband had given her. To the first child she gave the pipe. He was unable to light it. Both of them (the older brothers) tried it. Then the youngest tried it and now it was he who lit the pipe. Then the bow, not one of the two (older) of them could do anything with it.

[margin handwritten: Youngest Smartest]

Then they gave it to him (the youngest again) and it was he who did it. Now he had two pieces of property. Then the fire drill container, neither of them could do anything with it. But it was the youngest (again) who made a light (with) the fire drill. Now then they made preparations. "My relatives (parents) are very wealthy people. Let us go back to there. If they do not give compensation (for the murder of your father) we will take vengeance." That is what she said to her children. So then they fixed up a canoe, the canoe had limbs still on it (it was a large unfinished log).

Then early in the morning they came ashore at her parents' place. Now they saw a person come out of the house, he came down to the water, and when he saw the log on the beach he ran back to the house. "*Hô̄··* there is a (fine big) log beached." Now the people went down to the water, they were intending to cut off the limbs (to complete the log for a canoe). Now the boys got out of the canoe, and their mother too, and they stepped ashore. Now the parents saw the girl, and then all the people wept. Then they made a payment, they gave two women to each of her children, and so each of them had two wives. Then she explained to her parents thus, "My husband was not a dog. My husband was a person. He merely had gotten into the skin of my dog. That is why he resembled a dog, when you saw a dog. But it was not a dog, it was only a person inside the skin of my dog."

Now they all continued to live there.

That is all of that story of mine.

Notes

1. The translation of this one word of the song is in doubt; Mrs. Peterson was uncertain about its meaning. Ediphone record 14:14580:d; RCA Victor disc 14:14610B:b.

[handwritten at bottom: of embarrassed wish fulfillment for rebellious of]

24

The Person That Halloos

(Miluk Coos)

Annie Miner Peterson dictated the tale, "The Person that Halloos," in the Miluk Coos language to Melville Jacobs in 1933 at Charleston, Oregon. Mrs. Peterson also translated her narrative into English and the phonetically-recorded text and translation were published in *Coos Narrative and Ethnologic Texts* (Jacobs 1939, 51-52). Only the English translation is reprinted here. In a footnote to this text Jacobs wrote, "Coos of both dialects told this narrative excitedly. Mrs. Peterson heard it recounted by Taylor, Gabriel, Old Man Jackson and others. The Coos believed that in the ancient period, some generations ago when the episode transpired, the country was far hotter than it is now: food could be cooked by the heat of the sun; alligators (!) and other hot country animals such as the 'person that halloos' lived in the Coos territory. Incidentally, both Mrs. Peterson and Frank Drew, an ethnologic informant with whom I worked in 1932, believed that the 'person that halloos' must have been a rhinoceros!" (Jacobs 1939, 51). An Upper Coquille Athabaskan cognate text, "Hollering-Like-a-Person," was recorded by Elizabeth D. Jacobs (1935) from Coquelle Thompson, Sr. John P. Harrington recorded another version from the same consultant (1942).

T he people could never travel about in the woods because they feared the person that halloos. When you heard a person calling out, you did not answer, (because) maybe it was that thing. That is why they did not answer. One person was making a canoe. Now he heard a person calling out. But then the thing that was calling out was not quite a person when he got close to it. And then he saw that person that was calling out. Now he fled. He saw it could not get over a log. And that is how he could get quite a distance ahead of it because it could not jump over (logs). It went around them instead. That is why that person got far ahead of it. Indeed that is why he got away from it. Now he arrived at the beach, his canoe was not far away, and so he leaped into his canoe there. But the person that hallooed was also already there himself. He scrambled in haste over to there (to the far end of the canoe). Now he speared (horned) the canoe (through its center), he lifted it up on his head, and then the canoe was stuck over his head. That was how he ran (blindly) with the canoe covering his face. Then he (the man) ran to *waiqdi'* (village), people were there, and he said thus, "The person who halloos is pursuing me!" Now they asked some old woman. (She said,) "You can not kill it. You can not kill that even with a person's (largest) bow (for deer and elk hunting). Go get a crawfish digger (a sharp pole), (and) thrust it into his anus. That is the only way to kill it." They did that indeed, indeed they killed it. And they never saw one of them again, because that must have been the only one. They never saw another one of them again when they killed that one.

25

The Young Man Stepped on Snail's Back

(Miluk Coos)

Cannibalism is the dominant theme of the following tale, which explains the origin of a human cannibal (the accidental tasting of human blood, Thompson [1955-58] motif G36.2) and the necessity of killing such a dangerously antisocial individual. Annie Miner Peterson dictated "The Young Man Stepped on Snail's Back" in the Miluk Coos language to Melville Jacobs in 1933 at Charleston, Oregon. Mrs. Peterson also provided the English translation, and the phonetically-recorded text and translation were published in *Coos Narrative and Ethnologic Texts* (Jacobs 1939, 54-56). Only the English translation is reprinted below. In a note to the text Jacobs wrote: "Citing it as evidence from history, people avoided stepping on snail shells lest 'they go that way' again, becoming a dangerous being like the person in the narrative. Note the difference in emphasis from the Kwakiutl motif, where tasting blood causes cannibalism and that, rather than mashing a snail shell, is of primary interest" (Jacobs 1939, 54). An Upper Coquille Athabaskan cognate text, "Big Head," was recorded by Elizabeth D. Jacobs (1935) from Coquelle Thompson, Sr. John P. Harrington (1942) recorded an untitled version from the same consultant. Melville Jacobs (1935, 1938-1939) obtained a Galice Creek Athabaskan cognate, "Nothing But the Head Left," from Hoxie Simmons. See also Sapir (1909, 246-48) for a Wasco text recorded by Curtin, and Aoki (1979, 29-39) for a Nez Perce text, dealing with the same theme.

A young fellow was always going about here and there. His parents were dead. It was his older brother who raised him. One day he was running about, and then he stepped on a snail, and it broke the snail (shell). That was the way a tiny piece of it got stuck in his foot, and he was unable to get it out. Then he just gnawed at his foot, and while gnawing at it the blood got in his mouth. "Oh how sweet tasting that blood is!" (Unable to extract the piece of shell,) he just went back home. Now then he began to eat up his people. He ate up all the people in his village.

He had one younger sister. Now his younger sister arrived, and she saw no one (there). Only her younger brother was living there. The girl had a small baby. "Give the baby to me!" "Not just yet younger brother!" She deliberately pinched her baby, and indeed it cried. "I will give it to you after a while. I will nurse it first, then I will give it to you." She pinched her baby again, and indeed it cried. "He is so afraid of you, I will bathe him first. Then I will give him to you." She bathed it in the evening. Then she packed her baby, and now the girl fled. She went back to her husband.

Then she hallooed, "Come over quickly and get me! There is something pursuing me!" Indeed three persons went across by canoe so that they could get quickly to her there. Just as the canoe neared the beach the girl leaped immediately into the boat. "Go quickly. A dangerous being is pursuing me." Then indeed (they made haste) so. When they beached she told her husband. "My younger brother is a dangerous being. You will (have to) kill him. He ate up all the people. Then (they did) indeed (as she ordered).

He was already hallooing too (from the other side). Now they piled rocks onto the fire. And they dug a hole, and they got planks. Now the rocks were getting hot, so they put them down into the hole there, and they laid the boards over it. Now they went across to fetch that (dangerous) person. "Ho brother-in-law! You will eat well." Indeed they brought him back home, indeed they gave him food. Then in the middle of his eating they pulled off the lumber, and so indeed he tumbled into the hole. Now they piled up there on top of the lumber, now the people were on top of it there. Indeed he burned up (down in) there. That is how they killed him.

That is why the people fear snail shells.

References Cited

Aarne, Antti and Stith Thompson. 1961. *The Types of the Folktale.* FF Communications No. 184. Helsinki: Suomalainen Tiedeakatemia.

Adamson, Thelma. 1934. *Folktales of the Coast Salish.* Memoirs of the American Folk-Lore Society 27. New York: American Folklore Society.

Amoss, Pamela T. [1971.] [Reminiscences of Melville Jacobs, recorded by Pamela Amoss at the Jacobs house, Spring, 1971.] In Melville Jacobs Collection, University of Washington Libraries, Seattle.

Amoss, Pamela T. 1984. "A Little More than Kin, and Less than Kind: The Ambiguous Northwest Coast Dog," in *The Tsimshian and their Neighbors of the North Pacific Coast,* eds. Jay Miller and Carol M. Eastman, pp. 292-305. Seattle: University of Washington Press.

Amoss, Pamela T. 1990. "The Indian Shaker Church," in *Handbook of North American Indians, Vol. 7: Northwest Coast,* ed. Wayne Suttles, pp. 633-39. Washington, DC: Smithsonian Institution.

Aoki, Haruo. 1979. *Nez Perce Texts.* University of California Publications in Linguistics. Volume 90. Berkeley: University of California Press.

Ballard, Arthur. 1929. *Mythology of Southern Puget Sound.* University of Washington Publications in Anthropology 3.2, 31-150. Seattle: University of Washington Press.

Barnett, Homer G. 1957. *Indian Shakers: A Messianic Cult of the Pacific Northwest.* Carbondale: Southern Illinois University Press.

Beckham, Stephen D. 1977. *The Indians of Western Oregon: This Land Was Theirs.* Coos Bay: Arago Books.

Boas, Franz. 1898. "Traditions of the Tillamook Indians," *Journal of American Folklore* 11:23-38, 133-150.

Boas, Franz. 1916. *Tsimshian Mythology.* 31st Annual Report of the Bureau of American Ethnology for the Years 1909-1910. Washington, DC: Smithsonian Institution.

Boas, Franz. 1917. "The Origin of Death," *Journal of American Folklore* 30:486-491.

Boas, Franz. 1930. "Anthropology," in *Encyclopedia of the Social Sciences* 2, 73-110. New York: Macmillan.

Boas, Franz. 1940. *Race, Language and Culture.* New York: Macmillan.

Boyd, Robert. 1999. *The Coming of the Spirit of Pestilence: Introduced Infectious Diseases and Population Decline among Northwest Coast Indians, 1774-1874.* Seattle: University of Washington Press.

Countryman, Vern. 1951. *Un-American Activities in the State of Washington: The Work of the Canwell Committee.* Ithaca: Cornell University Press.

Diamond, Stanley, ed. 1960. *Culture in History: Essays in Honor of Paul Radin.* New York: Columbia University Press.

Drucker, Philip. 1951. *The Northern and Central Nootkan Tribes.* Bureau of American Ethnology Bulletin 144. Washington, DC: Smithsonian Institution.

Dundes, Alan. 1964. *The Morphology of North American Indian Folktales.* FF Communications No. 195. Helsinki: Suomalainen Tiedeakatemia.

Elmendorf, William W. 1960. *The Structure of Twana Culture.* Washington State University, Research Studies 28.3, Monographic Supplement 2. Pullman: Washington State University Press.

Elmendorf, William W. 1993. *Twana Narratives: Native Historical Accounts of a Coast Salish Culture.* Seattle: University of Washington Press.

Frachtenberg, Leo J. 1913. *Coos Texts.* Columbia University Contributions to Anthropology 1. New York: Columbia University Press.

Frachtenberg, Leo J. 1920. *Alsea Texts and Myths.* Bureau of American Ethnology, Bulletin 67. Washington, DC: Smithsonian Institution.

Frachtenberg, Leo J. 1922. "Coos," in *Handbook of American Indian Languages, vol. 2,* ed. Franz Boas, pp.297-429. Bureau of American Ethnology, Bulletin 40. Washington, DC: Smithsonian Institution.

Frank, Gelya. 1997. "Jews, Multiculturalism, and Boasian Anthropology," *American Anthropologist* 99.4:731-45.

Hajda, Yvonne. 1990. "Southwestern Coast Salish," in *Handbook of North American Indians, Vol. 7: Northwest Coast,* ed. Wayne Suttles, pp. 503-517. Washington, DC: Smithsonian Institution.

Harrington, John P. 1942. [Southwest Oregon Athabaskan.] Microfilm, Reel Nos. 025-027, John Peabody Harrington Papers, Alaska/Northwest Coast, in National Anthropological Archives, Smithsonian Institution, Washington, DC.

Hilbert, Vi, ed. 1995. *Aunt Susie Sampson Peter: The Wisdom of a Skagit Elder.* Seattle: Lushootseed Research.

Hollinger, David A. 1975. *Morris R. Cohen and the Scientific Ideal.* Cambridge: MIT Press.

Hunn, Eugene S. 1990. *Nch'i-Wána, "The Big River": Mid-Columbia Indians and Their Land.* Seattle: University of Washington Press.

Hymes, Dell H. 1965. "The Methods and Tasks of Anthropological Philology (Illustrated with Clackamas Chinook)," *Romance Philology* 19.2:325-40.

Hymes, Dell H. 1981. *"In Vain I Tried to Tell You": Essays in Native American Ethnopoetics.* Philadelphia: University of Pennsylvania Press.

Jacobs, Elizabeth D. [1935.] [Upper Coquille Athabaskan Linguistic and Ethnographic Notes, Folklore Texts (in English) from Fieldwork with Coquelle Thompson, Sr., Siletz, Oregon.] In Melville Jacobs Collection, University of Washington Libraries, Seattle.

Jacobs, Elizabeth D. 1990 [1959]. *Nehalem Tillamook Tales.* Corvallis: Oregon State University Press.

Jacobs, Melville. 1929. *Northwest Sahaptin Texts 1.* University of Washington Publications in Anthropology 2.6, 175-244. Seattle: University of Washington Press.

Jacobs, Melville. [1929-1930.] [Clackamas Chinook Field Notebooks, Based on Fieldwork with Victoria Howard, West Linn, Oregon.] In Melville Jacobs Collection, University of Washington Libraries, Seattle.

Jacobs, Melville. 1931. *A Sketch of Northern Sahaptin Grammar.* University of Washington Publications in Anthropology 4.2, 85-292. Seattle: University of Washington Press.

Jacobs, Melville. 1932. "Notes on the Structure of Chinook Jargon," *Language* 8.1:27-50.

Jacobs, Melville. 1934. *Northwest Sahaptin Texts, Part 1.* Columbia University Contributions to Anthropology 19.1, 1-291. New York: Columbia University Press.

Jacobs, Melville. [1935, 1938-1939.] [Galice Creek Athabaskan Linguistic Field Notebooks, Lexical File, Folklore Texts, Based on Fieldwork with Hoxie Simmons, Logsden, Oregon.] In Melville Jacobs Collection, University of Washington Libraries, Seattle.

Jacobs, Melville. 1936. *Texts in Chinook Jargon.* University of Washington Publications in Anthropology 7.1, 1-27. Seattle: University of Washington Press.

Jacobs, Melville. 1937. *Northwest Sahaptin Texts, Part 2.* Columbia University Contributions to Anthropology 19.2, 1-238. New York: Columbia University Press.

Jacobs, Melville. 1939. *Coos Narrative and Ethnologic Texts.* University of Washington Publications in Anthropology 8.1, 1-125. Seattle: University of Washington Press.

Jacobs, Melville. 1940. *Coos Myth Texts.* University of Washington Publications in Anthropology 8.2, 127-260. Seattle: University of Washington Press.

Jacobs, Melville. 1941a. "Racism and the Teacher," *University of Washington College of Education Record* 8:12-16.

Jacobs, Melville. 1941b. "Review of *Race: Science and Politics*, by Ruth Benedict, and *The Economic Life of Primitive Peoples*, by M.J. Herskovits," *American Teacher* 25:30.

Jacobs, Melville. 1942. "Jewish Blood and Culture," in *Jews in a Gentile World,* eds. I. Graeber and S.H. Britt, pp. 38-55. New York: Macmillan.

Jacobs, Melville. 1944. "Our High School Libraries and Racism," *University of Washington College of Education Record* 11:22-27.

Jacobs, Melville. 1945. *Kalapuya Texts.* University of Washington Publications in Anthropology 11, 1-394. Seattle: University of Washington Press.

Jacobs, Melville. [ca. 1945] "Handbook for Field Recording of Primitive Languages." Unpublished manuscript in Melville Jacobs Collection, University of Washington Libraries, Seattle.

Jacobs, Melville. 1946a. "An Anthropological View of Colonial and Race Questions," in *If Men Want Peace: The Mandates of World Order,* eds. J.B. Harrison, L.A. Mander, and N.H. Engle, pp. 97-111. New York: Macmillan.

Jacobs, Melville. 1946b. "Racism: A Program for Action," American Council on Race Relations, Pacific Coast Clearing House Release No. 8, pp. 1-8.

Jacobs, Melville. 1954. "The Areal Spread of Sound Features in the Languages North of California," in *Papers from the Symposium on American Indian Linguistics.* University of California Publications in Linguistics 10, 46-56.

Jacobs, Melville. 1955. "A Few Observations on the World View of the Clackamas Chinook Indians," *Journal of American Folklore* 68:283-89.

Jacobs, Melville. 1957. "Titles in an Oral Literature," *Journal of American Folklore* 70:157-72.

Jacobs, Melville. 1958. *Clackamas Chinook Texts, Part 1.* Indiana University Research Center in Anthropology, Folklore and Linguistics Publications 8. Bloomington: Indiana University.

Jacobs, Melville. 1959a. *Clackamas Chinook Texts, Part 2.* Indiana University Research Center in Anthropology, Folklore and Linguistics Publications 11. Bloomington: Indiana University.

Jacobs, Melville. 1959b. *The Content and Style of an Oral Literature: Clackamas Chinook Myths and Tales.* Chicago: University of Chicago Press.

Jacobs, Melville. 1959c. "Folklore," in *The Anthropology of Franz Boas,* ed. Walter Goldschmidt, pp. 119-38. American Anthropological Association, Memoir 89.

Jacobs, Melville. 1959d. [Unpublished Manuscript on Northwest States Indian Folklore.] In Melville Jacobs Collection, University of Washington Libraries, Seattle.

Jacobs, Melville. 1960a. *The People Are Coming Soon: Analyses of Clackamas Chinook Myths and Tales.* Seattle: University of Washington Press.

Jacobs, Melville. 1960b. "Humor and Social Structure in an Oral Literature," in *Culture in History: Essays in Honor of Paul Radin,* ed. Stanley Diamond, pp. 181-89. New York: Columbia University Press.

Jacobs, Melville. 1964. *Pattern in Cultural Anthropology.* Homewood, IL: The Dorsey Press.

Jacobs, Melville. 1966. "A Look Ahead in Oral Literature Research," *Journal of American Folklore* 79:413-427.

Jacobs, Melville. 1968. "An Historical Event Text from a Galice Athabaskan in Southwestern Oregon," *International Journal of American Linguistics* 34.3:183-91.

Jacobs, Melville. [1971.] "Notes for an obituary." Copy of unpublished manuscript in Seaburg's possession.

Jacobs, Melville. 1972. "Areal Spread of Indian Oral Genre Features in the Northwest States," *Journal of the Folklore Institute* 9.1:10-17.

Jenness, Diamond. 1955. *The Faith of a Coast Salish Indian.* Anthropology in British Columbia. Memoir No. 3. Victoria: British Columbia Provincial Museum.

Köngäs, Elli-Kaija and Pierre Maranda. 1962. "Structural Models in Folklore." *Midwest Folklore* 123: 133-92.

Kroeber, Alfred L. 1976. *Yurok Myths.* Berkeley: University of California Press.

Leach, Edmund. 1954. *Political Systems of Highland Burma.* Cambridge: Harvard University Press.

Lévi-Strauss, Claude. 1968. *The Savage Mind.* Chicago: University of Chicago Press.

Lévi-Strauss, Claude. 1995. *The Story of Lynx.* Chicago: University of Chicago Press.

Liljeblad, Sven. 1962. "*The People Are Coming Soon*: A Review Article," *Midwest Folklore* 12:93-103.

Mattina, Anthony. 1985. *The Golden Woman: The Colville Narrative of Peter J. Seymour.* Tucson: The University of Arizona Press.

Newman, Stanley. 1960. "Review of *The Content and Style of an Oral Literature: Clackamas Chinook Myths and Tales*, by Melville Jacobs," *Journal of American Folklore* 73:81-82.

Nichols, William. 1983. "'Badger and Coyote Were Neighbors': Comic Reconciliation in a Clackamas Chinook Myth," in *Smoothing the Ground: Essays on Native American Oral Literature,* ed. Brian Swann, pp. 301-8. Berkeley: University of California Press.

Olson, Ronald L. 1936. *The Quinault Indians.* University of Washington Publications in Anthropology 6.1, 1-194. Seattle: University of Washington Press.

Propp, Vladimir. 1958. *Morphology of the Folktale.* Publication 10 of the Indiana University Research Center in Anthropology. Folklore, and Linguistics.

Propp, Vladimir. 1968. *Morphology of the Folktale.* Second edition. Austin: University of Texas Press.

Randall, Betty U. 1949. "The Cinderella Theme in Northwest Coast Folklore," in *Indians of the Urban Northwest,* ed. Marian W. Smith, pp. 243-85. Columbia University Contributions to Anthropology 36. New York: Columbia University Press.

Ramsey, Jarold W. 1983. *Reading the Fire: Essays in the Traditional Indian Literatures of the Far West.* Lincoln: University of Nebraska Press.

Ramsey, Jarold. 1987. "Ti-Jean and the Seven-Headed Dragon: Instances of Native American Assimilation of European Folklore," in *The Native in Literature,* eds. Thomas King, Cheryl Calver, and Helen Hoy, pp. 206-24. Toronto: ECW Press.

Ramsey, Jarold. 1995. "Generic and Racial Appropriation in Victoria Howard's 'The Honorable Milt'," *Oral Tradition* 10.2:263-81.

Ray, Verne F. 1938. *Lower Chinook Ethnographic Notes.* University of Washington Publications in Anthropology 7.2, 29-165. Seattle: University of Washington Press.

Rubin, Rick. 1999. *Naked Against the Rain: The People of the Lower Columbia River, 1770-1830.* Portland: Far Shore Press.

Ruby, Robert H. and John A. Brown. 1976. *The Chinook Indians: Traders of the Lower Columbia River.* Norman: University of Oklahoma Press.

Ruby, Robert H. and John A. Brown. 1996. *John Slocum and the Indian Shaker Church.* Norman: University of Oklahoma Press.

Sapir, Edward. 1909. *Takelma Texts.* University of Pennsylvania. University Museum. Anthropological Publications 2.1:1-267. Philadelphia: University of Pennsylvania Press.

Seaburg, William R. 1982. *Guide to Pacific Northwest Native American Materials in the Melville Jacobs Collection and in Other Archival Collections in the University of Washington Libraries.* Seattle: University of Washington Libraries.

Seaburg, William R. 1992. "An Alsea Personal Narrative and Its Historical Context," *Western Folklore* 51.3/4:269-85.

Seaburg, William R. 1994. "Collecting Culture: The Practice and Ideology of Salvage Ethnography in Western Oregon, 1877-1942." Unpublished Ph.D. Dissertation in Anthropology, University of Washington, Seattle.

Senier, Siobhan. 1997. "American Indian Intellectuals in the Era of Assimilation: Victoria Howard's Oral Narratives," *Northwest Review* 35.3:46-56.

Sheppard, Janice R. 1983. "The Dog Husband: Structural Identity and Emotional Specificity in Northern Athapaskan Oral Narrative," *Arctic Anthropology* 20.1:89-101.

Silverstein, Michael. 1990. "Chinookans of the Lower Columbia," in *Handbook of North American Indians, Vol. 7: Northwest Coast,* ed. Wayne Suttles, pp. 533-46. Washington, DC: Smithsonian Institution.

Smith, Marian. 1940. *The Puyallup-Nisqually.* Columbia University Contributions to Anthropology 32. New York: Columbia University Press.

Snyder, Sally. 1964. "Skagit Society and Its Existential Basis: An Ethnofolkloristic Reconstruction." Unpublished Ph.D. Dissertation in Anthropology, University of Washington, Seattle.

Stross, Brian. 1972. "Serial Order in Nez Perce Myths," in *Toward New Perspectives in Folklore,* eds. Americo Paredes and Richard Bauman, pp. 104-13. Austin: University of Texas Press.

Suttles, Wayne P. 1955. *Katzie Ethnographic Notes.* Anthropology in British Columbia. Memoir No. 2. Victoria: British Columbia Provincial Museum.

Suttles, Wayne P. and Barbara Lane. 1990. "Southern Coast Salish," in *Handbook of North American Indians, Vol. 7: Northwest Coast,* ed. Wayne Suttles, pp. 485-502. Washington, DC: Smithsonian Institution.

Thompson, Laurence C. 1978. "Melville Jacobs, 1902-1971," *American Anthropologist* 80.3:640-646.

Thompson, Stith. 1929. *Tales of the North American Indian.* Cambridge: Harvard University Press.

Thompson, Stith. 1955-1958. *Motif-Index of Folk-Literature.* Six volumes. Bloomington: Indiana University Press.

Whorf, Benjamin Lee. 1956. *Language, Thought, and Reality: Selected Writings of Benjamin Lee Whorf.* Cambridge: The M.I.T. Press.

Wolfenstein, Martha. 1954. *Children's Humor: A Psychological Analysis.* Glencoe, IL: Free Press.

Youst, Lionel. 1997. *She's Tricky like Coyote: Annie Miner Peterson, an Oregon Coast Indian Woman.* Norman: University of Oklahoma Press.

Zenk, Henry. 1984. "Chinook Jargon and Native Cultural Persistence in the Grand Ronde Indian Community, 1856-1907: A Special Case of Creolization." Unpublished Ph.D. Dissertation in Anthropology, University of Oregon, Eugene.

Zenk, Henry. 1990a. "Siuslawans and Coosans," in *Handbook of North American Indians, Vol. 7: Northwest Coast,* ed. Wayne Suttles, pp. 572-79. Washington, DC: Smithsonian Institution.

Zenk, Henry. 1990b. "Kalapuyans," in *Handbook of North American Indians, Vol. 7: Northwest Coast,* ed. Wayne Suttles, pp. 547-53. Washington, DC: Smithsonian Institution.

INDEX

Actor personalities in oral literature content analysis, 51, 99-100
Adamson, Thelma, 11, 164, 225, 237
Albert, John, 281
Alsea Indians, 208, 282, 284
American Council of Learned Societies, 17
American Folklore Society, 27
Amoss, Harold, 3
Amoss, Pamela T., 163, 278, 288
Anatomical references in oral literature style analysis, 58-59, 99-100
Anger or depression, stylized, 155, 248
Animism, 71, 74
Anthropological folklore, 41-42
Anthropological linguists, 211
Antifeminism on the Northwest Coast, 116, 124, 179, 180, 192, 194, 199
Anus: assault with digging stick kills monster, 293; Coyote ties Skunk's, 255; turned inside out, 241
Aoki, Haruo, 294
Apachean, 210
Applegate Creek, Oregon, 210
Archetypes, 46-47, 50
Arrow-chain ladder to upper world, 241-43, 284, 285, 287
Arrows, as measure of trip length, 148-49, 156
Ashes, blown on child to avert ill fortune, 263
Athabaskan, 210, 211. *See also* Apachean, Chetco, Galice Creek, Navajo, Tolowa, Upper Coquille

Audience behavior. *See* Recitalist-audience behavior in oral literature style analysis
Australia, 22
Autonomy, 218

Baby: Coyote impersonates, 230-31; crying attracts Basket Ogress, 239; recognizes father, 134, 139, 143, 228; threatened by cannibal, 295. *See also* Infant picks out his unknown father motif
Babyland, 144, 195
Bachofen, Johann J., 47
Badger, 104
"Badger and Coyote Were Neighbors" (text and analysis), 104-18, 283
Ball game, 104, 110
Barnett, Homer G., 163, 278
Barrow, Susan, 11
Basket Ogress, 238, 252: steals child, 239; trees as relatives of, 241, 252
"Basket Ogress Took the Child, The" (text), 238-54
Beckham, Stephen D., 201
Beginnings (introductions) and endings in oral literature style analysis, 57, 97
Bellingham, Washington, 11
Bells, Shakers use, 279, 281 (note)
Benedict, Ruth, 8, 218
Bitterroot, 71
Blackberries, 68
Black bug, 283.
Black Louse, 252
Blind from weeping motif, 249, 253, 254
Blood: child mistakes for urine, 287; drinking of, 221, 295

Blood feud, 197, 205. *See also* Revenge on murderer of kin; Murder, compensation for
Blood money. *See* Murder, compensation for
Blue Jay, 248, 254
Boas, Franz, 3, 6, 8, 11-12, 15-19, 23-25, 30, 41, 47, 50, 54, 89, 93, 262, 282, 284, 288
Bond, Adeline, 276
Bond, Frank, 275-76
Bones: of Coyote's children come to life, 108-9, 114; of fish come to life, 119-20; sign of Cannibal's house, 149, 244. *See also* Jawbone; Knee cap
Bow breaks motif, 184, 186, 192, 195
Boyd, Robert, 64
Brandon, James, 9
Bremer, Washington, 163
Bride comes motif, 192
Brideprice, 193, 204, 212, 214-15
Brown, John A., 64, 104, 119, 163, 278
Buck, 256. *See also* Horned buck
Bug. *See* Black bug; Black louse; Centipede; Greyback louse
Burning. *See* Cannibalism
Butterworth, Joseph, 13
Buzzard, 136

Calling, dangerous being that calls, 166, 292
Camas, 65-66, 71, 172, 226, 230
Candles, Shakers use, 279
Cannibalism, 149-50, 156, 294-95; execution of cannibal, 295
Cannibal Persons, 253. *See also* Sky Cannibal Hunter
Canoe: as ferry, 286, 287; headless body in, 284;

302 |

magical expanding, 152; ocean-going, 207; stuck on head of monster, 293; unfinished log used as, 291

Canwell Committee, 7, 13-14

Cascade Mountains, 184

Cascades Chinook, 259

Castle Rock, Washington, 165

Catholic nun, 153, 154, 160

Caucasians. See Whites

Celibacy, as source of power, 153, 161

Centipede, 108, 114-17

Central Kalapuya language, 183

Centralia, Washington, 4

Charleston, Oregon, 18, 201, 284, 288, 292, 294

Chemawa, Oregon, 183

Chetco Athabaskan, 204, 205, 206, 209

Chetco River, Oregon, 202

Children, offer warnings that are ignored, 287

Chinook Jargon, 8, 92, 260-61, 282-83

Chinook salmon, 230ff

Chinookan Indians, 64, 132, 142, 161, 183, 207. See also Cascades; Clackamas; Wishram

Chokecherries, 68

Christianity, 163, 175, 176, 181, 278

Chub, 67, 71

Cispus River, Washington, 171

City College of New York, 6

Clackamas Chinook, 4-5, 26-29, 64-74, 104-18, 119-24, 125-31, 141, 156, 177, 238-54, 255-59, 260-61, 283, 284

Clackamas Chinook Texts, Part 1, 18, 255

Clackamas Chinook Texts, Part 2, 119, 125, 238

Class, social, 141, 143, 156, 183

Clear Fork, Washington, 172

Clothing: change of to impersonate owner, 286, 291; changes Grizzly to person, 185, 192; dentalia on shirt, 226, 229

Cohen, Morris R., 6, 8, 15

Columbia River, 4, 132, 178, 183, 210, 259

Columbia University, 6, 8

Committee on Research in Native American Languages, 11, 17

Communist Party, 7, 13-14

Companion. See Wishing for a companion

Compassion. See Generosity

Content analysis in oral literature, 48-54, 90

Content and Style of an Oral Literature, The, 27, 75, 104

Coos, 158, 201, 205, 282, 288, 292. See also Hanis; Miluk

Coos Myth Texts, 284, 288

Coos Narrative and Ethnologic Texts, 201, 292, 294

Corvallis, Oregon, 184

Cosmos, Washington, 168, 169

Costima, Lewy, 163, 164, 173, 174, 175, 176, 177, 178, 180, 181

Cottonwood bark, ashes burned to make snow, 120, 121-22

Co-wives, 131, 193, 194, 199

Cowlitz Creek, Washington, 169

Cowlitz Falls, Washington, 169, 171, 177

Cowlitz River, Washington, 165, 167, 168, 169, 173, 174, 176, 177, 224

Cowlitz Salish, 224, 237

Coyote, 68, 104, 113, 114-15, 164, 173, 174, 175, 176, 177, 178, 179, 180, 226, 255

"Coyote and Skunk. He Tied His Musk Sac" (text), 255-59

"Coyote, Eagle, and the Wolves" (text), 224-37

Coyote Jim, 282-83

"Coyote Made Everything Good" (text and analysis), 64-74

"Coyote's Journey" (text and analysis), 163-82

Crab apples, 68

Cradleboard, 230

Crane, 240

Crescent City, California, 202, 204

Cricket, 226

Crow, 164-65, 173

Cry: purchasing ability to, 251; of mourning, 186, 197, 289

Culture, differences between Coastal and Plateau groups. See Class, social

Curtin, Jeremiah, 294

Dam, for fish, origin of, 167, 176

Dangerous beings, 152, 159, 166, 292-93, 295. See also Cannibal Persons; Sky Cannibal Hunter

Darkness One. See Old Woman Darkness

Dead person spirit-power, 275-76

Death, origin of. See Origin of death

Deception, 212, 218, 226, 233-36, 286, 295

Dentalia (money beads), 206, 207, 209 (note),

215, 220, 221, 226, 244

Deprecation of females. *See* Antifeminism on the Northwest Coast

Depression. *See* Anger or depression, stylized

Derr, Elizabeth. *See* Jacobs, Elizabeth D.

Depression, Great (1929-35), 13, 17

Deserted: child, 145 (note); couple, 134; wife, 126

Determination of night and day motif, 243. *See also* Old Woman Darkness

Devil, 166, 175, 180

Diamond, Stanley, 75

Doe, 256

Dog: Dog husband motif, 288ff; dress in skin of, 289, 291; eating of is shameful, 120, 121; points to murderers of master, 284

Dove, 226

Dream: bad, 263-64; of kinsman's fate, 186, 194, 285

Dream-power: illness due to non-acceptance of new, 264-65; large black woodpecker, 275; taking from another person, 266; winter dances to strengthen, 268-69. *See also* Spirit-power

Drew, Frank, 292

Drowning, 278

Dundes, Alan, 49, 96, 97

Dust, raising to confound pursuers, 106, 111

Eagle, 226

Early-morning pedagogic sessions. *See* Pedagogy

Eby, Harold, 13

Ediphone wax cylinder recorder, 21

Eel, 67, 71

Effectiveness of repeated urging among Northwest States Indians, 154, 255

Elders, mixed feelings about, 142-43, 194

Elk, 258

Ellensburg, Washington, 225

Emetic root, 66, 70, 71

Encounter powers, 207

Epilogues in oral literature style analysis, 97

Ethel, Garland, 13

Ethical Culture movement, 6

Ethics of interfamilial relationships, 122

"Ethnographic Texts on Spirit-powers and Shamanism" (texts), 262-77

Eugene, Oregon, 184

Excrement as (spirit-power) advisor (helper), 232

Explanatory items in oral literature style analysis, 59-60, 98-99, 110, 115

Eyes: Coyote cures blindness, 166; water used to cure, 250. *See also* Blind from weeping motif

Eyley, Sam N., Jr., 132, 163, 224, 225 (photograph)

Famine, 72, 119-20, 122-24, 144

Fatalism, 218

Father-in-law, inimical to child's spouse, 149

Fawn, 227-29

Feather: as indicator of absent person's condition, 148, 156; as wealth, 226, 244

Feelings (sentiments). *See* Moods and feelings in oral literature style analysis

Fellatio, 196, 200

Females, deprecation of. *See* Antifeminism on the Northwest Coast

Fern roots. *See* Food

Ferry, in sky country, 286

Feuding, 202, 212, 215-16

Fire, for cooking, 167, 176

Firewood, 166

Flatus, 255ff, 258

Fleas, 243

Flowers, in girls' game, 260

Folklore, methodology in, 15, 41-42

Food: anthropomorphized, 68; cooked food, origins of, 167; fern roots, 288; gifts to elders, 286, 290; importance of productive sites, 174; kin to humans, 70, 158; non-human kinds of, 240; origin of, 165ff; Sun's children, 158; Tarweed, 184

Forbearance. *See* Generosity

Fornication. *See* Sexual relations

Frachtenberg, Leo J., 92, 93, 183, 281, 282, 284, 288

Frazer, Sir James G., 45, 46, 47

French Canadian tales, 92

Freudian psychology. *See* Psychoanalytic (Freudian) theory of folklore interpretation

Fuel, for fires, 166, 174

Galice Creek Athabaskan, 210-22, 294

Galice Creek, Oregon, 210

Games, girls', 260-61

Generosity, 136, 143, 145 (note), 178

Genres in Northwest States oral literatures, 88-93: acculturative genres, 92-93, 163-64, 201-2; post-white myth and tale genres, 91-93, 181, 182 (note); socio-cultural functions of, 90

Genres in oral literature style analysis, 57, 61-63

Ghost Dance (Warm House Dance), 277

Giantism, 204-5

"Girls' Game, A" (text), 260-61

"Girl Who Had a Dog Husband, The" (text), 288-91

Goat Creek, Washington, 169

God, 118, 176

Goldenweiser, Alexander A., 3

Grand Ronde, Oregon, 278

Greyback Louse, 242

Grimm brothers, 48

Grizzly woman, 184ff, 252

Grouse, 66-67, 71

Guardian-powers. See Spirit-powers

Gunlach, Ralph, 13

Gunther, Erna, 11-12

Hair: louse larvae infest, 242-43; magical regrowth, 148, 155; mark of worth, 154; pledge of marriage, 147-148; salient descriptor of appearance, 135, 208

Halloos. See Calling

Hanis Coos, 201, 284-87, 288

Harrington, John P., 292, 294

Hartless, William, 183, 184

Hawk. See Small Bird Hawk

Head: enemy's replaces victim's severed, 287; kept as trophy, 286; taken in raid, 284

Headmen, 111, 202, 204

Heredity, beliefs about, 143, 195

Hero's return, 152

Herskovits, Melville, 8

Herzog, George, 8

Heyerdahl, Thor, 208

Hilbert, Vi, 145

Historical event narratives, 88, 210, 278

Historico-geographical school of folklore, 39-40, 41, 48, 49, 89, 94, 98

Hoarded game. See Impounded fish

Hoijer, Harry, 210

Holy Ghost (Spirit), 176, 278

Horned Buck, 257

Household composition, 191

Howard, Victoria, 4, 21, 30, 65, 93, 104, 106 (photograph), 111, 112, 119, 125, 128, 238, 255, 258, 260

Huckleberry, 232: mountain, 68; small gray, 68

Hudson, Abe, 278

Hudson, John B., 183, 262, 273 (photograph), 276, 278

Hudson, Lloyd F., 278

Humor: caused by incongruous extrapolations from myths, 128; determined by a cluster of stimuli, 77; in Clackamas Chinook oral literature, 75-87; in myths vs. tales, 76; in oral literature content analysis, 52; in oral literature style analysis, 100; types and subtypes of humor stimulus, 77-82, 192

Hunn, Eugene, 132, 146, 163, 224

Hunt, Joe, 20, 132, 135 (photograph), 138, 144, 146, 153, 154

Husband: hidden from wife's father, 149; miraculous. See Milt

Husum, Washington, 132, 146

Hymes, Dell, 28-29, 284

Illinois Creek, Oregon, 210

Impounded fish motif, 230

Impounded fish released motif, 232

Impregnation with spittle motif, 138

Impromptu ethnographic texts, 262

Indian Shaker Church, 22, 91, 92, 163, 164, 173, 176, 177, 181, 278-81

Infant picks out his unknown father motif, 134, 139. See also Baby

In-laws: gifts to, 158, 193; rejection of, 123; tensions in relations among, 193, 213-14

Insane, Grizzly becomes, 198

Jackson, Tommy, 279

Jacobs, Alexander, 6

Jacobs Collection. See Melville Jacobs Collection

Jacobs, Elizabeth D. (Bess), 4, 9, 10 (photograph), 13, 21-22, 282, 284, 292, 294

Jacobs, Melville, 2 (photograph), 8 (photograph), 9 (photograph), 10 (photograph), 18 (photograph), 38, 64, 75, 104, 119, 125, 132, 146, 163, 183, 201, 210, 224, 238, 255, 260, 262, 282, 284, 288, 292, 294;

assessment of folklore research and publications, 26-30; career at University of Washington, 7-14; Communist Party membership, 7, 13; concern with racial issues, 5, 6; editing and publishing of folklore texts, 23-26; education, 6-8; fieldwork in the Northwest States, 16-19; fieldwork methodology, 20-22; Jewish background, 6; on Anthropology, 15-16; overview of academic career, 6-14; teaching English to immigrants, 7; theory of folklore interpretation, 25-26

Jacobs Research Fund, 11
Jacobs, Rose, 6, 11
Jacobsen, Philip A., 21
Japan, 203, 207, 208
Jawbone, of salmon, 191, 199
Jenness, Diamond, 182
Jesus, 164, 173-75
Jews, 6: Jewish intellectuals, 3
Johnson, Hank, 279
Johnson, Jakie, 279
Johnston, Orin, 18 (photograph), 21
Jung, Carl G., 45, 46, 47, 50

Kalapuya, 92, 183, 184, 282. See also Mary's River, Santiam, Tualatin, Yamhill, Yonkala
Kalapuya religion, 262
Kalapuya Texts, 262, 278
Katzie Coast Salish, 182
Kelso, Washington, 4, 165
Kiona Creek, Washington, 171
Klamath River, California, people, 211, 215, 217

"Klamath River Men Murdered a Shasta" (text and analysis), 210-22
Klikitat Creek, Washington, 165
Klikitat Sahaptin, 132-45, 146-62, 224, 255
Knee cap bone, breaks Grizzly's tooth, 186, 193
Köngäs, Elli-Kaija, 96
Kroeber, Alfred L., 3, 283
Kwakiutl, 294

Laconicism and speedy action in oral literature style analysis, 100, 215
Landers Creek, Washington, 168
Langdon, Elizabeth (Bess). See Jacobs, Elizabeth D.
Laughter: at the expense of whites, 128-29; as part of girls' game, 260-61
Lévi-Strauss, Claude, 96, 97, 132
Lewis, Washington, 172, 224
Li, Fang-Kuei, 210
Lice Women, 242, 252-53
Liljeblad, Sven, 27-28
Linguistic devices in oral literature style analysis, 54-56, 99, 211
Linguistics, structural, 15
Little Weasel, 136
Location (distance) references in oral literature style analysis, 58, 98
Logsden, Oregon, 210
Losing a husband to another woman, anxiety about, 130
Louse. See Black louse, Greyback louse; Hair: louse larvae infest
Lower Umpqua-Siuslaw language, 281
Lowie, Robert H., 3

Maranda, Pierre, 96
Marriage: initiated by woman, 184, 192; refusal by woman, 133, 147-48, 154-55; tensions attendant upon, 193
Mary's River Kalapuya, 183-200
Masculine dominance, 197
Mattina, Anthony, 93
Mayfield, Washington, 165
Mead, Margaret, 8
Melody contours and vocal mannerisms in oral literature style analysis, 99
Melville Jacobs Collection, 7, 237
Metaphors in oral literature style analysis, 100, 221
Metcalf, Leon, 145
Methodology, 15, 20-26
Milt, 125
Miluk Coos, 201-9, 288-91, 292-93, 294-95
Mink, 184
"Mink, Panther, and the Grizzly Sisters" (text and analysis), 183-200
Molale Indians, 274
Money beads. See Dentalia
Moods and feelings in oral literature style analysis, 99, 220
Moon, 149, 151-52
Morton, Washington, 7, 8, 132, 163, 165, 174, 177, 225
Mossy Rock prairie, Washington, 167, 168
Motifemes, 49, 50, 56, 96
Motifs, 39. See also Plot devices (motifs); and specific motifs
Mt. Adams, Washington, 169
Mt. Rainier, Washington, 169

Mt. St. Helens, Washington, 169

Mourning, 109, 113, 117, 187, 195

Mouse, 226

Movement and travel in oral literature style analysis, 99, 219

Movement, magical entry, 147, 154

Moving people. *See* Whites

Muddy Fork, Washington, 172

Mudfish, 67, 71

Murder, 212, 216; compensation for, 202-3, 205-6, 213, 219-20, 291

Musical compositions (songs) in oral literature content analysis, 54, 100

Myth Age (or Myth Era, pre-modern era, pre-cultural world), 71, 89, 109, 110, 118, 142, 153, 155, 157, 173, 175, 197, 253, 254

Myth genres vs. tale genres, 89, 202

National Anthropological Archives, 183

National Research Council, 21

Nature references in oral literature style analysis, 59, 99

Naturistic theories of folklore origins, 44

Navajo, 210

Neglected (abandoned) infant, 239

Nehalem Tillamook, 10

Nehalem Tillamook Tales, 10

Nesika, Washington, 168

Nets, dip, origin of, 168

New Critics, 45, 46, 47

Newman, Stanley, 27

New York City, 3, 6

Nez Perce, 294

Nichols, William, 104

Nit Girls, 242, 253

Nooksack language, 21

Nootka, 209

Northwest Sahaptin Texts, 120

Obsidian blade, 204

Obstacle flight, 189-90

Oedipal relationship, 109, 123-24

Ogress, 252. *See also* Basket Ogress

Ohanepecash, Washington, 172

Old age. *See* Elders

Old Dick, 284, 288

"Old Man and His Daughter-in-law, The. Her Fingers Stuck Together" (text and analysis), 119-24

Older men: cultural deprecation of, 194; fear of, 142-43

Oldest-dumbest motif, 179, 182

Old Woman Darkness, 243, 253

Olequa River, Washington, 165

Orality, 193, 196, 197-98

Oral literature: content analysis, 48-54; style analysis, 54-63, 94-102; theory of, 39-40

Oregon City, Oregon, 184, 259

Orifice: lacking, 166; restoring, 166. *See also* Sky Cannibal Hunter People

Origin of death, 115, 166, 175

"Origin of Death, The" (text), 282-83

Packstrap made of entrails, 229

Panther, 184

Paternity, proof of. *See* Infant picks out his unknown father motif

Pattern in Cultural Anthropology, 15, 38

Pattern number in oral literature style analysis, 57, 97, 155, 180, 200, 237

Pedagogy, early morning indoctrination of youth, 101, 102 (note), 199

Penis: Coyote borrows Wren's, 169-70, 177; Coyote makes a stone, 172; Grizzly keeps dead husband's, 187, 190, 195-96

Penutian, 183, 201

People Are Coming Soon, The, 119, 125

"Person That Halloos, The" (text), 292-93

Peterson, Annie Miner, 18 (photograph), 201, 207, 209, 284, 285 (photograph), 288; artifacts owned by, 290 (photograph), 294

Phillips, Herbert, 13

Phonograph recorder, portable electric, 18 (photograph), 21

Picimin, Jack, 274

Pine Nut, 232

Plot devices (expediters) in oral literature style analysis, 60-61, 98.

Plot ("architectural," "dramatic," "play") structures in oral literature style analysis, 61, 91, 96-97

Plunder shared within a raiding party, 113

Poison-powers, shamans extracting of, 269-70

Polygamy, 125

Polygyny, 205

Portland, Oregon, 4, 64

Pregnancy, magical causation. *See* Impregnation with spittle motif

Proper time/season for telling myths/tales in oral literature style analysis, 100

Propp, Vladimir, 49, 61, 96, 97
Psychoanalytic theories of folklore origins, 44-45
Psychoanalytic (Freudian) theory of folklore interpretation, 25-26, 29, 48, 154, 180, 196, 197
Puget Sound Salish, 179

Quail, 67, 71

Radin, Paul, 24
Rainy Creek, Washington, 168
Ramsey, Jarold, 93, 125, 284
Randall, Betty U., 132
Randle, Washington, 171, 172
Rape, 144, 179
Raspberries, 68
Ray, Verne, 17
Recitalist-audience behavior in oral literature style analysis, 57, 100
Reconciliation, with deserted couple, 136
Reichard, Gladys, 89
Rejection: of husband, 131; of wife, 120, 122. See also Suitors, rejection of
Rejuvenation, 135
Religious content in oral literature content analysis, 53-54
Requests, inability to refuse, 178
Resuscitation, 187: attempted, 107-9, 114-15; with new head, 287
Revenge: on murderer of kin, 187, 189, 213, 221; on rejecting woman, 152-53, 159-60
Riffe, Washington, 168
Ritual-to-myth theories of folklore origins, 45-46

Rogue River, Oregon, 204, 210, 214
Rogue River War, 215
Roheim, Geza, 44
Root digger breaks motif, 231
Rotten wood simulates a stolen infant motif, 239
Rubin, Rick, 64, 104, 119
Ruby, Robert H., 64, 104, 119,163, 278

Sagandahs Miluk Coos, 202
"Sagandahs People, The" (text and analysis), 201-9
Sahaptin, 8, 20, 146, 183, 224. See also Klikitat; Upper Cowlitz
Salem, Oregon, 279
Salish, 164, 174, 179, 224, 225. See also Cowlitz, Katzie, Nehalem Tillamook, Nooksack, Puget Sound, Skagit, Tillamook
Salkum, Washington, 165
Salmon, Chinook, 65
Salmon, Coyote creates, 172
Salmon Creek, Washington, 165
Santiam Kalapuya, 183, 262-77, 278-81
Sapir, Edward, 3, 255, 282, 283, 294
Science News Broadcasts, 7
Seaburg, William R., 88
Seattle, Washington, 9
Seduction by posing as a shaman, 170-71
Selky, Peter, 274
Senier, Siobhan, 30
Serviceberries, 68
Sexual relations: Coyote with girl in river, 169-70; long-distance, 170; prohibited to warriors, 286. See also Fellatio, Marriage, Rape, Seduction

Shakers. See Indian Shaker Church
Shamans, 179, 180, 216, 278: Americans prohibit killing of, 271-72; can tell about missing people, 262-63; could not kill Americans, 272; Coyote pretends to be, 170, 179-80; dreamed the earth became black, 275; extract poison-powers, 269-70; interlocutor-speaker for, 270; poisoning of drinking water, 271; power over rain and thunder, 276-77; predict death, 272; taking away of guardian-powers from others, 270-71; visiting paint their faces, 271, 277
Shame: caused by desertion, 126, 134; by rejection of suitor, 148; of refusal to grant request, 178; stylized response to, 155
Shasta Indians, 211, 214, 215
"She Deceived Herself with Milt" (text and analysis), 125-31
Sheppard, Janice R., 288
Shoshone, 27
Siamese twins, 247: separation of results in death, 251
Siletz, Oregon, 210, 279
Siletz Reservation, Oregon, 214, 216, 282
Silver Creek, Washington, 165, 171, 180
Silverstein, Michael, 64, 104, 119
Simmons, Hoxie, 210, 214, 215, 216, 219, 220, 221, 294
Sisters-in-law, 193, 194, 200

Skagit, 21, 29, 145

Skate Creek, Washington, 172

Sketch of Northern Sahaptin Grammar, A, 8

Skin color, preference for lighter, 126, 129

Skunk, 255: musk is lethal, 256

Sky Cannibal Hunter, 243, 253: Sky Cannibal Hunter people lack excretory and genital organs, 246, 253

Sky girls, 285

Sky rope motif, 249

Sky window motif, 248

Slaves, 238-39

"Small Bird Hawk Had His Head Cut Off" (text), 284-87

Smith, Sophie, 164

Smithsonian Institution, 183

Snail shell, danger of stepping on, 295

Snow, magically created to punish bad wife, 120

Snowstorm from cottonwood bark ashes motif, 121-22

Snyder, Sally, 21, 29-30, 179, 182

Social relationships in oral literature content analysis, 50

Soft Basket Person, 171-72, 180

"Some Shakers Find the Body of My Brother's Child" (text), 278-81

Songs in texts, 126, 128, 190, 226, 247, 255, 256, 257, 258, 289

Speedy action. *See* Laconicism and speedy action in oral literature style analysis

Spencer, J.J., 146

Spencer, M. Lyle, 11

Spider, 228, 249. *See also* Sky rope motif

Spier, Leslie, 11

Spirit-power, 196-97: and person relating as kin, 127; as romantic theme, 160-61, 162; canes and feathers for shamans', 269; of dead person, 275-76; dream, 194; losing of causing death, 259; need to relate to people, 70; of shamans, 266-68, 269; quest, 188, 196-97, 264, 277 (note); rejection and discarding of, 129; singing and dancing, 137, 238.

Starvation. *See* Famine

Sticky fingers: from eating old fish, 120; as reminder of story, 119

Strangers, fear of, 159

Structural linguistics. *See* Linguistics, structural

Structural mythology, 96, 132

Structural-psychological model of text interpretation, 5, 25

Sturgeon, 67, 71

Style analysis in oral literature, 54-63, 90, 94-102: terseness, 206

Suicide, 112-14: Coyote attempts, 107

Suitors, rejection of, 137-38, 153

Sun, 149, 251: is a cannibal, 156; daughter in announcer role, 156

"Sun and His Daughter" (text and analysis), 146-62

Suttles, Wayne, 182

Sweat house: Coyote pretends to doctor in, 170-71; used to transform disfigured person, 134-35, 139-40

Swing, catapults Grizzly to far north, 190, 198

Symbiotic relationship between foods, kin, spirit-powers, people, and headmen, 72-73

Tacoma, Washington, 4

Taitnapam, 7

Takelma, 282, 283

Tale genres. *See* Myth genres vs. tale genres

Taming, Panther tames Grizzly woman, 185

Tarweed. *See* Food

Technology, Coyote introduces tools, techniques, 167, 176

Testicles, 287

Texts in Chinook Jargon, 260, 282

Theft: of ball, 105-6, 110; of child, 239; of husband, 126, 130, 247; of wife, 130

Theodoratus, Robert, 8

Thompson, Coquelle, 282, 292, 294

Thompson, Laurence C. (Larry), 10, 94

Thompson, M. Terry, 10

Thompson, Stith, 98, 288, 294

Thorsen, Pamela 21. *See also* Amoss, Pamela T.

Tillamook, 96, 97, 115, 208, 284. *See also* Nehalem Tillamook

Tilton Creek, Washington, 165, 168

Time references in oral literature style analysis, 58, 98

Titles in oral literature style analysis, 100

Toledo, Washington, 165

Tolowa Athabaskan, 204

Toothed vagina motif, 171-72, 180

Toutle River, Washington, 165

Tragic, nature of the, 118

Translation, problems of, 23

Trap, fish, origin of, 168, 177

Travel. *See* Movement and travel in oral literature style analysis

Trout, 67, 71

Tualatin Kalapuya, 184
Turtle, 198
Turtle Dove, 226
Twins. *See* Siamese twins

University of Washington,
7-14, 16-18, 237;
Committee on Tenure
and Academic
Freedom, 14
Unmarried pregnant girl
and husband
abandoned, 139
Upper Coquille
Athabaskan, 282, 292,
294
Upper Cowlitz Sahaptin,
163-82, 224-37, 255
Urine (as shampoo, soap),
244, 246, 253. *See
also* Blood

Values in oral literature
content analysis, 52
Vancouver Island, 209
Vancouver, Washington, 4
Vengeance, for death of
relative. *See* Revenge;
Murder
Virginity, value of female,
178
Visit to the Sun, 156
Vocal mannerisms. *See*
Melody contours and
vocal mannerisms in
oral literature style
analysis
Vulva, 242. *See also*
Toothed vagina

War, return from dance,
285. *See also* Feud
Warm House Dance. *See*
Ghost Dance
Warnings, ignored, 185ff,
202, 212, 217-18
Wasco, 94
Wash, Percy, 211, 215,
217, 218, 219, 220,
221, 222
Washington, University of.
See University of
Washington
Watcheeno, Mrs., 128,
258, 259

Water of life motif, 187,
195, 250
Waterman, Richard, 22
Waterman, Thomas T., 11
Weltfish, Gene, 8
Weregild. *See* Murder,
compensation for
West Linn, Oregon, 104,
119, 238, 255
Whatcom Museum of
History and Art, 11
Whites: attitudes toward,
128-29; impervious to
shamans' powers, 272;
"moving people," 203;
suppress feuding, 216;
prohibit killing of
shamans, 271
Whorf, Benjamin Lee, 58
Widow, 125, 127
Wife: bad, 119-24; good,
213, 222. *See also*
Antifeminism on the
Northwest Coast
Wildcat, 133
"Wildcat" (text and
analysis), 132-45
Wild carrot, 66, 71
Wild Duck, 230-32
Wild strawberries, 68
Willamette River, 64, 184,
259
Williams, Lucy, 29
Winston Creek,
Washington, 165
Wishing for a companion,
125, 127
Wish projections
(fulfillments) in
Northwest Coast oral
literatures, 116, 127,
144
Wishram Chinook, 255
Withdrawal, stylized
response to shame, 155
Wolfenstein, Martha, 81
Wolves, 233-34
Women: attitudes toward,
161; positive
evaluation, 151, 161;
status of, 214. *See also*
Antifeminism on the
Northwest Coast

Wood, Oscar, 279
Woodpecker, large black
dream-power, 275
World view in oral
literature content
analysis, 26, 53, 157,
174, 180, 181, 218
World view of Clackamas
Chinook Indians, 64-
74, 118, 158
Wren, 169, 177, 178, 179

Yamhill Kalapuya, 184,
274, 275-76
Yamhill River, Oregon,
278
Yoke, Jim, 224, 225
Yonkalla Kalapuya,184,
274
"Young Man Stepped on
Snail's Back, The" (text),
294-95
Youngest-smartest motif,
109, 111, 195, 200
(note), 291
Youst, Lionel, 201
Yreka, California, 212,
214, 215
Yurok, 283

Zangretter, Joseph, 272-
74
Zenk, Henry, 183, 201